TRAINING

Solaris™ 2.6
Administrator Certification, Part II

*The single information source
for Solaris system administrators
who want to become certified*

M T P

Bill Calkins

Publisher	David Dwyer
Executive Editors	Laurie Petrycki
	Mary Foote
Acquisitions Editors	Stacey Beheler
	Dustin Sullivan
Product Marketing Manager	Stephanie Layton
Managing Editor	Sarah Kearns
Development Editor	Tina Oldham
Project Editor	Caroline Wise
Copy Editor	Christy Parrish
Technical Editor	Janice Winsor
Software Development Specialist	Craig Atkins
Proofreader	Debra Neel
Indexer	Lisa Stumpf
Compositor	Ron Wise

Copyright © 2000 by MTP

All rights reserved. No part of this book shall be reproduced, stored in a retrieval system, or transmitted by any means, electronic, mechanical, photocopying, recording, or otherwise, without written permission from the publisher. No patent liability is assumed with respect to the use of the information contained herein. Although every precaution has been taken in the preparation of this book, the publisher and author(s) assume no responsibility for errors or omissions. Neither is any liability assumed for damages resulting from the use of the information contained herein.

International Standard Book Number: 1-57870-086-8
Library of Congress Catalog Card Number: 61947200860
Printed in the United States of America
First Printing: February, 2000
03 02 01 00   7 6 5 4 3 2 1

Interpretation of the printing code: The rightmost double-digit number is the year of the book's printing; the rightmost single-digit number is the number of the book's printing. For example, the printing code 00-1 shows that the first printing of the book occurred in 2000.

Trademarks

All terms mentioned in this book that are known to be trademarks or service marks have been appropriately capitalized. MTP cannot attest to the accuracy of this information. Use of a term in this book should not be regarded as affecting the validity of any trademark or service mark. Solaris is a registered trademark of Sun Microsystems, Inc.

Warning and Disclaimer

Every effort has been made to make this book as complete and as accurate as possible, but no warranty or fitness is implied. The information provided is on an "as is" basis. The authors and the publisher shall have neither liability nor responsibility to any person or entity with respect to any loss or damages arising from the information contained in this book or from the use of the CD or programs accompanying it.

ABOUT THE AUTHOR

Bill Calkins is owner and president of Pyramid Consulting, a computer consulting firm located near Grand Rapids, Michigan, specializing in the implementation and administration of client-server systems. Bill is also the author of *Solaris 2.6 Administration Certification Training Guide, Part I*. He has over 16 years of experience in UNIX system administration and consulting at over 85 different companies. He has also worked as an instructor in both corporate and university settings, and has helped hundred of administrators get their certification. His experience covers all flavors of UNIX, including HP-UX, AIX, IRIX, Linux, and SCO. When he's not working in the field, he's conducting training and educational seminars on various topics in system administration. Bill draws on his many years of experience in system administration and training to provide a unique approach to computer training.

ACKNOWLEDGMENTS

I would like to thank MTP for all of their assistance in getting this book to print. They've assembled an incredible team to make certain that the technical information I present gets put to print in a clear and structured format. I thank Dustin Sullivan, Acquisitions Editor, and Mary Foote, Executive Editor, for cutting me slack when I missed a deadline. Thanks especially to Tina Oldham and Janice Winsor for helping me organize my ideas on paper and for being an integral part of this project. You've done a great job on both books, and I thank you. Thanks also to John Philcox for putting a careful eye to the processes and procedures that are outlined throughout this book. I also thank all of the other individuals that I did not have the opportunity to meet that were involved in getting this text to print.

DEDICATION

To Mom and Dad: Although you're not here to share in my achievement, you'll always be in my heart. I miss you. I sincerely want to thank God, who has made all things possible in my life and places no limitations on what I can achieve. I also thank my wife, Glenda, and my children William, Nicole, and Neil for putting up with this project on vacations, the cottage, the beach, and everywhere else we went. Although your names aren't on the cover, you're as much a part of this book as I was. Thank you also to my soon-to-be-born son (or daughter) for holding off on entering this world until after I finished this book. Finally, to my 15 brothers and sisters: Maybe someday I can write about our experiences growing up together.

CONTENTS AT A GLANCE

Chapter 1	Installing a Server	6
Chapter 2	JumpStart	36
Chapter 3	The Boot Process	72
Chapter 4	Device Configuration and Naming	106
Chapter 5	The Solaris File Systems	128
Chapter 6	The NFS Environment	154
Chapter 7	Name Services	184
Chapter 8	Solstice AdminSuite	210
Appendix A	Web Start	244
	Index	260

TABLE OF CONTENTS

Introduction		1
Conventions Used in This Book		4
Chapter 1	**Installing a Server**	**6**
The Server		7
Prerequisites for the Server		8
Installing Solaris 2.6 on the Server		8
Installing Software Using the Interactive Installation Program		10
Solstice AdminSuite		15
Host Management		16
User Management		16
Group Management		16
Administrative Data Management		16
Printer Management		16
Serial Port Management		16
Storage Management		17
Installing AdminSuite		18
Pre-Installation Checklist		18
Installation Process		19
Accessing the Server		21
Adding AutoClient Support		21
How an AutoClient System Works		24
Setting Up the AutoClient Server		25
Adding AutoClients to the Server		30
Starting Up an AutoClient System		32
Patching an AutoClient System		32
Chapter 2	**JumpStart**	**36**
Overview		37
Preparing for a Custom JumpStart Installation		38
What Happens During a Custom JumpStart Installation		38
Start Up Server		*39*
Setting Up the Startup Server		*39*
Install Server		*43*
Setting Up the Install Server		*43*
The Profile Server		44
Setting up the Profile Server		44
Setting Up a Profile Diskette		44

The rules File   45
   Validating the rules File   52
   Begin and Finish Scripts   54
Creating Profiles   55
   backup_media   56
   boot_device   56
   client_arch   57
   client_root   57
   client_swap   58
   cluster   58
   dontuse   59
   filesys   59
   install_type   61
   layout_constraint   61
   locale   63
   num_clients   63
   package   63
      partitioning   *63*
   root_device   64
   system_type   64
   usedisk   64
Testing Profiles   65
Setting Up Clients   67
Example JumpStart Installation   68
   Set Up the Installation Server   68
   Create the JumpStart Directory   68
   Setting Up a Profile Server   68
Set Up Clients   69
   Start Up the Clients   70

Chapter 3   The Boot Process   72
Power On   73
OpenBoot   74
   Device Names   77
   OpenBoot Device Aliases   80
   OpenBoot Non-Volatile RAM (NVRAM)   81
   OpenBoot Security   85
   OpenBoot Diagnostics   87
   Input and Output Control   89
   boot   90
kernel   95

Chapter 4 Device Configuration and Naming — 106
- Device Drivers — 107
- Physical Device Name — 108
- Device Auto-Configuration — 114
- Instance Name — 116
- Major and Minor Device Numbers — 120
- Logical Device Name — 122
- Meta Devices — 126

Chapter 5 The Solaris File Systems — 128
- Constructing a File System — 129
- Tuning File Systems — 133
- Large Versus Small Files — 136
- Mounting a File System — 136
  - /etc/mnttab — 139
- Unmounting a File System — 140
- Volume Manager — 142
  - Troubleshooting Volume Manager — 147
- Information on File Systems — 151

Chapter 6 The NFS Environment — 154
- Servers and Clients — 155
- NFS on Solaris — 156
  - NFS Daemons — 158
  - Setting Up NFS — 158
  - NFS Security — 161
- Mounting a Remote File System — 162
- WebNFS — 166
  - How to Enable WebNFS Access — 168
  - Using a Browser to Access a NFS URL — 168
- Autofs — 169
  - Autofs Maps — 172
- Master Map — 172
  - Direct Map — 175
- Indirect Map — 179
- When to Use Automount — 182

Chapter 7 Name Services — 184
- /etc Files — 186
- NIS — 186
  - Structure of the NIS Network — 186
    - *Determining the Number of NIS Servers You Need* — *188*
    - *Determining Which Hosts Will Be NIS Servers* — *188*
  - Information Managed by NIS — 188

Planning Your NIS Domain	191
Configuring a NIS Master Server	192
Creating the Master passwd File	*194*
Creating the Master group File	*195*
Creating the Master hosts File	*196*
Other Source Files	*197*
Preparing the Makefile	*198*
Setting Up the Master Server with ypinit	*198*
Starting and Stopping NIS on the Master Server	*199*
Name Service Switch	*200*
Setting Up NIS Clients	201
Setting Up NIS Slave Servers	202
NIS+	203
Hierarchical Namespace	204
NIS+ Tables	204
NIS+ Security	206
Authentication	206
Authorization	206
DES Authentication	207
DNS	208
Chapter 8 Solstice AdminSuite	**210**
Solstice AdminSuite and the Command-Line Equivalents	211
Starting the Solstice AdminSuite Tools	212
Customizing the Launcher Window	214
Using the Solstice AdminSuite Tools	215
Host Manager	216
User Manager	216
Setting Up User Account Defaults	*217*
Adding a New User Account	*219*
Modify a User Account	*221*
Delete a User Account	*221*
Group Manager	222
Serial Port Manager	224
Print Client Software	228
The Print Server	*228*
The Print Client	*229*
Processing a Print Request	*230*
Printer Manager	*230*
Installing a Printer	*231*
Modify a Printer	*235*
Delete a Printer	*235*
Database Manager	236
Storage Manager	239

Appendix A   Web Start   244

Minimum System Requirements for Solaris
Web Start   245
Modes of Operation   245
    Local Mode   246
    Client-Server Mode   246
Web Start Default Installation Selection   250
Limitations of the Default Installation   251
Web Start Custom Installation   252
When to Lay Out File Systems Manually   255
Web Start Helpful Information   256

Index   260

TELL US WHAT YOU THINK!

As the reader of this book, *you* are our most important critic and commentator. We value your opinion and want to know what we're doing right, what we could do better, what areas you'd like to see us publish in, and any other words of wisdom you're willing to pass our way.

As the Executive Editor for the Certification team at MTP, I welcome your comments. You can fax, email, or write me directly to let me know what you did or didn't like about this book—as well as what we can do to make our books stronger.

Please note that I cannot help you with technical problems related to the topic of this book, and that due to the high volume of mail I receive, I might not be able to reply to every message.

When you write, please be sure to include this book's title and author, as well as your name and phone or fax number. I will carefully review your comments and share them with the author and editors who worked on the book.

Fax: 317-581-4663

Email: nrfeedback@newriders.com

Mail: Laurie Petrycki
Executive Editor
Certification
201 West 103rd Street
Indianapolis, IN 46290 USA

INTRODUCTION

This book is designed for Solaris system administrators who want to become certified. It is a training and study guide for the Solaris Certified Administrator Examination, Part II, Sylvan exam number 310-008. Use it to study for the topics that will be presented on the exam. This book is designed to complement my previous book, the *Solaris 2.6 Administrator Certification Training Guide, Part I*. In addition to using them as study guides for the exams, I encourage you to keep both of these books on your bookshelf as reference guides to assist you in your daily system administration tasks.

This book is not a cheat sheet for the exam, it is a training manual. In other words, it does not merely give answers to the questions you will be asked on the exam. I have made certain that both books, address the exam objectives in detail, from start to finish. If you are unsure about the objectives on the exam, this book will teach you what you need to know. After reading this book, test your knowledge using the sample exams on the CD-ROM. The test CD will prepare you for the questions that you might see on the exam, and it will thoroughly test your knowledge on all the exam objectives. If you're weak in any area, the tests will identify it so that you can go back to that chapter and study the topic.

This book expands on topics discussed in *Solaris 2.6 Administrator Certification Training Guide, Part I*; therefore, make sure you've read, and are familiar with, the material covered in *Part I*. Some of the questions on Exam #2 are covered in *Part I* of the training guide. Although this book takes you through all the objectives covered on the Certified Solaris Administrator Examination for Solaris 2.6, Part II, it does not repeat material covered in *Part I*, which does include fundamentals you'll need to know for both exams, Parts 1 and 2.

The following list outlines the test objectives for Exam #2; it then recommends the chapter(s) in this book that you should study to gain a firm grasp of those objectives.

- The Solaris 2.6 Network Environment
- Installing a Server

    Study Chapter 1, "Installing a Server."

- Solstice AdminSuite

    Study Chapter 8, "Solstice AdminSuite."

- The Startup PROM *

    Study Chapter 3, "The Boot Process."

- The Startup Process *

    Study Chapter 3.

- Changing Run Levels *

- Device Configuration and Naming

    Study Chapter 4, "Device Configuration and Naming."

- Disks, Partitions, and Format *

    Study Chapter 5, "The Solaris File Systems."

- The Solaris File Systems *

    Study Chapters 5 and 6, "The NFS Environment."

- Mounting File Systems *

    Study Chapters 5 and 6.

- Configuring the NFS (Networked File Systems) Environment

    Study Chapter 6.

- Using Automount

    Study Chapter 6.

- Naming Services

    Study Chapter 7, "Name Services."

- Adding Network Clients

    Study Chapter 1.

- JumpStart—Automatic Installation

    Study Chapter 2, "JumpsStart."

- Network Devices

    Study Chapter 4.

* These objectives are covered in detail in the *Solaris 2.6 Administrator Certification Training Guide, Part I,* and they are not repeated in this book.

To take the exam, purchase an examination voucher from your local Sun Educational Services office by calling 1-800-USA-SUN or visiting their Web site. Go to www.pdesigninc.com for the latest link to the Sun certification Web site. You will need to purchase a voucher from Sun for $150. The exam number is 310-008, and it has approximately 72 questions, which comprise multiple choice and multiple short answer questions. After you have received your voucher number, contact your Authorized Prometric Testing Center (APTC) to locate the testing center nearest to you and to schedule your examination. The APTC needs 24 hours to prepare for your exam.

Go to the APTC and take your examination. You'll have 90 minutes to complete the test. You will not be able to bring any reference materials with you. At the end of the examination, you will receive your pass/fail grade, score, and feedback on your exam results. Keep this report so that you know what areas you need to improve. If it shows that you are weak in a particular topic, review the chapter in this book that covers that subject. A score of 70 percent is required to pass the exam.

After you have completed your examination, your exam information will be loaded into the Sun Educational Services Certification Database within eight working days. You can view your information after that time.

In addition, watch my Web site, www.pdesigninc.com, where you'll find:

> Late breaking changes that Sun might make to the exam or the objectives. Make sure you check here first, before taking the exam.
>
> A FAQ page with frequently asked questions regarding this book or the exams.
>
> Links to other informative Web sites.

You can also email me directly from this Web site.

After you are confident, take the test and become certified. Drop me an email and let me know how you did on the exam.

Bill Calkins (www.pdesigninc.com)

Conventions Used in This Book

Commands—In the steps and examples, the commands entered by you are displayed in a special font. For example: "Type: `ls -l <return>`." The `<return>` means to press the Return key to enter the command. Only press Return if instructed to do so.

Arguments and Options—When describing command syntax, command options and arguments are shown in *italics* and enclosed with "< >" For example,

```
lp -d<printer name> <filename> <return>
```

Using the Mouse—When using menus and windows, you will be selecting items with the mouse. Here is the default mapping for a 3-button mouse:

Left button	SELECT
Middle button	TRANSFER/ADJUST
Right button	MENU

The SELECT button is used to select unselected objects and to activate controls. The middle mouse button is configured for either TRANSFER or ADJUST. By default, it is setup for TRANSFER, which means the mouse button is used to drag or drop list or text items. Use the first mouse button to highlight text, use the middle button to move it to another window or to reissue a command. The middle button can also be used to move windows around on the screen. The third mouse button is the MENU button. Use this button to display and choose options from pop-up menus.

CHAPTER

1

Installing a Server

The following test objectives are covered in this chapter:

- Definition of a server, client, AutoClient, standalone
- The installation process
- Minimum system requirements for a server installation
- Using the interactive installation program to install server software
- Installing Solstice Adminsuite
- Setting up an AutoClient server and clients

n Part I, setting up a single standalone system was discussed. In this chapter, the emphasis is on installing and configuring the server. I begin by describing a server, its role, and its relationship to other systems on the network. Next, I describe how to install the operating system and some of the additional software packages that differentiate a server from a standalone system.

The Server

A server is a system that provides services and/or file systems, such as home directories or mail files, for other systems on the network. An operating system (OS) server is a server that provides the Solaris software for other systems on the network. For diskless clients, OS servers provide /usr, root (/), and swap file systems. For AutoClient systems, an OS server provides all system software required to set up the individual root (/) and /usr file systems required for local swapping and caching.

There are file servers, startup servers, database servers, license servers, print servers, installation servers, and even servers for particular applications. Systems that rely on servers are called clients. In other words, a client is a system that uses remote services from a server. Some clients have limited disk storage capacity, or perhaps none at all, and they have to rely on remote file systems from a server to function. Diskless and AutoClient clients are examples of this type of client. Other clients might use remote services, such as installation software, from a server. These clients don't rely on a server to function, and they are referred to as standalone systems. System types are defined by how they access the root (/) and /usr file systems, including the swap area. Standalone and server systems mount these file systems from a local disk, whereas diskless and AutoClient clients mount the file systems remotely, relying on servers to provide these services. A standalone system has all its Solaris software on its local disk and does not require services from an OS server. Both networked and non-networked systems can be standalone systems in the Solaris operating environment. Here is a brief description of the various clients you'll find in the Solaris 2.6 environment:

- *Diskless Client*—A client that has no local disk or file systems. These are accessed from the server across the network.

- *JavaStation*—A client that has no local file system and its /home is accessed from a server across the network. The JavaStation runs only applications that are 100 percent pure Java. All data, applications, and configuration information reside on a centralized server that is running Netra J software, a Solaris operating environment. Java applications are downloaded on demand and executed locally.

- *Dataless Client*—A client that has a local root (/), file system, and a local swap partition. The /usr and data directories are accessed across the network from a server.

- *AutoClient*—A client system type that caches (locally stores copies of data as it is referenced) all its needed system software from a server. The AutoClient system has a local disk, but the root (/) and /usr file systems are accessed across the network from a server and are loaded in a local disk cache. Files in the / and /usr file systems are copied to the cache disk as they are referenced. If a Solstice AutoClient client accesses an application that is not already in its disk cache, that application is downloaded. If the application already resides in the client's disk cache, the application is accessed locally. AutoClient has replaced the dataless client in Solaris 2.6.

Prerequisites for the Server

The server must meet a few minimum requirements before Solaris 2.6 can be installed. The Solaris 2.6 release supports all sun4c and sun4d platforms. Most sun4u and sun4m platforms are also supported, but check with your hardware vendor for exceptions.

To run a graphical user interface (GUI) installation, the system must have a minimum of 32MB of RAM. As a server, however, it is typical to have 256MB of RAM or more.

The disk needs to be large enough to hold the Solaris OS, swap, and the additional software, such as Solstice AdminSuite and AutoClient. You'll also need to allocate additional disk space on an OS server in the /export file system for diskless clients or Solstice AutoClient systems.

Plan on a minimum of 1GB of disk, but realistically you should have 2GB or more.

Installing Solaris 2.6 on the Server

Before beginning the installation, let's do a pre-installation checklist. First, gather the system identification information about your server. If the system is running, you can gather all the information by using the commands in Table 1-1.

Table 1-1   System Identification Information

Information Required	Command Used to Gather the Information
System name	/usr/bin/uname -u
Primary network interface	ifconfig -a
IP address	ypmatch <system_name> host nismatch <system_name> more /etc/inet/hosts

Information Required	Command Used to Gather the Information
Domain name	`/usr/bin/domainname`
Whether part of a subnet	`more /etc/netmasks`
What name service is used	`more /etc/nsswitch.conf`

Next, verify that you have enough disk space for Solaris 2.6 and all the co-packaged and third party software that you plan to add. Use Table 1-2 as a guide. In addition, you need to check with your software vendor regarding space requirements for your third-party software packages, as well as swap space requirements.

Table 1-2 Disk Space Requirements

Software	Size (MB)
Entire Distribution Plus OEM	651
Entire Distribution	633
Developer System Support	565
End User System Support	305
Core System Support	116

In addition, make sure you have enough disk space if you plan to run the following software:

- Solstice AdminSuite
- Solstice DiskSuite
- Solstice Backup
- Desktop Power Pack
- Sun Hardware AnswerBook
- Solaris 2.6 Documentation
- Solstice AutoClient
- AnswerBook2
- ODBC Driver Manager
- OpenGL
- Sun MediaCenter One
- Sun WebServer
- Internet Mail Service

Contact Sun to obtain current disk space requirements for each of these packages.

Software can be installed from a local CD or from a CD-ROM located on a system connected to the network. However, for speed, I recommend loading the software from a local CD-ROM drive.

Installing Software Using the Interactive Installation Program

You are now prepared to install your software. I recommend one of two methods to install the operating system: interactive or Web Start. The interactive installation process is described in this chapter. The interactive installation option gives the most flexibility when installing the OS. Web Start, described in Appendix A, "Web Start," does not let you set up additional disks, only the system disk. Use the Web Start option if you don't have a bit-mapped system console attached to your system but you have access to a Web browser attached to the same network. The following steps provide an overview of the software installation procedure.

1. Insert the Solaris 2.6 Software CD in the CD-ROM drive.

2. At the OpenBoot ok prompt, type: boot cdrom

    The system starts up from the CD-ROM, and after a few minutes, you'll enter the system identification section of the installation. Follow the system prompts, entering the information as it is presented. You are asked to enter your system's Hostname, IP Address, and Network information.

3. After the system identification section, you'll see the following dialog:

    ```
    Solaris Interactive Installation:

    This system is upgradeable, so you have two options for installing Solaris
    software.

    The upgrade option updates the Solaris software on the system to the new release,
    saving as many modifications as possible that you've made to the previous version
    of Solaris software. You should back up the system before using the upgrade
    option.

    The initial option overwrites the system's disks with the new version of Solaris
    software. Backing up any modifications that you've made to the previous version
    of Solaris software is recommended before starting the initial option. This
    option also lets you preserve any existing file systems.

    After selecting an option and completing the tasks that follow, a summary of your
    selections will be displayed.

        F2_Upgrade    F4_Initial    F5_Exit    F6_Help
    ```

Installing Software Using the Interactive Installation Program   11

CAUTION! *All data on the OS partitions will be lost. These partitions include / (root), /usr, /opt, and /var.*

4. Press F4 to select a complete reinstallation of the software. You'll see the following dialog:

   ```
   You'll be using the initial option for installing Solaris software on the system.
   The initial option overwrites the system's disks when the new Solaris software is
   installed.

   On the following screens, you can accept the defaults or you can customize how
   Solaris software will be installed by:

         - Allocating space for diskless clients or AutoClient systems
         - Selecting the type of Solaris software to install
         - Selecting disks to hold software you've selected
         - Specifying how file systems are laid out on the disks

   After completing these tasks, a summary of your selections (called a profile)
   will be displayed.
   ```

5. Press F2 to continue. You'll see the following dialog:

   ```
   Allocate Client Services?

   Do you want to allocate space for diskless clients and/or AutoClient systems?

     F2_Continue    F3_Go Back    F4_Allocate    F5_Exit    F6_Help
   ```

6. Press F2. Setting up client services is discussed in the section titled "Adding AutoClient Support." You'll see the following dialog:

   ```
   Select Software:

   Select the Solaris software to install on the system.

   NOTE: After selecting a software group, you can add or remove software by
   customizing it. However, this requires understanding of software dependencies
   and how Solaris software is packaged.

        [ ]   Entire Distribution plus OEM support .. 656MB
        [X]   Entire Distribution ................... 637MB (F4 to Customize)
        [ ]   Developer System Support .............. 572MB
        [ ]   End User System Support ............... 313MB
        [ ]   Core System Support ................... 117MB


     F2_Continue    F3_Go Back    F4_Customize    F5_Exit    F6_Help
   ```

NOTE. *By pressing F4, you are brought to an interactive menu that allows you to select and deselect software packages within a particular cluster.*

7. Select the software cluster that you want to install and press F2. For a server, I recommend selecting the Entire Distribution cluster. You'll see the following dialog:

```
Select Disks:
On this screen you must select the disks for installing Solaris software.
Start by looking at the Suggested Minimum field; this value is the approximate
space needed to install the software you've selected. Keep selecting disks until
the Total Selected value exceeds the Suggested Minimum value.

        Disk Device (Size)         Available Space
        ==========================================
        [X] c0t0d0   (2046 MB) boot disk      2046MB   (F4 to edit)
        [X] c0t1d0   (1001 MB)                1001MB

                          Total Selected:    3047MB
                          Suggested Minimum:  487MB



        F2_Continue    F3_Go Back    F4_Edit    F5_Exit    F6_Help
```

8. Select your disks and press F2. You'll see the following dialog:

```
Preserve Data?
Do you want to preserve existing data? At least one of the disks you've selected
for installing Solaris software has file systems or unnamed slices that you may
want to save.




        F2_Continue    F3_Go Back    F4_Preserve    F5_Exit    F6_Help
```

9. Press F2, and the data on all file systems is erased. You'll see the following dialog:

```
Automatically Layout File Systems?

Do you want to use auto-layout to automatically layout file systems? Manually
laying out file systems requires advanced system administration skills.



        F2_Auto Layout    F3_Go Back    F4_Manual Layout    F5_Exit    F6_Help
```

Installing Software Using the Interactive Installation Program 13

10. Press F2. The system automatically lays out the file systems. Sizes are determined by the software packages you selected. If you plan to add additional software, you can modify the file system sizes later. You'll see the following dialog:

```
Automatically Layout File Systems

On this screen you must select all the file systems you want auto-layout to
create, or accept the default file systems shown.

NOTE: For small disks, it may be necessary for auto-layout to break up some of
the file systems you request into smaller file systems to fit the available disk
space. So, after auto-layout completes, you may find file systems in the layout
that you did not select from the list below.

            File Systems for Auto-layout
            =========================================
            [X]  /
            [ ]  /opt
            [X]  /usr
            [ ]  /usr/openwin
            [ ]  /var
            [X]  swap



    F2_Continue    F5_Cancel    F6_Help
```

11. Make your selection(s) and press F2. I recommend adding /var and /opt as separate file systems if you expect to have large spool files and to add additional software products. For this example, I won't select these file systems. You'll see the following dialog:

```
File System and Disk Layout

The summary below is your current file system and disk layout, based on the
information you've supplied.

NOTE: If you choose to customize, you should understand file systems, their
intended purpose on the disk, and how changing them may affect the operation of
the system.

File system/Mount point          Disk/Slice            Size
============================================================
/                                c0t0d0s0              69MB
swap                             c0t0d0s1              79MB
overlap                          c0t0d0s2              2046MB
/usr                             c0t0d0s6              44MB
/export/home                     c0t0d0s7              1852MB



    F2_Continue    F3_Go Back    F4_Customize    F5_Exit    F6_Help
```

12. Press F2 to continue. You'll see the following dialog:

    ```
    Mount Remote File Systems?

    Do you want to mount software from a remote file server? This may be necessary if
    you had to remove software because of disk space problems.




    F2_Continue   F3_Go Back   F4_Remote Mounts   F5_Exit   F6_Help
    ```

13. Press F2 to continue, unless you want to setup remote mounts. I usually wait until after the initial software installation to setup these mounts.

    ```
    Profile
    The information shown below is your profile for installing Solaris software. It
    reflects the choices you've made on previous screens.
    ==================================================================

                     Installation Option: Initial
                             Boot Device: c0t0d0s0
                         Client Services: None
                                Software: Solaris 2.6, Entire Distribution

    File System and Disk Layout:
    /                     c0t0d0s0      69MB
    swap                  c0t0d0s1      79MB
    /usr                  c0t0d0s6      44MB
    /export/home          c0t0d0s7      1852MB



    F2_Continue    F4_Change    F5_Exit    F6_Help
    ```

14. Verify the information and press F2 if you agree. You'll see the following dialog:

    ```
    Reboot After Installation?

    After Solaris software is installed, the system must be rebooted. You can choose
    to have the system automatically reboot, or you can choose to manually reboot the
    system if you want to run scripts or do other customizations before the reboot.
    You can manually reboot a system by using the reboot(1M) command.



                    [X] Auto Reboot
                    [ ] Manual Reboot



    F2_Begin Installation    F5_Cancel
    ```

15. Make your selection and press F2 to begin the installation. This completes the interactive installation.

With the interactive installation complete, you can now install the Solstice AdminSuite package.

Solstice AdminSuite

By now, you should be familiar with AdminTool. I have described it several times as an easy to use graphical interface for user, printer, and serial device administration. Solstice AdminSuite is similar to AdminTool in that it provides an easy-to-use GUI to facilitate routine server administration tasks. AdminSuite provides a unified suite of tools for administering your Solaris systems and for managing such functions as user accounts, hosts, groups, administrative data, printers, file systems, disks, and serial ports. AdminSuite is co-packaged with the Solaris Operating Environment Application and Enterprise servers. You start Solstice AdminSuite by typing `solstice` from the command prompt and pressing return. The Solstice Launcher window is shown in Figure 1-1.

Figure 1-1
The Solstice Launcher window.

AdminTool is used to manage a standalone system, whereas AdminSuite addresses your needs for reducing the cost and complexity of managing distributed systems. AdminSuite can assist you in administering your network in the following ways:

- It offers local administration of Solaris workgroups by using network services, such as Network Information Service (NIS). This centralizes desktop administration and makes remote management painless.

- It automates routine administration tasks, such as host setup, printer setup, and user setup.

- It provides easy-to-use system administration tools consisting of an extensive GUI to facilitate centralized setup and maintenance of the network environment. Administration is done without requiring root privileges, making centralized administration a reality.

The next few sections cover the facilities provided by Solstice AdminSuite.

Host Management

Host Manager enables you to manage information about clients on the network without manually creating or editing files. It is used for connecting client systems onto the network as well as modifying and deleting them. Host Manager also allows you to add and delete OS services and to set up remote installation services. You can also use Host Manager on a local server to manage support for clients that need remote file resources and disk storage space. Supported client types include standalone, diskless, and AutoClient.

User Management

User Manager allows easy set up and maintenance of user accounts. This includes adding new users, removing users, and updating user information. Some of the defaults that can be set include login shell, password policy, and identifying the user's mail server.

Group Management

The Group Manager adds, displays, modifies, and deletes groups in the NIS name service environment, on a local system, or on a remote system (/etc files) in the same way that AdminTool manages local groups. The Group Manager can also be used to add and change group passwords.

Administrative Data Management

Database Manager is used to manage system files, such as /etc/passwd and /etc/hosts, on the local system, a remote system, or in the NIS database if you have appropriate access privileges.

Printer Management

Printer Manager is a GUI that enables you to install, modify, and delete printers on an LP print server. Furthermore, if your site uses NIS, Printer Manager can provide centralized print administration.

Centralized print administration means that you don't have to individually configure remote printers for each print client on the network. If you use Printer Manager to install a printer, the printer is added to the name service and it becomes available to all SunSoft print clients in the name service. Printer Manager and printers are discussed in Chapter 8, "Solstice AdminSuite."

Serial Port Management

Serial Port Manager is used for adding and maintaining port services for terminals and modems. Using Serial Port Manager to configure serial ports enables you to set up terminals and modems without having to edit and create the necessary files manually. It can display serial port information and facilitate port set up, modification, or deletion. It also provides templates for common terminal and modem configurations.

You can use Serial Port Manager to manage serial port information on the local system or on a remote system if you have the appropriate access privileges.

Storage Management

The Storage Manager consists of two components, File System Manager and Disk Manager. These components enable you to manage the file systems and disk configurations for the systems on your network.

File System Manager enables the file system management of a server or a group of clients on a server. The Disk Manager enables management of disk slices and fdisk partitions on a single disk or a group of equivalent disks. Storage Manager also supports management of High Sierra file system CD-ROMs.

With File System Manager, you can perform the following tasks:

- Create new file systems
- Modify file system options in the /etc/vfstab file
- Manage /etc/vfstab files on a single client, a group of diskless clients, or on an AutoClient system
- Mount or unmount file systems
- Share or unshare directories
- Include a file system in existing automounter maps
- Convert a directory into a mount point

With Disk Manager, you can perform the following tasks:

- Assign a name to a disk
- View and change fdisk partitions on x86 platforms
- Show and set the active fdisk partition on x86 platforms
- View and change slice geometry on SPARC and x86 platforms
- Copy a disk's characteristics to one or more disks of the same type
- Edit disks of the same type simultaneously (or in batches)

All the preceding features of AdminSuite are discussed in more detail in Chapter 8.

After installing the AdminSuite package, install any additional Solaris software packages using AdminTool. This procedure is described in *Solaris 2.6 Administrator Certification Training Guide, Part I.*

Installing AdminSuite

AdminSuite comes with only the Server edition of the Solaris software distribution, and it only runs on Solaris revision 2.4 or higher. The software is on the CD-ROM labeled "Solaris Server Intranet Extension" and is described in Chapter 8.

Pre-Installation Checklist

To perform a full installation of the Solstice AdminSuite software, you need 35MB of free disk space for the spooled software area and an additional 15MB of disk space for each client architecture that you plan to support.

The following software packages need to be already installed on your system: SUNWadmc, SUNWadmfw, SUNWsadml, and SUNWmfrun. If these packages are not already installed, go back to the Solaris CD-ROM and install them.

Before installing the AdminSuite software, you must remove any old versions of AdminSuite. Check to see if AdminSuite is already installed using the `pkginfo` command as follows:

```
pkginfo|grep -i adminsuite
```

The system responds with the following output if AdminSuite already exists:

```
system      SUNWadmsm    Solstice AdminSuite Storage Manager Application
system      SUNWsadma    Solstice AdminSuite Applications
system      SUNWsadmb    Solstice AdminSuite CLI
system      SUNWsadmc    Solstice AdminSuite Core Methods
system      SUNWsadmm    Solstice AdminSuite man pages
system      SUNWsadmo    Solstice AdminSuite Object Libraries
system      SUNWsadmp    Solstice AdminSuite Data Files
system      SUNWspapp    Solstice AdminSuite print application
```

If a previous version of AdminSuite exists, remove it as follows:

1. Log in as root.

2. Change directories to the /cdrom/cdrom0 directory.

3. Type: `./rm_admin -v 2.2 -d /opt`

   Where options are

-v	Represents the version of AdminSuite you want to remove.
-d	Represents the directory in which the AdminSuite software is installed.
-f	Forces the removal of software with no confirmation prompt (optional, but recommended).

To install the AdminSuite software, you must be a member of the sysadmin group for each host that you specify during installation. The following procedure describes how to become a member of the sysadmin group:

1. Log in as root to the system.

2. Edit the /etc/group file, adding the users you want to be authorized to install the AdminSuite software. A sample entry is as follows:

   ```
   sysadmin::14:bcalkins, bholzgen, sburge
   ```

   In this example, bcalkins, bholzgen, and sburge represent the users you are adding to the sysadmin group. You must be a member of the sysadmin group to install the AdminSuite software.

3. Verify that the user is a member of the sysadmin group by entering the following commands:

   ```
   su - sburge
   groups
       staff sysadmin
   exit
   ```

   Perform this step for each user you add to the system.

You are now ready to proceed with the installation of Solstice AdminSuite 2.3.

Insert the CD-ROM labeled "Solaris Server Intranet Extension." If your system is not running Volume Management, you must mount the CD with the following commands before accessing it:

```
mkdir /cdrom
mount -F hsfs -o ro /dev/dsk/<c?t?d0s0> /cdrom
```

where the c?t?d?s0 represents the CD-ROM device on your system. Usually, it is set to c0t6d0s0.

The AdminSuite software is installed using the admin_install script found in the /AdminSuite directory on the CD-ROM. You can use the installation script to install the software on systems on the network as well as standalone systems. Help is available when you run the script, and the script dialog makes it easy for you to install the product.

Installation Process

The following section describes the options presented by the script during the installation process. To install the AdminSuite software, follow these steps:

1. Change to the directory on the CD-ROM that contains the admin_install script. On a system running Volume Manager, the mount point is:
   /cdrom/solaris_srvr_intranet_ext_1_0/AdminSuite_2.3+AutoClient_2.1.

2. Type: `./admin_install`

   The system responds:

   ```
   Welcome to the Solstice Installation Program ...
   To exit the installation process at any time, type 0
   and press the Return key.
           1. Install AdminSuite 2.3 and AutoClient 2.1
           2. Install SunSoft Print Client (Solaris 2.3 - 2.5.1 only)
           3. Install Software Usage Monitoring Toolkit
           4. Set up systems to use AdminSuite and AutoClient
           5. Installation Help
   Enter the number for one or more choices, separated by a space and
   then press the Return key.
   [default: 1]>>>
   ```

3. Enter option 1—Install AdminSuite 2.3 and AutoClient 2.1—and press Return.

   The AdminSuite Software Location information appears as follows:

   ```
   AdminSuite Software Location
   1. /opt
   Choose this option if you intend to support only one architecture of the software.

   2. /export/opt
   Choose this option if you need to support multiple architectures and if you will
   set up other systems that will NFS mount AdminSuite.

   3. Specify location
   Choose this option if you intend to set up other systems to NFS mount AdminSuite
   but you do not want to install the software in /export/opt.

   4. Installation Help
   Type 1, 2, 3, or 4 and press the Return key.
   [default: 1]>>>
   ```

4. Choose the following option that installs the software in the appropriate directory.

   Option 1: /opt

   This installation directory is the recommended directory. With this option, only one architecture can be used with the software. After this option has been chosen, the following installation summary appears:

   ```
   After confirming that the directory and host are correct, enter 1 to continue
   with the installation. You will see a scrolling list of the log activities. If
   the installation is successful, the following message will display in your
   installation window:
   Successfully installed product: AdminSuite/AutoClient
   ```

```
==== Installation Summary ====
Product(s):      AdminSuite/AutoClient
Install Directory:      /opt
Host(s):         your_host_name
Start Installation
-----------------

Do you want to start the installation?
1. Start installation
2. Cancel installation

>>>
```

5. Verify the information provided in the Installation Summary; type 1 and press Return to continue with the installation.

   You will see a scrolling list of log activities. If the installation is successful, the following message displays:

   `Successfully installed product: AdminSuite/AutoClient`

6. Update your shell search path to include the location of the AdminSuite commands.

   If you use either the Bourne or the Korn shell, type:

   ```
   PATH = $PATH:/opt/SUNWadm/bin
   MANPATH = $MANPATH:/opt/SUNWadm/man
   ```

   Enter these changes into your .profile startup file to make them permanent.

7. Start the Solstice Launcher with the following command:

   `/usr/bin/solstice &`

The launcher should now contain the Solstice AdminSuite applications.

Accessing the Server

Standalone systems and clients access the server for various reasons. A standalone system accesses the server for data, whereas a client accesses the server to obtain its operating system as well as data. The following sections describe each of these scenarios.

Adding AutoClient Support

After the AdminSuite software is installed, as described in the previous section, the Solstice AutoClient support software is also installed on the server. AutoClient software reduces the cost of desktop management and is a key component to centralized administration by providing the following benefits:

- *Hands-Off Installation*—System administrators no longer need to visit each desktop to install software. They can configure the Solstice AutoClient client on the server, and after an initial `boot net`, the operating system is automatically cached to the desktop. AutoClient provides an alternative to the traditional push method of software, eliminating the need to explicitly install software on the desktop.

- *Field Replaceable Units*—Solstice AutoClient clients hold only cached data; the server holds all original data where it can be securely managed. In the event of an AutoClient desktop hardware failure, the machine can be replaced and started up via the network. The user's downtime is significantly reduced.

- *Enhanced Server Scalability*—In contrast to the dataless client, Solstice AutoClient reduces NFS reads and network traffic, improving the NFS server scalability. The client/server ratio of AutoClient workgroups is much higher than diskless or dataless workgroups.

- *Disconnectable Option*—This option allows an AutoClient to continue to operate if the server is unavailable, providing a higher level of availability for the client.

- *Command-Line Interface*—Allows administrators to choose between the graphical user interface (GUI) or Command-Line Interface (CLI) to perform operations.

- *Efficient System-Wide Restart*—Clients restart directly from cache, reducing the network traffic during a system-wide restart.

- *Centralized Client Patching*—Patching of Solstice AutoClients is centralized. All patches are applied once on the server. For example, if you add a software patch to an AutoClient system, you don't actually install the patch on the client, because its local disk space is reserved for caching. Instead, you add the patch to the server or to the client's root file system (which resides on the server), or both. This process is discussed later in this section.

- *Remote Halting and Remote Starting of Clients*—Solstice AutoClient allows the system administrator to remotely halt clients and start them up, providing administrative control from a management console.

- *Operation Logging*—Creates a log entry for each major operation completed with the host manager, providing a record of past transactions for diagnostic purposes.

Solstice AutoClient turns the desktop's disk into a cache for the operating system, applications, and user data. If an AutoClient client accesses an application that is not already in its disk cache, the application is downloaded. If the application already resides in the client's disk cache, the application is accessed locally. Following the initial read of data into the desktop's disk cache, network traffic and CPU load are reduced, allowing a higher client/server ratio than diskless or dataless client types.

Table 1-3 lists the disk space requirements for AutoClient servers and AutoClient systems.

Table 1-3 Disk Space Requirements for AutoClient Servers and AutoClient Systems

File System	Minimum Disk Space Requirements
Servers of AutoClient Systems	
root (/)	1MB
/usr	4MB
/var	7.5MB
/export	17MB per OS service
	20MB for each AutoClient system (typically in /export)
AutoClient Systems	
Cache for root (/) and /usr	70MB minimum

NOTE. *If you add an AutoClient system to a server, the /export/root directory is specified on the server by default to store the 20MB for each AutoCient system. However, you can specify any directory that has available disk space. Make sure the server has enough space for this directory.*

Unlike diskless clients, AutoClient systems do not require their swap space to be allocated on the server.

After the Solstice AutoClient software is installed on the server, AutoClient systems are installed, configured, and maintained with the command-line interface or with Host Manager. Host Manager is part of the AdminSuite package and is a graphical user interface that allows for greater efficiency and ease of use in administering your AutoClient systems in a network environment. Using AdminSuite's Host Manager to administer your AutoClients is the method described in this chapter. Host Manager enables system administrators to perform the following tasks:

- Add, modify, display, or remove AutoClient system support on a server
- Convert existing generic, standalone, and dataless systems to the AutoClient system type
- Change information about multiple AutoClient systems in one operation

How an AutoClient System Works

The CacheFS technology is the important component of AutoClient systems. A cache is a local storage area for data. A cached file system is a local file system that stores files in the cache as they are referenced. Subsequent references to the same files are satisfied from the cache rather than retrieving them across the network from the server again. This functionality reduces the load on the network and the server, and it results in faster access for the AutoClient system. If the cache becomes full, space is reclaimed on a least recently used (LRU) basis. Files that have not been referenced for the longest time are discarded from the cache to create free space for the files that are currently being referenced.

An AutoClient system uses its local disk for swap space and to cache its individual root (/) and /usr file system from the server's back file system. The back file system is the AutoClient's file system located back on the server and is usually located in /export/root/<*hostname*>. An AutoClient system uses consistency checking to keep a cached file system synchronized with its back file system.

By default, files that are updated in the server's back file systems are updated on the AutoClient system's cached file systems within 24 hours. However, if the update needs to occur sooner, you can use the `autosync` command. This command initiates consistency checking that synchronizes an AutoClient system's cached file systems with its server's back file systems. In addition, each time an AutoClient system is started, its cached file systems are checked for consistency and updated with its server's back file systems.

Using `autosync`, you can update individual AutoClient systems or all local AutoClient systems in your network to match their corresponding back file systems. You should do this update if you add a new package in the shared /usr directory, in one or more system / (root) directories, or if you add a patch. The following procedures, issued from the server, illustrate the use of the `autosync` command:

Autosync	Updates all AutoClient systems.
autosync –h <*hostname*>	Use the –h option to specify a specific AutoClient system to update.
autosync –h <*hostname*> /usr	Update only the cached file system /usr on a specific AutoClient system.

The system responds with the names of any systems that failed to be updated. No system response means the updates were all successful. If the update fails, you will receive a message similar to this:

```
sparc4:: failed:
```

Consistency checking for an AutoClient system is different from a system running CacheFS. AutoClient files (/ and /usr) are not likely to change often, so consistency checking does not need to occur as frequently on an AutoClient system as it does on a system running CacheFS. This reduces traffic on your AutoClient network. Also, if you add new files to an AutoClient system, its server's back file systems are updated immediately, because an AutoClient system uses a write-through cache. A write-through cache is one that immediately updates its back file system as data is changed or added to the cache.

Setting Up the AutoClient Server

As described in the section "Installing AdminSuite," the installation of Solstice AutoClient was completed. After installing AutoClient, you must follow the setup procedure described next to set up the server as an OS server for the AutoClient systems.

1. On the AutoClient server, type the following command to start the Solstice Launcher:

    /usr/bin/solstice &

    The Solstice Launcher window opens.

2. Click on the Host Manager icon in the Solstice Launcher window.

    The Host Manager: Select Naming Service window is displayed as shown in Figure 1-2. If you are using a Naming Service, it shows the server's domain name, or if you are using local files, the system name is displayed.

Figure 1-2
The Host Manager: Select Naming Service window.

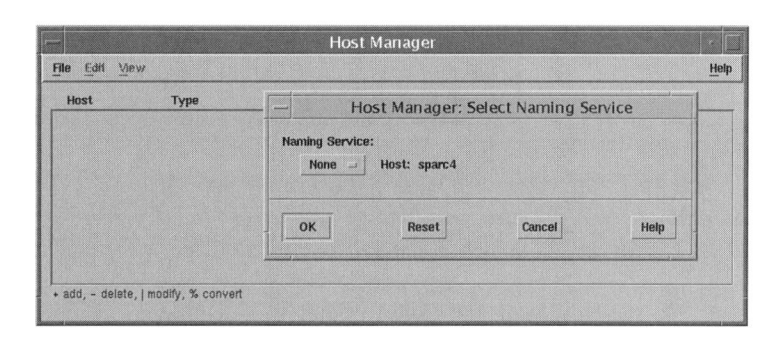

3. Choose a Naming Service and click on OK. (In the example, I'm not running a Naming Service, so I chose None.)

    The Host Manager window is displayed as shown in Figure 1-3.

Figure 1-3
The Host Manager window.

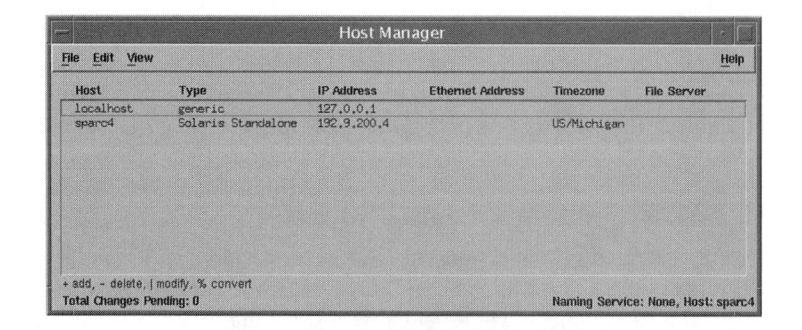

4. Select the system that you want to convert to an OS server from the Host Manager main window. Click on Edit from the toolbar, slide down the menu and select Convert, and then select "to OS server..." from the pop-up menu (see Figure 1-4).

Figure 1-4
The Host Manager Edit window.

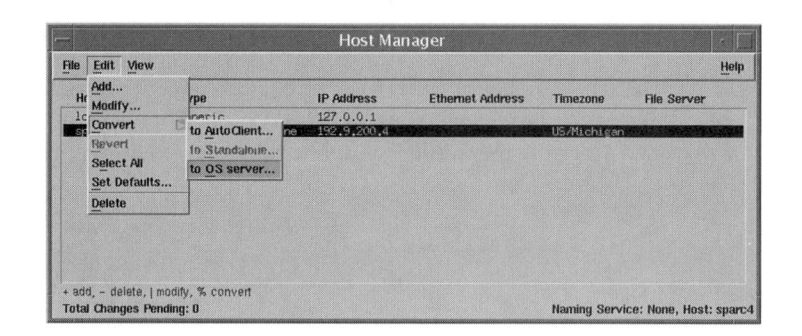

NOTE. *As shown in Figure 1-4, when the pop-up menu appears, AutoClient is automatically selected, scroll down and select "to OS server..." In the example, I chose sparc4 as the OS server that supports the AutoClient systems.*

The Host Manager: Convert window is displayed as shown in Figure 1-5.

ADDING AUTOCLIENT SUPPORT   27

Figure 1-5

The Host Manager: Convert window.

5. In the Host Manager: Convert window, below the OS Services box, select Add... The Set Media Path window is displayed as shown in Figure 1-6.

Figure 1-6

The Set Media Path window.

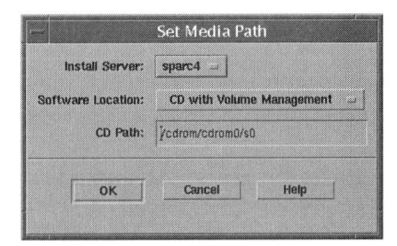

Fill in the Set Media Path window, following these guidelines:

- If you are using the Solaris CD-ROM as the Solaris CD-ROM image, and the CD-ROM is managed by Volume Management, enter the path:
  /cdrom/cdrom0/s0.

- If you mounted the CD-ROM manually, enter the path: `<mount point to the CD>`.

- If you are using a copy of the Solaris CD-ROM image on the install server's hard disk, enter the path: `<directory where the image is loaded>`.

Click on OK after you've finished filling in the options.

The Add OS Services window opens as shown in Figure 1-7.

Figure 1-7

The Add OS Services window.

6. In the Add OS Services window, choose the distribution type—the default distribution type is Entire Distribution. Select the platform of the AutoClient system that you plan to support and click on Add. The Add OS Services window closes. If you want to add more services for other platforms, repeat this step.

NOTE. *To support clients of a different platform group, you must add an OS service for that platform. For example, if a server with Sun4m kernel architecture needs to support an AutoClient system with Sun4c kernel architecture, client support for the Sun4c kernel architecture must be added to the server.*

In addition, for clients that require a different Solaris release from the OS server, you must have the appropriate Solaris CD-ROM image to add this OS service. For example, if you have an OS server running Solaris 2.6 and you want it to support AutoClients running Solaris 2.5, then you must add the Solaris 2.5 OS services to the OS server.

7. The Host Manager: Convert window reopens. Figure 1-8 shows an example of a completed Add OS Services window. Click on OK.

ADDING AUTOCLIENT SUPPORT   29

Figure 1-8

*The Host Manager:
Convert window.*

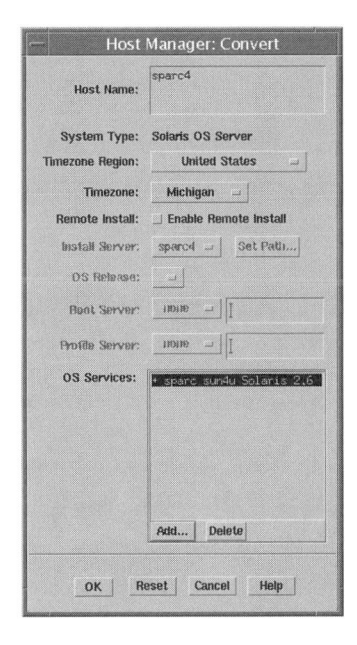

The Host Manager window opens as shown in Figure 1-9, and the bottom of the window reads: Total Changes Pending: 1.

Figure 1-9

The Host Manager window.

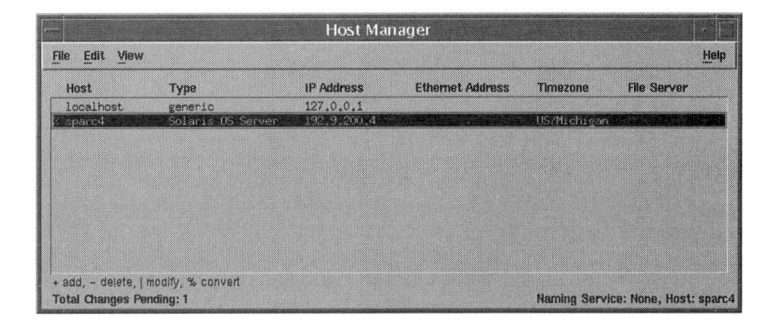

8. Select File from the toolbar and then select Save Changes.

To verify that all the OS services have been added, make sure the status line at the bottom of the main window says All changes successful.

Adding AutoClients to the Server

After adding AutoClient OS services to the OS Server, you now need to add each AutoClient system. If an AutoClient is not listed in Host Manager, it cannot start up from the OS server. You'll use Solstice Host Manager to do this. The steps are as follows:

1. In the Host Manager main window, select Edit and then Add... from the toolbar as shown in Figure 1-10.

Figure 1-10

The Host Manager main window.

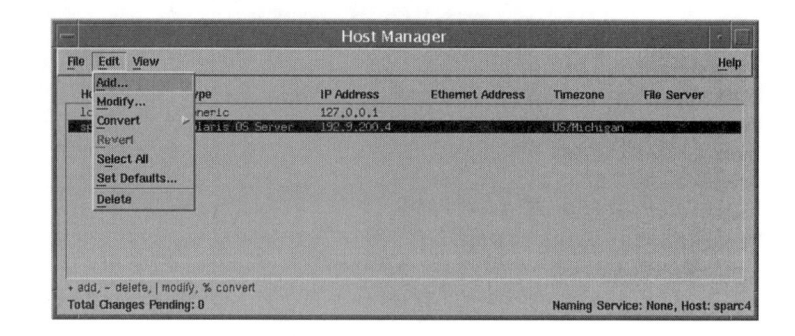

The Host Manager: Add window opens as shown in Figure 1-11.

Figure 1-11

The Host Manager: Add window.

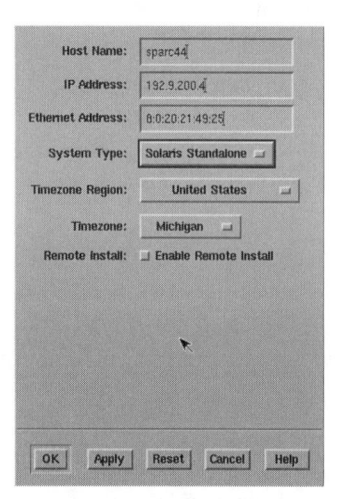

2. Fill in the system information for the AutoClient system. The System Type is Solaris Standalone. Change the System Type to Solstice AutoClient as shown in Figure 1-12.

Figure 1-12
Select System Type.

The Host Manager: Add window changes to look like Figure 1-13.

Figure 1-13
The Host Manager: Add window.

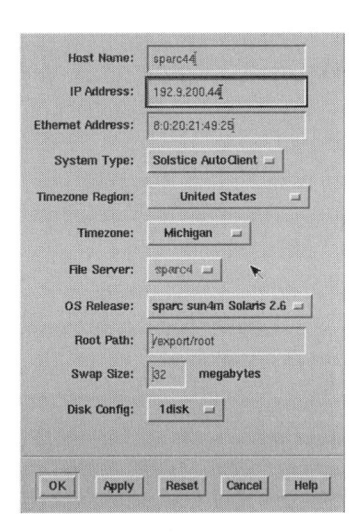

After entering the required information, click on OK.

You'll return to the Host Manager main window as shown in Figure 1-14.

Figure 1-14

The Host Manager main window.

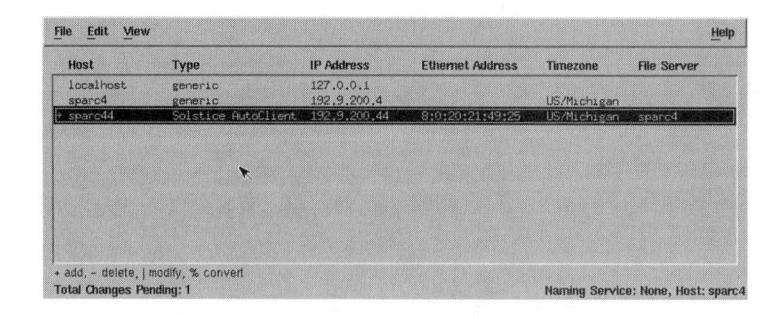

File Edit View						Help
Host	Type	IP Address	Ethernet Address	Timezone	File Server	
localhost	generic	127.0.0.1				
sparc4	generic	192.9.200.4		US/Michigan		
sparc44	Solstice AutoClient	192.9.200.44	8:0:20:21:49:25	US/Michigan	sparc4	

+ add, – delete, | modify, % convert
Total Changes Pending: 1   Naming Service: None, Host: sparc4

Repeat steps 1 and 2 to add subsequent AutoClient systems.

3. When you are ready to confirm the addition of all the AutoClient systems listed in the Host Manager window, choose Save Changes from the File menu.

Starting Up an AutoClient System

On an AutoClient system, the operating system and application software is installed on the workstation by performing a `boot net` at the `ok` OpenBoot prompt on the workstation. The following command is used to start up the AutoClient system for the first time:

```
ok boot net <cr>
```

The first time the AutoClient system is started up, you'll be prompted to provide system configuration information for the AutoClient system. You'll also be prompted to create a root password.

Much like the Solaris JumpStart product, described in Chapter 2, "JumpStart," the client's disk and software are automatically set up and installed, but now, instead of requiring the ongoing administration of each client as a standalone, all the files used by the desktop are preserved on a network server.

After it is up and running, any changes made on the client are also written back to the server. Should the desktop system experience a component failure, a similarly configured system can be put in its place and brought back up in a matter of minutes. The net effect is that the desktop is a field replaceable unit (FRU) and both backups and hardware maintenance have a reduced impact on the system administrator's time.

Patching an AutoClient System

As stated in *Solaris 2.6 Administrator Certification Training Guide, Part I*, a software patch is a collection of files and directories, which replace or update existing files and directories that are preventing proper execution of the software. On diskless clients and AutoClient systems, all software resides on the server. If you add a software patch to an AutoClient system, you don't actually install the patch on the client because its local disk space is reserved for caching. Instead, you add the patch to the server, to the client's root file system (which resides on the server), or to both. An AutoClient system's root file system is typically in /export/root/<*hostname*> on the server.

Applying patches to clients is typically complicated because the patch might place software partially on the client's root file system and partially on the OS service used by that client. To reduce the complexity of installing patches on diskless clients and AutoClient systems, the Solstice AutoClient product includes the `admclientpatch` command. The options and uses of the `admclientpatch` command are as follows:

-a *patch_dir/patch_id*	Add a patch to a spool directory on the server. *patch_dir* is the source directory where patches reside on a patch server. *patch_id* is a specific patch ID number, as in 102209-01.
-c	List all diskless clients, AutoClient systems, and OS services along with patches installed on each that are served by this server.
-p	List all currently spooled patches.
-r *patch_id*	Remove the specified *patch_id* from the spool directory.
-s	Synchronize all AutoClients so that the patches they are running match the patches in the spool directory.

The `admclientpatch` command provides a way to manage patches on all AutoClient systems. You can use `admclientpatch` to initially establish a patch spool directory on the OS server. The spool directory is /opt/SUNWadmd/2.3/Patches. Then, by using `admclientpatch` with the -s option, you synchronize patches running on the clients (and their associated services in /usr) so that they match the revisions of the patches in the spool directory.

The general procedure for maintaining patches on AutoClient systems is as follows:

Use `admclientpatch` -a or -r to create or update a spool directory of all appropriate patches on the local machine as follows:

```
admclientpatch -a /tmp/106828-01 <cr>
```

The system responds:

```
Copying the following patch into spool area: 106828-01 . done
```

If the patch being added to the spool directory makes any existing patches obsolete, `admclientpatch` archives the old patches in case they need to be restored.

On any client server, use `admclientpatch` -s to synchronize those patches installed on clients with those patches in the spool directory as follows. The -v option reports whether `admclientpatch` is adding new patches or backing out unwanted patches.

```
admclientpatch -s -v
Synchronizing service: Solaris_2.6
    Removing patches installed but not spooled.
    To find currently spooled patches, run 'admclientpatch -p'
        105654-03          .
    Installing patches spooled but not installed
        106828-01          ..................................
Synchronizing client: sparc44
    Installing patches spooled but not installed
        106828-01          .........

All done synchronizing patches to existing clients and OS services.
Note: The following machines were affected by these patches
and should be rebooted: sparc44
```

The `admclientpatch` command is a front-end to the standard patch utilities, `installpatch` and `backoutpatch`. Using these utilities, installing a patch and backing out a patch are distinct tasks. However, by using `admclientpatch -s`, you do not need to be concerned about whether you are installing or backing out a patch. The `-s` option ensures that `admclientpatch` takes the appropriate actions. It either installs the patch on the server and in the client's own file systems on the server or it backs out the patch from the client and server and re-installs the previous version of that patch. This is what is meant by synchronizing patches installed on the clients with patches in the patch spool directory.

If you use Host Manager to add new diskless clients and AutoClient systems to a network's configuration files, it automatically sets up those new clients with the patches in the patch spool directory. Host Manager might detect that the installation of a patch in an OS service area might have made all other clients of that service out-of-sync with the patch spool directory. If so, Host Manager issues a warning for you to run `admclientpatch -s` to synchronize the patches that are installed on existing diskless clients or on AutoClients with the patches in the patch spool directory.

Use the following command to verify that the patch has been added to the default patch spool directory:

```
admclientpatch -p
```

The system responds with a list of patches installed, for example:

```
Solaris 2.4 sparc
102755-01      SunOS 5.4_x86: rpld fixes
101945-13      SunOS 5.4: jumbo patch for kernel
102039-04      SunOS 5.4: jumbo patch for package installation utilities
102066-02      SunOS 5.4: sendmail bug fixes

106828-01          SunOS:5.6: /usr/bin/date patch
```

```
Solaris 2.5 i386
102939-06    AutoClient 1.1: allow disconnected CacheFS mounts
Solaris 2.5 sparc
102906-06    AutoClient 1.1: allow disconnected CacheFS mounts
Solaris 2.5.1 i386
103007-06    AutoClient 1.1: allow disconnected CacheFS mounts
Solaris 2.5.1 ppc
102940-06    AutoClient 1.1: allow disconnected CacheFS mounts
Solaris 2.5.1 sparc
103006-06    AutoClient 1.1: allow disconnected CacheFS mounts
Solaris 2.5.1_ppc ppc
102940-06    AutoClient 1.1: allow disconnected CacheFS mounts
Solaris 2.6 sparc
106828-01    SunOS 5.6: /usr/bin/date patch
```

To verify that the patches in the Solstice AutoClient patch spool directory are running on diskless clients and AutoClient systems, use the `admclientpatch` command with the -c option as follows:

```
admclientpatch -c
```

The system responds with:

```
Clients currently installed are:
        sparc44              Solaris, 2.6, sparc
            Patches installed :
OS Services available are:
        Solaris_2.6
            Patches installed :   105654-03
```

This general procedure for maintaining patches assumes the OS server (that is, the server providing OS services to clients) is the same system with the patch spool directory. If, however, your site has several OS servers for your AutoClient systems, you might want to use a single file server for the patch spool directory, and then mount that directory on the OS servers using NFS.

CAUTION! *Do not manually add or remove patches from the spool directory. Instead, use the* `admclientpatch` *command for all your patch administration tasks.*

Whenever you use AdminSuite Host Manager to add new clients, Host Manager consults the patch spool directory and automatically installs any relevant patches on those new clients.

This concludes our discussion on setting up the server. Many additional tasks take place, such as setting up the NIS and the network environment. These topics are covered in their respective chapters. Next, we will take a look at setting up the server to support standalone installations using the JumpStart utility.

CHAPTER 2

JumpStart

The following test objectives are covered in this chapter:

- Definition of JumpStart
- Preparing a JumpStart installation
- Configuring the install and boot servers
- Creating the configuration directory and customization files
- Setting up and booting install clients

As I described in the *Solaris 2.6 Administrator Certification Training Guide, Part I*, there are four methods of installing the Solaris software on a system: interactive installation, custom JumpStart, Web Start, and installation over the network. To install the operating system (OS) on a server, you'll use the interactive method described in Chapter 1. This chapter describes how to install the Solaris operating system (OS) on the clients using the custom JumpStart method.

Overview

There are two methods of JumpStart: JumpStart and custom JumpStart. JumpStart enables you to automatically install the Solaris software on a new SPARC-based system just by inserting the Solaris CD and powering on the system. You do not need to specify the `boot` command at the PROM. The software that is installed is specified by a default profile that is picked based on the system's model and the size of its disks; you don't have a choice of the software that is installed.

The custom JumpStart method of installing the OS provides a way to install groups of systems automatically and identically. If you use the interactive method to install the OS, you must carry on a dialog with the installation program by answering various questions. At a large site with several systems that are to be configured exactly the same, this task can be monotonous and time consuming. In addition, there is no assurance that each system is set up the same. Custom JumpStart solves this problem by providing a method to create sets of configuration files beforehand so that the installation process can use them in configuring each system.

Custom JumpStart requires up-front work, creating custom configuration files before the systems can be installed, but it's the most efficient way to centralize and automate the OS installation at large enterprise sites. Custom JumpStart can be set up to be completely "hands off."

The custom configuration files that need to be created for JumpStart are the rules and profile files. Both of these files consist of several keywords and values that are described in this chapter.

The various commands that are introduced in this chapter are

Solstice Host Manager	A GUI used to set up restart services for the clients.
`setup_install_server`	This sets up an installation server to provide the OS to the client during a JumpStart installation.
`add_install_client`	Sets up the remote workstations to install Solaris from the install server.
`check`	Validates the information in the rules file.
`pfinstall`	Performs a "dry run" installation to test the profile.

Preparing for a Custom JumpStart Installation

The first step when preparing a custom JumpStart installation is to decide how you want the systems at your site to be installed. Questions that need to be answered before you begin include

- Will the installation be an initial installation or an upgrade?
- What applications will the system be supporting?
- Who will be using the system?
- How much swap space is required?

These questions will help you in grouping the systems together when you create the profile and rules files later in this chapter.

Additional questions to be answered include what software packages need to be installed and what size to make the disk partitions. After answering these questions, group systems according to their configuration as shown in the example of a custom JumpStart at the end of this chapter.

The next step when preparing a custom JumpStart installation is to create the configuration files that are used during the installation: the rules.ok file (a validated rules file) and a profile file for each group of systems. The rules.ok file is a text file that should contain a rule for each group of systems that you want to install. Each rule distinguishes a group of systems based on one or more system attributes. The rule links each group to a profile, which is a text file that defines how the Solaris software is installed on each system in the group. Both the rules.ok file and the profiles must be located in a JumpStart directory that you define.

The custom JumpStart configuration files that you need to set up can be located on either a diskette (called a profile diskette) or a server (called a profile server). Use a profile diskette when you want to perform custom JumpStart installations on non-networked, standalone systems. Use a profile server when you want to perform custom JumpStart installations on networked systems that have access to the server. This chapter covers both procedures.

What Happens During a Custom JumpStart Installation

This section provides a quick overview of what takes place during a custom JumpStart installation. Each step is described in detail in this chapter.

To prepare for the install, you'll create a set of JumpStart configuration files, the rules file and profile, on a server that is located on the same network as the client you are installing.

Next, you set up the server to provide a startup kernel which is passed to the client across the network. This is called the "startup server."

After the client starts up, the startup server directs the client to the JumpStart directory, which is usually located on the startup server. The configuration files in the JumpStart directory direct and automate the entire Solaris installation on the client.

To be able to startup and install the OS on a client, you need to set up three servers: a startup server, an install server, and a profile server. These can be three separate servers; however, in most cases, one server provides all these services.

Start Up Server

The startup server is where the client systems access the startup files. This server must be on the local subnet (not across routers). When a client is first turned on, it does not have an OS installed or an IP address assigned, therefore, when the client is first started up, the startup server provides this information. The startup server supplies an IP address to the client by answering reverse ARP (Address Resolution Protocol), or RARP, requests from clients. Reverse ARP is a method by which a client is assigned an Internet (IP) address based on a lookup of its Ethernet address. After supplying an IP address, the startup server transmits a "miniroot" kernel to the client via trivial file transfer program (tftp). This "miniroot" is used by the client to start up.

Setting Up the Startup Server

The startup server is set up to answer RARP requests from clients using either the `add_install_client` command or the Host Manager. Before a client can start up from a startup server however, the `setup_install_server` command is used to set up the startup server. Follow these steps to set up the startup server:

1. On the system that is the startup server, log in as root.

2. Insert and mount the Solaris 2.6 Hardware/Software CD into the CD-ROM drive. Change the directory to the mounted CD, for example:

    ```
    cd /cdrom/sol_2_6_hw2_sparc_smcc_dt/s0/Solaris_2_6/Tools
    ```

3. Use the `setup_install_server` command to set up the startup server. The -b option copies just the startup software from the Solaris CD to the local disk. Enter this command:

    ```
    ./setup_install_server -b <boot_dir_path>
    ```

    Where

-b	Specifies that the system is set up as a startup server.
<boot_dir_path>	Specifies the directory where the kernel architecture is copied. You can substitute any directory path.

For example, the following command copies the kernel architecture information necessary for starting up SPARC sun4c systems to be installed over the network:

```
./setup_install_server -b /export/install
```

The system responds:
```
Verifying target directory...
Calculating space required for the installation boot image
Copying Solaris_2.6 Tools hierarchy...
Install Server setup complete
```

Now that you've installed the client's startup files, you're ready to use Host Manager to set up the startup server to handle RARP requests from the clients. Host Manager is an easy-to-use graphical user interface, and it is the easiest method available. If Host Manager is not available, I suggest adding it to your server by installing Solstice AdminSuite. The installation is described in Chapter 1, "Installing a Server."

You'll start Host Manager by starting up Solstice AdminSuite using the following command:

```
/usr/bin/solstice &
```

When the Solstice Launcher window opens, click on the Host Manager icon shown in Figure 2-1.

Figure 2-1
The Solstice Launcher window.

The Host Manager window opens asking you to select a naming service as shown in Figure 2-2. (For this example, I selected None and then selected OK.)

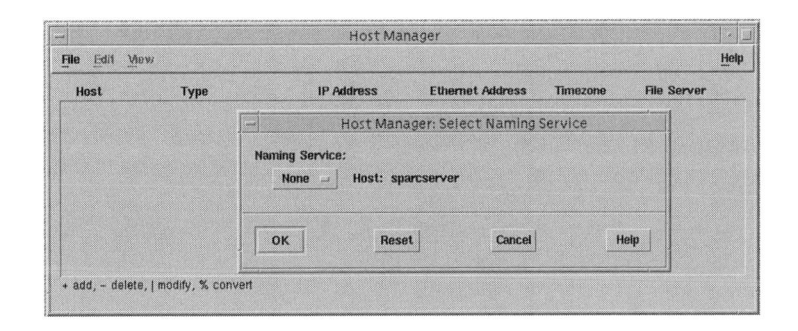

Figure 2-2
Select a naming service.

The Host Manager window opens as shown in Figure 2-3.

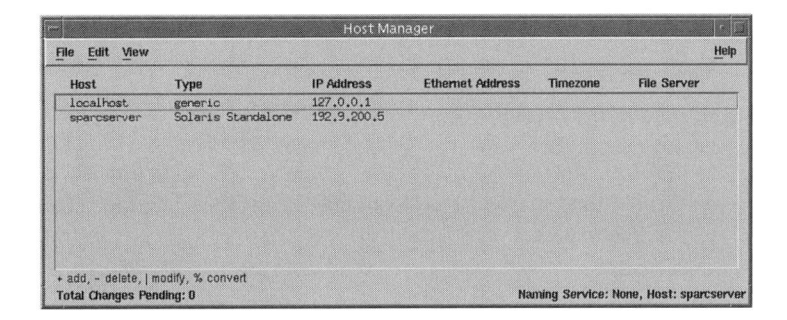

Figure 2-3
The Host Manager window.

Now you need to add information for the client. Select Edit and then Add from the Host Manager window as shown in Figure 2-4.

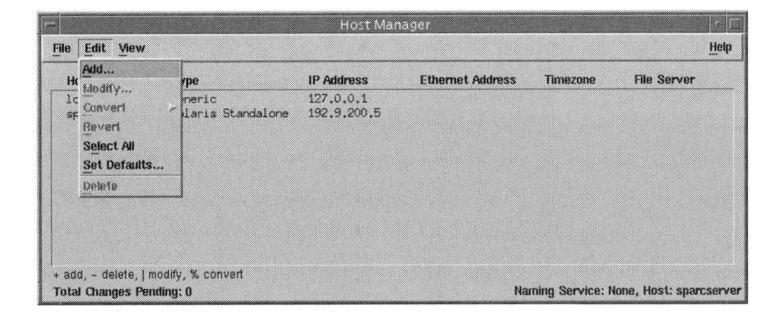

Figure 2-4
The Host Manager Edit menu.

The Host Manager: Add window opens as shown in Figure 2-5.

Figure 2-5

The Host Manager: Add window.

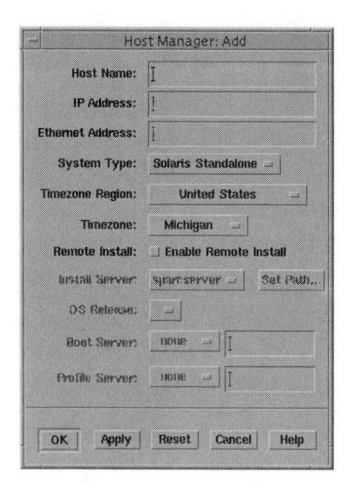

In the Host Manager: Add window, complete all fields described as follows and then click on the OK button. Enter the Hostname, IP address, and the Ethernet address of the host you would like to add.

Host Name	Specify the host name of the client to be installed over the network. This is not the host name of the install server.
IP Address	Specify the IP address to be assigned to the client (example: 192.9.200.5).
Ethernet Address	Specify the hexadecimal Ethernet address of the client (example: 8:0:20:1a:c7:e3).
System Type	Specify whether the client is a standalone or server.
Timezone Region	Enter your time zone.
Remote Install	Enable Remote Install. This allows the client to startup from the specified install server.
Install Server	Specifies the install server and path to where the software resides. Default is the current server and the CD-ROM.
OS Release	Specify the client architecture and Solaris release.
Boot Server	Specify the startup server if not using the current server.
Profile Server	Specify the profile server and path to the installation configuration information.

The startup server is set up and ready to provide startup services to a client.

Install Server

The install server, sometimes called a media server, supplies the OS during a JumpStart installation. An install server can use either the Solaris CD image in its CD-ROM drive or a copy of the Solaris CD, which you can copy to the install server's hard disk. Network installations that use a Solaris CD image copied on an install server's hard disk are faster than installations from a CD-ROM drive.

Setting Up the Install Server

Creating an install server involves these steps:

1. Choosing a system with a CD-ROM drive to be the install server

2. Mounting the Solaris CD

    Using the `setup_install_server` command, copy the Solaris CD to the install server's local disk. (This is an optional step, but by loading the CD image to the server's hard disk, the client install is much quicker.) To load the Solaris CD onto a local disk, follow these steps:

    a. On the system that is going to be the install server, log in as `root`.

    b. Insert and mount the Solaris CD into the CD-ROM drive.

    c. Change to the following directory on the mounted CD:

    ```
    cd /cdrom/sol_2_6_hw2_sparc_smcc_dt/s0/Solaris_2.6/Tools
    ```

    d. Use the `setup_install_server` command to copy the contents of the Solaris CD to the install server's local disk: `./setup_install_server <path>`

    <path> specifies the local directory where the Solaris CD image is copied on the install server. You can specify any directory path. For example, the following command copies the CD image from the Solaris CD to the /export/install directory on the local disk:

    ```
    ./setup_install_server /export/install
    ```

    NOTE. *The `setup_install_server` command indicates if you do not have enough disk space to copy the CD image from the Solaris CD.*

3. After copying the Solaris CD, you can use the `patchadd -c` command to patch the Solaris CD image on the install server's hard disk so that every client does not need to be patched after the install.

The Profile Server

If you are setting up custom JumpStart installations for systems on the network, you have to create a directory on a server called a JumpStart directory. This directory contains all the essential custom JumpStart configuration files for example, the rules file, the rules.ok file, and the profile.

The server that contains a JumpStart directory is called a profile server, which is usually the same system as the install or startup server, although it can be a completely different server. The JumpStart directory on the profile server should be owned by root and have permissions set to 755.

Setting up the Profile Server

To set up a profile server, follow these steps:

1. Pick the system that acts as the server and log in as root.
2. Create the JumpStart directory anywhere on the server: for example: mkdir /jumpstart
3. To be certain this directory is shared across the network, edit the /etc/dfs/dfstab file and add the following entry: share -F nfs -o ro,anon=0 /jumpstart
4. Type: shareall and press return.
5. Place the JumpStart files (that is, rules, rules.ok, and profiles) in the /jumpstart directory.

When you create a profile server, you must make sure systems can access it during a custom JumpStart installation. Every time you add a system for network installation, you'll need to do one of the following tasks. You either have to use the -c option of the add_install_client command or specify the profile server in Host Manager. The example located at the end of this chapter describes how to specify the profile server in Host Manager to setup your clients for a network installation.

Setting Up a Profile Diskette

An alternative to setting up a profile server is to create a profile diskette, provided the system to be installed has a diskette drive. If you use a diskette for custom JumpStart installations, the essential custom JumpStart files, such as the rules file, the rules.ok file, and the profiles, must reside in the root directory on the diskette. The diskette that contains JumpStart files is called a profile diskette. The custom JumpStart files on the diskette should be owned by root and have permissions equal to 755. The steps to create a profile diskette are as follows:

1. Format the diskette: fdformat -U

2. Create a UFS file system on the diskette. Assuming your system uses Volume Management mount the diskette.

3. Create a file system on the diskette by issuing the `newfs` command: `newfs /vol/dev/aliases/floppy0`

   The `newfs` command is covered in Chapter 5, "The Solaris File Systems."

4. Eject the diskette: `eject floppy`

5. Insert the formatted diskette back into the diskette drive.

6. Use the `volcheck` command to make sure Volume Management knows about the diskette.

You have completed the creation of a profile diskette. Now you can create the rules file and create profiles on the profile diskette to perform custom JumpStart installations.

The rules File

The rules file is a text file that should contain a rule for each group of systems you want to install automatically. Each rule distinguishes a group of systems based on one or more system attributes and links each group to a profile, which is a text file that defines how the Solaris software is installed on each system in the group.

After deciding how you want each group of systems at your site to be installed, you need to create a rules file for each specific group of systems to be installed. The rules.ok file is a generated version of the rules file that the Solaris installation program uses to perform a custom JumpStart installation.

After you create the rules file, validate it with the check script by changing into the /jumpstart directory and issuing the `check` command. If the check script runs successfully, it creates the rules.ok file. During a custom JumpStart installation, the Solaris installation program reads the rules.ok file and tries to find the first rule that has a system attribute matching the system being installed. If a match occurs, the installation program uses the profile specified in the rule to install the system.

An example rules file for a Sparcstation LX is shown in Listing Table 2-1. Each line in the code table has a rule keyword and a valid value for that keyword. The Solaris installation program scans the rules file from top to bottom. If the program matches a rule keyword and value with a known system, it installs the Solaris software specified by the profile listed in the profile field.

Listing 2.1   Sample rules File for Sparcstation LX

```
#
#           @(#)rules 1.12 94/07/27 SMI
#
# The rules file is a text file used to create the rules.ok file for
# a custom JumpStart installation. The rules file is a lookup table
# consisting of one or more rules that define matches between system
# attributes and profiles.
#
# This example rules file contains:
#    o syntax of a rule used in the rules file
#    o rule_keyword and rule_value descriptions
#    o rule examples
#
# See the installation manual for a complete description of the rules file.
#
#
###########################################################################
#
# RULE SYNTAX:
#
# [!]rule_keyword rule_value [&& [!]rule_keyword rule_value]... begin profile finish
#
#      "[ ]"   indicates an optional expression or field
#      "..."   indicates the preceding expression may be repeated
#       "&&"   used to "logically AND" rule_keyword and rule_value pairs together
#        "!"   indicates negation of the following rule_keyword
#
#   rule_keyword    a predefined keyword that describes a general system
#                   attribute. It is used with the rule_value to match a
#                   system with the same attribute to a profile.
#
#   rule_value      a value that provides the specific system attribute
#                   for the corresponding rule_keyword. A rule_value can
#                   be text or a range of values (NN-MM).
#                   To match a range of values, a system's value must be
#                   greater than or equal to NN and less than or equal to MM.
#
#   begin           a file name of an optional Bourne shell script
#                   that will be executed before the installation begins.
#                   If no begin script exists, you must enter a minus sign (-)
#                   in this field.
#
#   profile         a file name of a text file used as a template by the
#                   custom JumpStart installation software that defines how
#                   to install Solaris on a system.
#
#   finish          a file name of an optional Bourne shell script
#                   that will be executed after the installation completes.
#                   If no finish script exists, you must enter a minus sign (-)
#                   in this field.
```

```
#
# Notes:
# 1. You can add comments after the pound sign (#) anywhere on a line.
# 2. Rules are matched in descending order: first rule through the last rule.
# 3. Rules can be continued to a new line by using the backslash (\) before
#    the carriage return.
# 4. Don't use the "*" character or other shell wildcards, because the rules
#    file is interpreted by a Bourne shell script.
#
#
############################################################################
#
# RULE_KEYWORD AND RULE_VALUE DESCRIPTIONS
#
#
# rule_keyword      rule_value Type        rule_value Description
# ------------      ---------------        ----------------------
# any               minus sign (-)         always matches
# arch              text                   system's architecture type
# domainname        text                   system's domain name
# disksize          text range             system's disk size
#                                              disk device name (text)
#                                              disk size (MBytes range)
# hostname          text                   system's host name
# installed         text text              system's installed version of Solaris
#                                              disk device name (text)
#                                              OS release (text)
# karch             text                   system's kernel architecture
# memsize           range                  system's memory size (MBytes range)
# model             text'                  system's model number
# network           text                   system's IP address
# totaldisk         range                  system's total disk size (MBytes range)
#
#
############################################################################
#
# RULE EXAMPLES
#
# The following rule matches only one system:
#

#hostname sample_host      -         host_class       set_root_pw

# The following rule matches any system that is on the 924.222.43.0 network
# and has the sun4c kernel architecture:
#    Note: The backslash (\) is used to continue the rule to a new line.

#network 924.222.43.0 && \
#         karch sun4c        -         net924_sun4c        -
```

continues

Listing 2.1 Sample rules File for Sparcstation LX (continued)

```
# The following rule matches any sparc system with a c0t3d0 disk that is
# between 400 to 600 MBytes and has Solaris 2.1 installed on it:

#arch sparc && \
#        disksize c0t3d0 400-600 && \
#        installed c0t3d0s0 solaris_2.1 - upgrade    -
#
# The following rule matches all x86 systems:

#arch i386    x86-begin    x86-class    -
#
# The following rule matches any system:

#any -    -    any_machine    -
#
# END RULE EXAMPLES
#
#
hostname pyramid2            -          sparc_lx -
```

The following table describes the syntax that the rules file must follow.

!	Use before a rule keyword to indicate negation.
[ ]	Use to indicate an optional expression or field.
...	Use to indicate the preceding expression might be repeated.
rule_keyword	A predefined keyword that describes a general system attribute, such as host name (*hostname*) or memory size (*memsize*). It is used with the rule value to match a system with the same attribute to a profile. The complete list of rule_keywords is described in Table 2-1.
rule_value	Provides the specific system attribute value for the corresponding rule keyword. See Table 2-1 for the list of rule values.
&&	Use to join rule keyword and rule value pairs together in the same rule (a logical AND). During a custom JumpStart installation, a system must match every pair in the rule before the rule matches.
begin	A name of an optional Bourne shell script that can be executed before the installation begins. If no begin script exists, you must enter a minus sign (–) in this field. All begin scripts must reside in the JumpStart directory. See the section titled "Begin and Finish Scripts" for more information.
profile	A name of a text file that defines how the Solaris software is installed on the system if a system matches the rule. The information in a profile consists of profile

finish	A name of an optional Bourne shell script that can be executed after the installation completes. If no finish script exists, you must enter a minus sign (–) in this field. All finish scripts must reside in the JumpStart directory. See the section titled "Begin and Finish Scripts" for more information.

keywords and their corresponding profile values. All profiles must reside in the JumpStart directory. Profiles are described in the "Creating Profiles" section of this chapter.

The rules file must have the following:

- At least one rule
- The name "rules"
- At least a rule keyword, a rule value, and a corresponding profile
- A minus sign (-) in the begin and finish fields if there is no entry

The rules file should be saved into the JumpStart directory, should be owned by root, and should have permissions equal to 644.

The rules.ok file allows

- A comment after the pound sign (#) anywhere on a line. If a line begins with a "#", the entire line is a comment line. If a "#" is specified in the middle of a line, everything after the "#" is considered a comment.
- Blank lines.
- Rules to span multiple lines. You can let a rule wrap to a new line, or you can continue a rule on a new line by using a backslash (\)before the Return.

Table 2-1 Describes the various rule_keywords and rule_values that were introduced earlier.

Table 2-1 Rule Keyword and Rule Value Descriptions

Rule Keyword	Rule Value	Description
any	minus sign (–)	Match always succeeds.
arch	processor_type The following table lists the valid values for processor_type: platform processor_type SPARC sparc x86 i386	Matches a system's processor type. The uname -p command reports the system's processor type.
domainname	domain_name	Matches a system's domain name, which controls how a name service determines information. If you have a system already installed, the domainname command reports the system's domain name.

continues

Table 2-1 Rule Keyword and Rule Value Descriptions (continued)

Rule Keyword	Rule Value	Description
disksize	<disk_name> <size_range> <disk_name> - A disk name in the form cxtydz, such as c0t3d0, or the special word rootdisk. If rootdisk is used, the disk to be matched is determined in the following order: ■ The disk that contains the pre-installed boot image (new SPARC based system with factory JumpStart installed) ■ The c0t3d0s0 disk, if it exists ■ The first available disk (searched in kernel probe order) <size_range> - The size of the disk, which must be specified as a range of MB (xx-xx).	Matches a system's disk (in MB). Example: `disksize c0t3d0 250-300` The example tries to match a system with a c0t3d0 disk that is between 250 and 300MB. Note - When calculating size_range, remember that a Mbyte equals 1,048,576 bytes. A disk may be advertised as a "535MB" disk, but it may have only 510 million bytes of disk space. The Solaris installation program will actually view the "535MB" disk as a 510MB disk because 535,000,000 / 1,048,576 = 510. So, a "535MB" disk would not match a size_range equal to 530-550.
hostaddress	IP_address	Matches a system's IP address.
hostname	host_name	Matches a system's host name. If you have a system already installed, the uname -n command reports the system's host name.
installed	slice version slice - A disk slice name in the form cwtxdysz, such as c0t3d0s5, or the special words any or rootdisk. If any is used, all of the system's disks will try to be matched (in kernel probe order). If rootdisk is used, the disk to be matched is determined in the following order: ■ The disk that contains the pre-installed boot image (new SPARC based system with factory JumpStart installed) ■ The c0t3d0s0 disk, if it exists ■ The first available disk (searched in kernel probe order)	Matches a disk that has a root file system corresponding to a particular version of Solaris software. Example: `installed c0t3d0s1 Solaris_2.5` The example tries to match a system that has a Solaris 2.5 root file system on c0t3d0s1.

Rule Keyword	Rule Value	Description
	version - A version name, Solaris_2.x, or the special words any or upgrade. If any is used, any Solaris or SunOS release is matched. If upgrade is used, any upgradable Solaris 2.1 or greater release is matched. Matches a disk that has a root file system corresponding to a particular version of Solaris software.	
karch	platform_group Valid values are sun4d, sun4c, sun4m, sun4u, i86pc, or prep.	Matches a system's platform group. If you have a system already installed, the `arch -k` command or the `uname -m` command reports the system's platform group.
memsize	physical_mem The value must be a range of MB (xx-xx) or a single MB value.	Matches a system's physical memory size (in MB). Example: `memsize 16-32` The example tries to match a system with a physical memory size between 16 and 32MB. If you have a system already installed, the output of the `prtconf` command (line 2) reports the system's physical memory size.
model	platform_name	Matches a system's platform name. Any valid platform name will work. To find the platform name of an installed system, use the `uname -i` command or the output of the `prtconf` command (line 5). Note - If the platform_name contains spaces, you must enclose it in single quotes ('). For example: 'SUNW,Sun 4_50'
network	network_num	Matches a system's network number, which the Solaris installation program determines by performing a logical AND between the system's IP address and the subnet mask. Example: `network 193.144.2.0` The example tries to match a system with a 193.144.2.0 IP address (if the subnet mask were 255.255.255.0).

continues

Table 2-1 Rule Keyword and Rule Value Descriptions (continued)

Rule Keyword	Rule Value	Description
osname	Solaris_2.x	Matches a version of Solaris software already installed on a system. Example: `osname Solaris_2.5` The example tries to match a system with Solaris 2.5 already installed.
totaldisk	size_range The value must be specified as a range of MB (xx-xx).	Matches the total disk space on a system (in MB). The total disk space includes all the operational disks attached to a system. Example: `totaldisk 300-500` The example tries to match a system with a total disk space between 300 and 500MB.

During a custom JumpStart installation, the Solaris installation program attempts to match the system being installed to the rules in the `rules.ok` file in order: first rule through the last rule. A rule match occurs when the system being installed matches all the system attributes defined in the rule. As soon as a system matches a rule, the Solaris installation program stops reading the `rules.ok` file and begins to install the software based on the matched rule's profile.

For example, the rule —karch sun4cbasic_prof—specifies that the Solaris installation program automatically installs any system with the sun4c platform group based on the information in the basic_prof profile.

Validating the rules File

Before the rules file can be used, you must run the `check` script to validate that this file is set up correctly. If all the rules are valid, the rules.ok file is created, which is required by the custom JumpStart installation software to match a system to a profile.

To validate the rules file, make sure that the `check` script resides in the JumpStart directory. The `check` script is provided in the Solaris_2.6/Misc/jumpstart_sample directory on the Solaris CD.

Change the directory to the JumpStart directory and run the `check` script to validate the rules file.

Syntax: `./check [-p path] [-r file_name]`

Where

-p <path>	Validates the rules file by using the check script from a specified Solaris 2.6 CD image, instead of the check script from the system you are using. <path> is the pathname to a Solaris installation image on a local disk or a mounted Solaris CD. Use this option to run the most recent version of check if your system is running a previous version of Solaris.
-r <file_name>	Specifies a rules file other than a file named "rules." Using this option, you can test the validity of a rule before integrating it into the rules file.

When you use check to validate a rules file, the following happens:

- The rules file is checked for syntax. check makes sure that the rule keywords are legitimate, and the begin, class, and finish fields are specified for each rule.

- If no errors are found in the rules file, each profile specified in the rules is checked for syntax.

- If no errors are found, check creates the rules.ok file from the rules file, removing all comments and blank lines, retaining all the rules, and adding the following comment line to the end:

    ```
    version=2 checksum=num
    ```

- As the check script runs, it reports that it is checking the validity of the rules file and the validity of each profile. If no errors are encountered, it reports: "The custom JumpStart configuration is ok."

Here is a sample session using check to validate a rules file. I named it rulestest temporarily and I am using the -r option. With -r, the rules.ok file is not created and only the rulestest file is checked.

```
# ./check /tmp/rulestest
Usage: check [-r <rules filename>] [-p <Solaris 2.x CD image path>]
# ./check -r /tmp/rules
Validating /tmp/rulestest...
Validating profile host_class...
Validating profile net924_sun4c...
Validating profile upgrade...
Validating profile x86-class...

Error in file "/tmp/rulestest", line 113
        any - - any_maine -
ERROR: Profile missing: any_maine
```

In the preceding example, the check script found a bad option. I misspelled "any_machine" as "any_maine." The check script reported this error.

In the next example, I fixed the error, copied the file from rulestest to rules, and re-ran the `check` script.

```
#cp rulestest rules
# ./check
Validating /tmp/rules...
Validating profile host_class...
Validating profile net924_sun4c...
Validating profile upgrade...
Validating profile x86-class...
Validating profile any_machine...
The custom JumpStart configuration is ok.
```

As the `check` script runs, it reports that it is checking the validity of the rules file and the validity of each profile. If no errors are encountered, it reports: `The custom JumpStart configuration is ok`. The rules file is now validated.

After the rules.ok file is created, verify that it is owned by root and has permissions equal to 644.

Begin and Finish Scripts

A begin script is a user-defined Bourne shell script, specified within the rules file, which performs tasks before the Solaris software is installed on the system. You could setup begin scripts to perform the following tasks:

- Backing up a file system before upgrading
- Saving files to a safe location
- Loading other applications

Output from the begin script goes to /var/sadm/begin.log.

Be careful that you do not specify something in the script that would prevent the mounting of file systems onto /a during an initial or upgrade installation. If the Solaris installation program cannot mount the file systems onto /a, an error occurs and the installation fails.

Begin scripts should be owned by root and have permissions equal to 644.

In addition to begin scripts, you can also have finish scripts. A finish script is a user-defined Bourne shell script, specified within the rules file, which performs tasks after the Solaris software is installed on the system, but before the system restarts. Finish scripts can be used only with custom JumpStart installations. You could set up finish scripts to perform the following tasks:

- Moving saved files back into place

- Adding packages or patches
- Setting the system's root password

Output from the finish script goes to /var/sadm/finish.log.

When used for adding patches and software packages, begin and finish scripts can ensure the installation is consistent between all systems.

Creating Profiles

A profile is a text file that defines how to install the Solaris software on a system. Every rule in the rules file specifies a profile that defines how a system is installed when the rule is matched. You usually create a different profile for every rule; however, the same profile can be used in more than one rule.

A profile consists of one or more profile keywords. Their values are described in the section titled "Profile Keywords." Each profile keyword is a command that controls one aspect of how the Solaris installation program installs the Solaris software on a system. Use the vi editor to create a profile in the JumpStart directory. You can create a new profile or edit one of the sample profiles located in /cdrom/cdrom0/s0/Solaris_2.6/Misc on the Solaris CD. The profile can be named anything, but it should reflect the way in which it installs the Solaris software on a system. Example names are: basic_install, eng_profile, or accntg_profile.

A profile must have

- The install_type profile keyword as the first entry
- Only one profile keyword on a line
- The root_device keyword if the systems being upgraded by the profile have more than one root file system that can be upgraded.

A profile allows

- A comment after the pound sign (#) anywhere on a line. If a line begins with a '#', the entire line is a comment line. If a '#' is specified in the middle of a line, everything after the '#' is considered a comment.
- Blank lines.

The profile is made up of profile keywords and their values, which are described in the following sections.

backup_media

backup_media defines the media that is used to back up file systems if they need to be reallocated during an upgrade because of space problems. If multiple tapes or disks are required for the backup, you are prompted to insert these during the upgrade. The backup_media syntax is described as follows.

Syntax: `backup_media <type> <path>`

Where *type* can be one of the following keywords:

local_tape	Specifies a local tape drive on the system being upgraded. The *path* must be the character (raw) device path for the tape drive, such as /dev/rmt/0.
local_diskette	Specifies a local disk drive on the system being upgraded. The *path* is the local disk, such as /dev/rdiskette0. The disk must be formatted.
local_filesystem	Specifies a local file system on the system being upgraded. The *path* can be a block device path for a disk slice or the absolute *path* to a file system mounted by the /etc/vfstab file. Example *paths* are /dev/dsk/c0t0d0s7 or /home.
remote_filesystem	Specifies an NFS file system on a remote system. The *path* must include the name or IP address of the remote system (host) and the absolute *path* to the NFS file system. The NFS file system must have read/write access. An example path could be sparc1:/home.
remote_system	Specifies a directory on a remote system that can be reached by a remote shell (rsh). The system being upgraded must have access to the remote system through the remote system's .rhosts file. The *path* must include the name of the remote system and the absolute path to the directory. If a user login is not specified, the login is tried as root. An example path could be: bcalkins@sparc1:/home.

Examples:

```
backup_media local_tape /dev/rmt/0
backup_media local_diskette /dev/rdiskette0
backup_media local_filesystem /dev/dsk/c0t3d0s7
backup_media local_filesystem /export
backup_media remote_filesystem sparc1:/export/temp
backup_media remote_system bcalkins@sparc1:/export/temp
```

backup_media must be used only with the upgrade option when disk space reallocation is necessary.

boot_device

boot_device designates the device where the installation program installs the root file system and consequently what the system's startup device is. The eeprom value also enables you to update the system's EEPROM if you change its current startup device so that the system can automatically start up from the new startup device.

Syntax: boot_device <*device*> <*eeprom*>

Where

device	Specifies the startup device. *device* specifies a disk slice, such as c0t1d0s0. It can be the keyword "existing," which places the root file system on the existing startup device, or the keyword "any," which lets the installation program choose where to put the root file system.
eeprom	Specifies whether you want to update the system's EEPROM to the specified startup device. *eeprom* specifies the value "update," which tells the installation program to update the system's EEPROM to the specified startup device, or "preserve," which leaves the startup device value in the system's EEPROM unchanged.
	Example: boot_device c0t1d0s0 update

The installation program installs the root file system on c0t1d0s0 and updates the EEPROM to start up automatically from the new startup device.

client_arch

client_arch indicates that the OS server supports a different platform group than its own. If you do not specify client_arch, any diskless client or Solstice AutoClient system that uses the OS server must have the same platform group as the server. client_arch can be used only when system_type is specified as the server. You must specify each platform group that you want the OS server to support.

Syntax: `client_arch karch_value [karch_value...]`

Values for *karch_value* include sun4d, sun4c, sun4m, sun4u, or i86pc.

Example: `client_arch sun4m`

client_root

client_root defines the amount of root space, in MB, to allocate for each client. If you do not specify client_root in a server's profile, the installation software automatically allocates 15MB of root space per client. The size of the client root area is used in combination with the num_clients keyword to determine how much space to reserve for the /export/root file system.

Syntax: `client_root root_size`

root_size is specified in MBs.

Example: `client_root 20`

client_swap

client_swap defines the amount of swap space, in MB, to allocate for each diskless client. If you do not specify client_swap, 32MB of swap space is allocated. Physical memory plus swap space must be a minimum of 32MB. If a profile does not explicitly specify the size of swap, the Solaris installation program determines the maximum size that the swap file can be, based on the system's physical memory. The Solaris installation program makes the size of swap no more than 20 percent of the disk where it resides, unless there is free space left on the disk after laying out the other file systems.

Syntax: `client_swap swap_size`

swap_size is specified in MB.

Example: `client_swap 64`

The example specifies that each diskless client has a swap space of 64MB.

cluster

cluster designates what software group to add to the system. The software groups are

Software Group	group_name
Core	SUNWCreq
End user system support	SUNWCuser
Developer system support	SUNWCprog
Entire distribution	SUNWCall
Entire distribution plus OEM support (SPARC-based systems only)	SUNWCXall

You can specify only one software group in a profile, and it must be specified before other cluster and package entries. If you do not specify a software group with cluster, the end user software group, SUNWCuser, is installed on the system by default.

Syntax: `cluster group_name`

Example: `cluster SUNWCall`

The example specifies the Entire Distribution group to be installed.

The cluster keyword can also be used to designate whether a cluster should be added or deleted from the software group that was installed on the system. add or delete indicates whether the cluster should be added or deleted. If you do not specify add or delete, add is set by default.

Syntax: `cluster cluster_name [add | delete]`

cluster_name must be in the form SUNWCname. To view detailed information about clusters and their names, start AdminTool on an installed system and choose Software from the Browse menu.

dontuse

dontuse designates one or more disks that you don't want the Solaris installation program to use. By default, the installation program uses all the operational disks on the system. *disk_name* must be specified in the form cxtydz or cydz, for example, c0t0d0.

Syntax: `dontuse disk_name [disk_name...]`

Example: `dontuse c0t0d0 c0t1d0`

NOTE. *You cannot specify the usedisk keyword and the dontuse keyword in the same profile.*

filesys

filesys sets up the installed system to mount remote file systems automatically when it starts up. You can specify filesys more than once. The following describes using filesys to setup mounts to remote systems.

Syntax: `filesys <server>:<path> <server_address> <mount_pt_name> [mount_options]`

Where

server:	The name of the server where the remote file system resides. Don't forget to include the colon (:).
path	The remote file system's mount point name.
server_address	The IP address of the server specified in *server:path*. If you don't have a name service running on the network, this value can be used to populate the /etc/hosts file with the server's IP address, you must specify a minus sign (–).
mount_pt_name	The name of the mount point that the remote file system is mounted on.

continues

continued

mount_options	One or more mount options that are added to the /etc/vfstab entry for the specified *mount_pt_name*. If you need to specify more than one mount option, the mount options must be separated by commas and no spaces. For example: ro,quota

Example: `filesys zeus:/export/home/user1 192.9.200.1 /home ro,bg,intr`

filesys can also be used to create local file systems during the installation by following the syntax described as follows.

Syntax: `filesys <slice> <size> [file_system] [optional_parameters]`

The following values can be used for *slice*:

any	This variable tells the installation program to place the file system on any disk.
c?t?d?s? or c?d??z	The disk slice where the Solaris installation program places the file system, for example, c0t0d0s0.
rootdisk.*sn*	The variable that contains the value for the system's root disk, which is determined by the Solaris installation program. The *sn* suffix indicates a specific slice on the disk.

size can be

num	The size of the file system is set to num (in MB).
existing	The current size of the existing file system is used.
auto	The size the file system is automatically determined depending on the selected software.
all	The specified slice uses the entire disk for the file system. When you specify this value, no other file systems can reside on the specified disk.
free	The remaining unused space on the disk is used for the file system.
start:size	The file system is explicitly partitioned: start is the cylinder where the slice begins; size is the number of cylinders for the slice.

file_system is an optional field when slice is specified as 'any' or c?t?d?s?. If *file_system* is not specified, unnamed is set by default, but then you can't specify the optional_parameters value. The value for *file_system* can be one of the following:

mount_pt_name	The file system's mount point name, for example, /opt.
swap	The specified slice is used as swap.

overlap	The specified slice is defined as a representation of the whole disk. *overlap* can be specified only when *size* is *existing*, *all*, or *start:size*.
unnamed	The specified slice is defined as a raw slice, and so the slice does not have a mount point name. If *file_system* is not specified, unnamed is set by default.
ignore	The specified slice is not used or recognized by the Solaris installation program. This can be used to ignore a file system on a disk during an installation so that the Solaris installation program can create a new file system on the same disk with the same name. *ignore* can be used only when existing partitioning is specified.

In the following example, the size of swap is set to 32MB, and it is installed on c0t3d0s1:

```
filesys          c0t3d0s1 32 swap
```

In the next example, /usr is based on the selected software and the installation program determines what disk to put it on when you specify the "any value":

```
filesys          any auto /usr
```

The `optional_parameters` field can be one of the following options:

preserve	The file system on the specified slice is preserved. preserve can be specified only when size is existing and slice is c?t?d?s?.
mount_options	One or more mount options that are added to the /etc/vfstab entry for the specified *mount_pt_name*.

install_type

install_type defines whether to perform the initial installation option or the upgrade option on the system. install_type must be the first profile keyword in every profile.

Syntax: `install_type [initial_install | upgrade]`

Select either initial_install or upgrade.

Example: `install_type initial_install`

layout_constraint

layout_constraint designates the constraint that auto-layout has on a file system if it needs to be reallocated during an upgrade because of space problems. layout_constraint can be used only for the upgrade option when disk space reallocation is required.

With layout_constraint, you'll specify the file system and the constraint you want to put on it.

Syntax: `layout_constraint <slice> <constraint> [minimum_size]`

The *slice* field specifies the file-system disk slice on which to specify the constraint. It must be specified in the form c?t?d?s? or c?d?s?.

What follows describes keywords for the layout_constraint syntax and options.

changeable	Auto-layout can move the file system to another location and can change its size.
	You can change the file system's size by specifying the minimum_size value. When you mark a file system as changeable and minimum_size is not specified, the file system's minimum size is set to 10 percent greater than the minimum size required. For example, if the minimum size for a file system is 100MB, the changed size would be 110MB. If minimum_size is specified, any free space left over (original size minus minimum size) is used for other file systems.
movable	Auto-layout can move the file system to another slice on the same disk or on a different disk, and its size stays the same.
available	Auto-layout can use all the space on the file system to reallocate space. All the data in the file system is then lost. This constraint can only be specified on file systems that are not mounted by the /etc/vfstab file.
collapse	Auto-layout moves (collapses) the specified file system into its parent file system.
	You can use this option to reduce the number of file systems on a system as part of the upgrade. For example, if the system has the /usr and /usr/openwin file systems, collapsing the /usr/openwin file system would move it into /usr (its parent).
minimum_size	This value lets you change the size of a file system by specifying the size that you want it to be after auto-layout reallocates. The size of the file system might end up being more if unallocated space is added to it, but the size is never less than the value you specify. You can use this optional value only if you have marked a file system as changeable. The minimum size cannot be less than the file system needs for its existing contents.

Examples:

```
layout_constraint c0t3d0s1 changeable 200
```

The file system c0t3d0s1 can be moved to another location and its size can be changed to more than 200MB, but no less than 200MB.

```
layout_constraint c0t0d0s4 movable
```

The file system on slice c0t0d0s4 can move to another disk slice, but its size stays the same.

```
layout_constraint c0t2d0s1 collapse
```

c0t2d0s1 is moved into its parent directory to reduce the number of file systems.

locale

locale designates which language or locale packages should be installed for the specified locale_name. A locale determines how online information is displayed for a specific language or region, for example, date, time, spelling, and monetary value. Therefore, if you want English as your language but you also want to use the monetary values for Australia, you would choose the Australia locale value (en_AU) instead of the English language value (C).

The English language packages are installed by default. You can specify a locale keyword for each language or locale you need to add to a system.

Syntax: `locale locale_name`

Example: `locale es`

The example specifies Spanish as the language package that you want installed.

num_clients

When a server is installed, space is allocated for each diskless client's root (/) and swap file systems. num_clients defines the number of diskless clients that a server supports. If you do not specify num_clients, five diskless clients are allocated.

Syntax: `num_clients client_num`

Example: `num_clients 10`

In this example, space is allocated for 10 diskless clients.

package

package designates whether a package should be added to, or deleted from, the software group that is installed on the system. add or delete indicates the action required. If you do not specify add | delete, add is set by default.

Syntax: `package package_name [add | delete]`

`package_name` must be in the form SUNW*name*.

Example: `package SUNWxwman delete`

In this example, SUNWxwman (X Window online man pages) is not installed on the system.

partitioning

partitioning defines how the disks are divided into slices for file systems during the installation. If you do not specify partitioning, the default is set.

Syntax: `partitioning default|existing|explicit`

Where

`default`	The Solaris installation program selects the disks and creates the file systems where the specified software is installed. Except for any file systems specified by the filesys keyword, rootdisk is selected first. Additional disks are used if the specified software does not fit on rootdisk.
`existing`	The Solaris installation program uses the existing file systems on the system's disks. All file systems except /, /usr, /usr/openwin, /opt, and /var are preserved. The installation program uses the last mount point field from the file system superblock to determine which file system mount point the slice represents. When specifying the filesys profile keyword with partitioning, "existing" must be specified.
`explicit`	The Solaris installation program uses the disks and creates the file systems specified by the filesys keywords. If you specify only the root (/) file system with the filesys keyword, all the Solaris software is installed in the root file system. When you use the explicit profile value, you must use the filesys profile keyword to specify which disks to use and what file systems to create.

root_device

root_device designates the system's root disk.

Syntax: `root_device slice`

Example: `root_device c0t3d0s2`

system_type

system_type defines the type of system being installed. If you do not specify *system_type* in a profile, standalone is set by default.

Syntax: `system_type [standalone | server]`

Example: `system_type server`

usedisk

usedisk designates one or more disks that you want the Solaris installation program to use when partitioning default is specified. By default, the installation program uses all the operational disks on the system. disk_name must be specified in the form c?t?d? or c?d?, for example, c0t0d0. If you specify the usedisk profile keyword in a profile, the Solaris installation program only uses the disks that you specify with the usedisk profile keyword.

Syntax: `usedisk disk_name [disk_name]`

Example: `usedisk c0t0d0 c0t1d0`

NOTE. *You cannot specify the usedisk keyword and the dontuse keyword in the same profile.*

Testing Profiles

After you create a profile, you can use the `pfinstall` command to test the profile. Testing a profile is sometimes called a "dry run" installation. By looking at the installation output generated by `pfinstall`, you can quickly determine whether a profile is going to do what you expected. For example, you can determine if a system has enough disk space to upgrade to a new release of Solaris before you actually perform the upgrade on the system.

To test a profile for a particular Solaris release, you must test a profile within the Solaris environment of the same release. For example, if you want to test a profile for Solaris 2.6, you have to run the `pfinstall` command on a system running Solaris 2.6.

To test the profile, change to the JumpStart directory that contains the profile and type:

pfinstall -d

or

pfinstall -D

CAUTION! *Without the* -d *or* -D *option,* pfinstall *performs an actual installation of the Solaris software on the system by using the specified profile, and the data on the system is overwritten.*

The command syntax for the `pfinstall` command is described as follows.

Syntax: /usr/sbin/install.d/pfinstall [-D | -d] *disk_config* [-c *path*] *profile*

Where

-D	Tells `pfinstall` to use the current system's disk configuration to test the profile against.
-d disk_config	Tells `pfinstall` to use a disk configuration file, disk_config, to test the profile against. If disk_config file is not in the directory where `pfinstall` is run, you must specify the path. This option cannot be used with an upgrade profile (install-type upgrade). You must always test an upgrade profile against a system's disk configuration (-D option). A disk configuration file represents a structure of a disk. It describes a disk's bytes/sector, flags, and slices. See the example following the table on how to create the disk_config file.
-c path	Specifies the path to the Solaris CD image. This is required if the Solaris CD is not mounted on /cdrom. For example, use this option if the system is using Volume Management to mount the Solaris CD.

continues

continued

profile   Specifies the name of the profile to test. If profile is not in the directory where `pfinstall` is being run, you must specify the path.

A *disk_config* file can be created by issuing the following command:

```
prtvtoc /dev/rdsk/device_name > disk_config
```

Where: /dev/rdsk/*device_name* is the device name of the system's disk. device_name must be in the form c?t?d?s2 or c?d?s2.

disk_config is the name of the disk configuration file.

Example: `prtvtoc /dev/rdsk/c0t3d0s2 >test`

The file named 'test' created by the previous example would be your disk_config file, and it would look like this:

```
* /dev/rdsk/c0t3d0s2 partition map
*
* Dimensions:
*     512 bytes/sector
*     126 sectors/track
*       4 tracks/cylinder
*     504 sectors/cylinder
*    4106 cylinders
*    4104 accessible cylinders
*
* Flags:
*    1: unmountable
*   10: read-only
*
*                          First     Sector    Last
* Partition   Tag   Flags  Sector    Count     Sector    Mount Directory
       0       2     00         0    268632    268631    /
       1       3     01    268632    193032    461663
       2       5     00         0   2068416   2068415
       3       0     00    461664    152712    614375    /export
       4       0     00    614376    141624    755999    /export/swap
       6       4     00    756000   1312416   2068415    /usr
```

NOTE. *If you want to test installing Solaris software on multiple disks, concatenate single disk configuration files together and save the output to a new file.*

The following example tests the sparc10_prof profile against the disk configuration on a Solaris 2.6 system where `pfinstall` is being run. The sparc10_prof profile is located in the

/jumpstart directory, and the path to the Solaris CD image is specified because Volume Management is being used.

In addition, if you want to test the profile for a system with a specific system memory size, set SYS_MEMSIZE to the specific memory size in MB as follows:

```
SYS_MEMSIZE=memory_size
export SYS_MEMSIZE
cd /jumpstart
/usr/sbin/install.d/pfinstall -D -c /cdrom/cdrom0/s0 sparc10_prof
```

The system tests the profile and displays several pages of results. Look for the following message that indicates that the test was successful:

```
Installation complete
Test run complete. Exit status 0.
```

Setting Up Clients

Now you need to set up the clients to install over the network. After setting up the /jumpstart directory and appropriate files, use the `add_install_client` command on the install server to set up remote workstations to install Solaris from the install server. The steps are as follows:

```
cd /export/install/sparc_2.6/Solaris_2.6/Tools
./add_install_client -c <servername>:/jumpstart <clientname> sun4m
```

Syntax: add install client [options]

Where

servername	The name of the installation server
clientname	The hostname for each workstation
-c	Specifies the server (servername) and path (/jumpstart) to the JumpStart directory
sun4m	Specifies the platform group of the systems that uses *servername* as an install server

For additional options to the `add_install_client` command, see the Solaris online manual pages.

Example JumpStart Installation

The following example shows how you would set up a custom JumpStart installation for a fictitious site. The network consists of an Enterprise 3000 server and five Sparc10 workstations.

Set Up the Installation Server

The first step is to set up the installation server. You'll choose the enterprise server. This is where the contents of the Solaris CD are located. The contents of the CD can be made available by either loading the CD in the CD-ROM drive or copying the CD to the server's local hard drive. For this example, you are copying the files to the local hard drive. Use the setup_install_server command to copy the contents of the Solaris CD to the server's local disk. Files are copied to the /export/install directory. Follow these steps to create the install server:

1. Insert the Solaris CD into the server's CD-ROM drive

2. Type:

   ```
   cd /CD_mount_point/Solaris_2.6/Tools
   ./setup_install_server /export/install/sparc_2.6
   ```

Create the JumpStart Directory

After you've installed the install server, you'll need to set up a JumpStart directory on the server. This directory holds files necessary for a custom JumpStart installation of Solaris software. You set up this directory by copying the sample directory from one of the Solaris CD images that has been put in /export/install. Do this by typing the following:

```
mkdir /jumpstart
cp -r /export/install/sparc_2.6/Solaris_2.6/Misc/jumpstart_sample /jumpstart
```

Any directory name can be used. You'll use /jumpstart for this example.

Setting Up a Profile Server

The next step is to set up a profile server. Follow these steps:

1. Log in as root on the server where you want the JumpStart directory to reside.

2. Edit the /etc/dfs/dfstab file. Add the following entry:
   ```
   share -F nfs -o ro,anon=0 /jumpstart
   ```

3. Type `shareall` and press Return. This makes the contents of the /jumpstart directory accessible to systems on the network.

4. Add the profile and rules files to the JumpStart directory. You can copy example custom JumpStart files from the directory containing the Solaris CD image. These files are located in /export/install/sparc_2.6/Solaris_2.6/Misc. These are only sample files, and they must be modified for your installation. To copy them into the /jumpstart directory, type:

```
cd /export/install/sparc_2.6/ Solaris_2.6/Misc
cp -r jumpstart_sample/* /jumpstart
```

For this example, the profile is named engrg_prof and looks like this:

```
#Specifies that the installation will be treated as an initial
#installation, as opposed to an upgrade.
install_type initial_install
#Specifies that the engineering systems are standalone systems.
system_type standalone
#Specifies that the JumpStart software uses default disk
#partitioning for installing Solaris software on the engineering
#systems.
partitioning default
#Specifies that the developer's software group will be
#installed.cluster
SUNWCprog
#Specifies that each system in the engineering group will have 50
#Mbytes of swap space.
filesys any 50 swap
```

The rules file looks like the following code:

```
network 192.9.200.0 - engrg_prof -
```

This rules file states that systems on the 192.9.200.0 network is installed using the engrg_prof profile.

Validate the rules and profile files as follows:

```
cd /jumpstart
./check
```

If `check` doesn't find any errors, it creates the rules.ok file. You are finished creating the profile server.

Set Up Clients

Now, on the install server, set up each client as follows:

```
cd /export/install/sparc_2.6/Solaris_2.6/Tools
./add_install_client -c sparcserver:/jumpstart sparc1 sun4m
./add_install_client -c sparcserver:/jumpstart sparc2 sun4m
```

The previous example sets up two engineering workstations, sparc1 and sparc2, so that they can be installed over the network from the install server named "sparcserver".

Start Up the Clients

After the setup is complete, you can start up the engineering systems by using the following startup command at the ok (PROM) prompt of each system:

```
boot net - install
```

The client reads the rules.ok and profile files on the server. You are then asked to input the time zone, name service, subnet, and date and time information. The system then automatically installs the Solaris operating environment.

This completes the JumpStart configuration.

CHAPTER 3

The Boot Process

The following test objectives are covered in this chapter:

- The OpenBoot environment
- The boot process
- Device names
- The EEPROM
- The kernel

Part 1 of *The Solaris 2.6 Administrator Certification Training Guide* provided a general overview of the startup process, including specifics on /sbin/init, run levels, and run control scripts. You might want to review Part I before proceeding. Also, see Figure 3-1 for a review of the default startup sequence. This chapter will provide more details on those topics, specifically OpenBoot and kernel loading.

Figure 3-1
Default startup sequence.

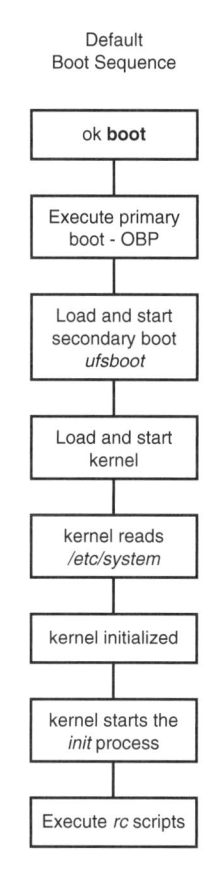

Default Boot Sequence

```
ok boot
   │
Execute primary
boot - OBP
   │
Load and start
secondary boot
   ufsboot
   │
Load and start
kernel
   │
kernel reads
/etc/system
   │
kernel initialized
   │
kernel starts the
init process
   │
Execute rc scripts
```

Power On

Before powering on the system, make sure that all your connections are secure. Check the SCSI cables that connect your external disk drives, tape drives, and CD-ROM to the system to make sure they are properly connected. Check your network connection. Also, make sure that the keyboard and monitor are connected properly. Loose cables can cause your system to fail the startup process.

CAUTION! *Always connect your cables* before *turning on the hardware, or you could damage your system.*

The correct sequence for powering on your equipment is to first turn on all your peripherals, such as external disk drives, tapes drives, and CD-ROM. Turn on power to the monitor, and finally, turn on power to the system.

OpenBoot

The hardware-level user interface that you see before the operating system has been started is called the OpenBoot PROM (OBP). OpenBoot is based on an interactive command interpreter that gives you access to an extensive set of functions for hardware and software development, fault isolation, and debugging. The OBP firmware is stored in the socketed startup PROM (Programmable Read-Only Memory). The OpenBoot PROM consists of two chips on each system board; the startup PROM itself, which contains extensive firmware allowing access to user-written startup drivers and extended diagnostics; and a NVRAM (Nonvolatile Random Access Memory) chip.

The NVRAM chip has user-definable system parameters and writable areas for user-controlled diagnostics, macros, and device aliases. The NVRAM is where the system identification information is stored, such as the hostid. Many software packages use this hostid for licensing purposes; therefore, it is important that this chip be removed and replaced into any replacement system board.

OpenBoot is currently at version 3, which is the version I describe in this chapter. Depending on the age of your system, you could have OpenBoot version 1, 2, or 3 installed.

You can get to the OpenBoot environment in the following ways:

- By halting the operating system.
- By pressing the Stop and A keys simultaneously.
- When the system is initially powered on. If your system is not configured to start up automatically, it will stop at the user interface. If automatic starting up is configured, you can make the system stop at the user interface by pressing the Stop and A keys from the keyboard after the display console banner is displayed, but before the system begins starting up the operating system.
- If the system hardware detects an error from which it cannot recover (this is known as a Watchdog Reset).

CAUTION! *Using the Stop+A key sequence abruptly breaks execution of the operating system, and it should be used only as a last effort to restart the system.*

The primary tasks of the OpenBoot firmware are to

- Test and initialize the system hardware.
- Determine the hardware configuration.
- Start up the operating system from either a mass storage device or from a network.
- Provide interactive debugging facilities for testing hardware and software.
- Allow modification and management of system start-up configuration, such as NVRAM parameters.

Specifically, OpenBoot will perform the tasks necessary to initialize the operating system kernel, which include the following:

1. Display system identification information and then run self-test diagnostics to verify the system's hardware and memory. These checks are known as POST (Power On Self Test).
2. Load the primary startup program, bootblk, from the default startup device.
3. The bootblk program finds and executes the secondary startup program, ufsboot, and loads it into memory.
4. The ufsboot program loads the operating system kernel.

The OpenBoot architecture provides an increase in functionality and portability as compared with the proprietary systems of some other hardware vendors. Although this architecture was first implemented by Sun Microsystems as OpenBoot on SPARC (Scaleable Processor Architecture) systems, its design is processor-independent. Some notable features of OpenBoot firmware include:

- *Plug-in device drivers*—A device driver that can be loaded from a plug-in device, such as an SBus card. This feature enables the input and output devices to evolve without changing the system PROM.
- *FCode interpreter*—Plug-in drivers are written in a machine-independent interpreted language called FCode. Each OpenBoot system PROM contains an FCode interpreter. This allows the same device and driver to be used on machines with different CPU instruction sets.
- *Device tree*—Devices, called nodes, are attached to a host computer through a hierarchy of interconnected buses on the device tree. A node representing the host computer's main physical address bus forms the tree's root node. Both the user and the operating system can determine the hardware configuration of the system by viewing the device tree.

Nodes with children usually represent buses and their associated controllers, if any. Each such node defines a physical address space that distinguishes the devices connected to the node from one another. Each child of that node is assigned a physical address in the parent's address space. The physical address generally represents a physical characteristic unique to the device (such as the bus address or the slot number where the device is installed). The use of physical addresses to identify devices prevents device addresses from changing when other devices are installed or removed.

- *Programmable user interface*—The OpenBoot User Interface is based on the interactive programming language Forth. Forth provides an interactive programming environment and is a language that's used for direct communication between human beings and machines. It can be quickly expanded and adapted to special needs and different hardware systems. You'll see Forth used not only by Sun, but also other hardware vendors, such as Hewlett-Packard.

Refer to ANSI X3.215-1994 (American National Standard for Information Systems) if you're interested in more information on Forth.

At any time you can obtain help on the various Forth commands supported in OpenBoot by using the `help` command. The syntax for using help from the `ok` prompt is any of the choices below:

help	List main help categories.
help *category*	Show help for all commands in the *category*. Use only the first word of the category description.
help *command*	Show help for an individual *command* (where available).

The following example shows the `help` command with no arguments:

```
ok help
```

The system responds with:

```
Enter 'help command-name' or 'help category-name' for more help
(Use ONLY the first word of a category description)
Examples: help select   -or-   help line
     Main categories are:
File download and boot
Resume execution
Diag (diagnostic routines)
Power on reset
>-prompt
Floppy eject
Select I/O devices
Ethernet
System and boot configuration parameters
Line editor
```

```
Tools (memory,numbers,new commands,loops)
Assembly debugging (breakpoints,registers,disassembly,symbolic)
Sync (synchronize disk data)
Nvramrc (making new commands permanent)
```

This example shows the use of the `help` command with a *category* argument:

```
ok help diag
    Category: Diag (diagnostic routines)
test    device-specifier ( -- ) run selftest method for specified device
    Examples:
        test /iommu/sbus/ledma@f,400010/le     - test net
        test net           - test net  (device-specifier is an alias)
        test scsi          - test scsi (device-specifier is an alias)
        test floppy        - test floppy disk drive
watch-clock         ( -- )  - show ticks of real-time clock
watch-net           ( -- )  - monitor broadcast packets using auto-selected interface
watch-aui           ( -- )  - monitor broadcast packets using AUI interface
watch-tpe           ( -- )  - monitor broadcast packets using TPE interface
watch-net-all       ( -- )  - monitor broadcast packets on all net interfaces
probe-scsi          ( -- )  - show attached SCSI devices
probe-scsi-all      ( -- )  - show attached SCSI devices for all host adapters
test-all            ( -- )  - execute test for all devices with selftest method
test-memory         ( -- )  - test all memory if diag-switch? is true, otherwise test
➥memory specified by selftest-#megs
```

Device Names

OpenBoot deals directly with hardware devices in the system. Each device has a unique name representing both the type of device and the location of that device in the system addressing structure. The following example shows a full device pathname:

`/sbus@1f,0/esp@0,40000/sd@3,0:a`

A full device pathname is a series of node names separated by slashes (/). The root of the tree is the machine node, which is not named explicitly but is indicated by a leading slash (/). Each device pathname has the form:

driver-name@unit-address:device-arguments

The components of the device pathname are described in Table 3-1.

Table 3-1   Device Pathname Parameters

Parameter	Description
driver-name	A human-readable string consisting of one to 31 letters, digits, and the following punctuation characters: , . _ + - Uppercase and lowercase characters are distinct. In some cases, the driver name includes the name of the device's manufacturer and the device's model name, separated by a comma. Typically, the manufacturer's uppercase, publicly listed stock symbol is used as the manufacturer's name (that is, SUNW,sd). For built-in devices, the manufacturer's name is usually omitted (that is, sbus). @ must precede the address parameter and serves as a separator between the driver name and unit address.
unit-address	A text string representing the physical address of the device in its parent's address space. The exact meaning of a particular address depends on the bus to which the device is attached. In the previous example: /sbus@1f,0/esp@0,40000/sd@3,0:a 1f,0 represents an address on the main system bus, because the SBus is directly attached to the main system bus in this example. 0,40000 is an SBus slot number. The example shows that the device is in SBus slot 0 and the offset is 40000. 3,0 is a SCSI target and logical unit number. In the example, the disk device is attached to a SCSI bus at target 3, logical unit 0.
device-arguments	A text string, whose format depends on the particular device. It can be used to pass additional information to the device's software. In the example: /sbus@1f,0/scsi@2,1/sd@3,0:a the argument for the disk device is "a". The software driver for this device interprets its argument as a disk partition, so the device pathname refers to partition "a" on that disk.

The OpenBoot command, show-devs, is used to obtain information about devices and to display device pathnames. This command displays all the devices known to the system directly beneath a given device in the device hierarchy. show-devs used by itself shows the entire device tree.

The syntax is: show-devs [*device path*]

Example:

```
ok show-devs
```

The system outputs the following information:

```
/TI,TMS390Z50@f,f8fffffc
/eccmemctl@f,0
/virtual-memory@0,0
/memory@0,0
/obio
/iommu@f,e0000000
/openprom
/aliases
/options
/packages
/obio/power@0,a01000
/obio/auxio@0,800000
/obio/SUNW,fdtwo@0,700000
/obio/interrupt@0,400000
/obio/counter@0,300000
/obio/eeprom@0,200000
/obio/zs@0,0
/obio/zs@0,100000
/iommu@f,e0000000/sbus@f,e0001000
/iommu@f,e0000000/sbus@f,e0001000/cgsix@2,0
/iommu@f,e0000000/sbus@f,e0001000/SUNW,DBRIe@f,8010000
/iommu@f,e0000000/sbus@f,e0001000/SUNW,bpp@f,4800000
/iommu@f,e0000000/sbus@f,e0001000/ledma@f,400010
/iommu@f,e0000000/sbus@f,e0001000/espdma@f,400000
/iommu@f,e0000000/sbus@f,e0001000/SUNW,DBRIe@f,8010000/mmcodec
/iommu@f,e0000000/sbus@f,e0001000/ledma@f,400010/le@f,c00000
/iommu@f,e0000000/sbus@f,e0001000/espdma@f,400000/esp@f,800000
/iommu@f,e0000000/sbus@f,e0001000/espdma@f,400000/esp@f,800000/st
/iommu@f,e0000000/sbus@f,e0001000/espdma@f,400000/esp@f,800000/sd
/packages/obp-tftp
/packages/deblocker
/packages/disk-label
```

Commands used to examine the device tree are listed in Table 3-2.

Table 3-2 Commands for Browsing the Device Tree

Command	Description
.properties	Display the names and values of the current node's properties.
dev device-path	Choose the specified device node, making it the current node.
dev node-name	Search for a node with the specified name in the sub-tree below the current node, and choose the first such node found.
dev ..	Choose the device node that is the parent of the current node.

continues

Table 3-2 Commands for Browsing the Device Tree (continued)

Command	Description
dev /	Choose the root machine node.
device-end	Leave the device tree.
"*device-path*" find-device	Choose the specified device node, similar to dev.
ls	Display the names of the current node's children.
pwd	Display the device pathname that names the current node.
see *wordname*	De-compile the specified word.
show-devs [*device-path*]	Display all the devices known to the system directly beneath a given device in the device hierarchy. show-devs used by itself shows the entire device tree.
words	Display the names of the current node's methods.
"device-path" select-dev	Select the specified device and make it the active node.

OpenBoot Device Aliases

Device pathnames can be long and complex to enter. The concept of device aliases, like the UNIX alias, allows a short name to be substituted for a long name. For example, an alias called disk0 can be used to represent the device pathname /sbus@1f,0/esp@0,40000/sd@3,0. Systems usually have predefined device aliases for the most commonly used devices, so you rarely need to type a full device pathname. However, if you add disk drives or change the target of the startup drive you may need to modify these device aliases. The following table describes the devalias command, which is used to examine, create, and change OpenBoot aliases.

devalias	Display all current device aliases.
devalias *alias*	Display the device pathname corresponding to *alias*.
devalias *alias device-path*	Define an *alias* representing *device-path*.

NOTE. *If an alias with the same name already exists, the new value overwrites the old.*

The following example creates a device alias named disk3, which represents a SCSI disk with a target ID of 3 on a sparc10 system:

```
devalias disk3 /iommu/sbus/espdma@f,400000/esp@f,800000/sd@3,0
```

To confirm the alias, type `devalias` and the system will print out all the aliases:

```
ok devalias
screen      /iommu@f,e0000000/sbus@f,e0001000/cgsix@2,0
disk5       /iommu/sbus/espdma@f,400000/esp@f,800000/sd@0,0
floppy      /obio/SUNW,fdtwo
scsi        /iommu/sbus/espdma@f,400000/esp@f,800000
net-aui     /iommu/sbus/ledma@f,400010:aui/le@f,c00000
net-tpe     /iommu/sbus/ledma@f,400010:tpe/le@f,c00000
net         /iommu/sbus/ledma@f,400010/le@f,c00000
disk        /iommu/sbus/espdma@f,400000/esp@f,800000/sd@3,0
cdrom       /iommu/sbus/espdma@f,400000/esp@f,800000/sd@6,0:d
tape        /iommu/sbus/espdma@f,400000/esp@f,800000/st@4,0
tape0       /iommu/sbus/espdma@f,400000/esp@f,800000/st@4,0
tape1       /iommu/sbus/espdma@f,400000/esp@f,800000/st@5,0
disk3       /iommu/sbus/espdma@f,400000/esp@f,800000/sd@3,0
disk2       /iommu/sbus/espdma@f,400000/esp@f,800000/sd@2,0
disk1       /iommu/sbus/espdma@f,400000/esp@f,800000/sd@1,0
disk0       /iommu/sbus/espdma@f,400000/esp@f,800000/sd@3,0
ttyb        /obio/zs@0,100000:b
ttya        /obio/zs@0,100000:a
keyboard!   /obio/zs@0,0:forcemode
keyboard    /obio/zs@0,0
```

User-defined aliases are lost after a system reset or power cycle, unless you create a permanent alias. If you want to create permanent aliases, you can either manually store the `devalias` command in a portion of non-volatile RAM (NVRAM) called nvramrc or use the `nvalias` and `nvunalias` commands. The following section describes how to configure permanent settings in the NVRAM on a Sun system.

OpenBoot Non-Volatile RAM (NVRAM)

System configuration variables are stored in the system NVRAM. These OpenBoot variables determine the startup machine configuration and related communication characteristics. You can modify the values of the configuration variables, and any changes you make remain in effect even after a power cycle. Configuration variables should be adjusted cautiously, however. Table 3-3 describes OpenBoot's NVRAM configuration variables, their default values, and a brief description of their function.

Table 3-3   NVRAM Variables

Variable	Default	Description
auto-boot?	true	If true, start up automatically after power on or reset.
boot-command	boot	Command that is executed if auto-boot? is true.
boot-device	disk or net	Device from which to start up.

continues

Table 3-3 NVRAM Variables (continued)

Variable	Default	Description
boot-file	empty string	Arguments passed to started program.
diag-device	net	Diagnostic startup source device.
diag-file	empty string	Arguments passed to startup program in diagnostic mode.
diag-switch?	false	If true, run in diagnostic mode.
fcode-debug?	false	If true, include name fields for plug-in device FCodes.
input-device	keyboard	Console input device (usually keyboard, ttya, or ttyb).
nvramrc	empty	Contents of NVRAMRC.
oem-banner	empty string	Custom OEM banner (enabled by oem-banner? true).
oem-banner?	false	If true, use custom OEM banner.
oem-logo	no default	Byte array custom OEM logo (enabled by oem-logo? true). Displayed in hexadecimal.
oem-logo?	false	If true, use custom OEM logo (else, use Sun logo).
output-device	screen	Console output device (usually screen, ttya, or ttyb).
screen-#columns	80	Number of on-screen columns (characters/line).
screen-#rows	34	Number of on-screen rows (lines).
security-#badlogins	no default	Number of incorrect security password attempts.
security-mode	none	Firmware security level (options: none, command, or full).
security-password	no default	Firmware security password (never displayed).
use-nvramrc?	false	If true, execute commands in NVRAMRC during system startup.
sbus-probe-list	0123	Which SBus slots to probe and in what order.

NOTE. Older SPARC systems, because they use older versions of OpenBoot, might use different defaults and/or different configuration variables. As mentioned earlier, this text describes OpenBoot version 3.

The NVRAM configuration variables can be viewed and changed using the commands listed in Table 3-4.

Table 3-4 Viewing or Modifying Configuration Variables

Command	Description
printenv	Displays the variable, the current value, and the default value to show the current value of the named variable, type: printenv *variable*
setenv *variable value*	Set variable to the given decimal or text value. Changes are permanent, but often take effect only after a reset.
set-default *variable*	Reset the value of variable to the factory default.
set-defaults	Reset variable values to the factory defaults.
password	Set security-password.

The following examples illustrate the use of the commands described in Table 3-4.

All commands are entered at the ok OpenBoot prompt.

```
ok printenv
```

The system responds with:

Parameter Name	Value	Default Value
tpe-link-test?	true	true
output-device	screen	screen
input-device	keyboard	keyboard
sbus-probe-list	f0123	f0123
keyboard-click?	false	false
keymap		
ttyb-rts-dtr-off	false	false
ttyb-ignore-cd	true	true
ttya-rts-dtr-off	false	false
ttya-ignore-cd	true	true
ttyb-mode	9600,8,n,1,-	9600,8,n,1,-
ttya-mode	9600,8,n,1,-	9600,8,n,1,-
fcode-debug?	false	false
diag-file		
diag-device	net	net
boot-file		
boot-device	disk5	disk
auto-boot?	true	true
watchdog-reboot?	false	false
local-mac-address?	false	false
screen-#columns	80	80
screen-#rows	34	34
selftest-#megs	1	1
scsi-initiator-id	7	7
use-nvramrc?	true	false
nvramrc	devalias	disk5 /iommu/sbus/espdma@f, 400000/esp@f,800000/sd@0,0

continues

Parameter Name	Value	Default Value *(continued)*
sunmon-compat?	false	false
security-mode	none	none
security-password		
security-#badlogins	0	<no default>
oem-logo		<no default>
oem-logo?	false	false
oem-banner		<no default>
oem-banner?	false	false
hardware-revision		<no default>
last-hardware-update		<no default>
testarea	0	0
mfg-switch?	false	false
diag-switch?	false	false
ok		

To set the auto-boot? variable to false, type:

`ok setenv auto-boot? false`

Verify the setting by typing:

`ok printenv auto-boot?`

The system will respond with:

`auto-boot?     false     true`

To reset the variable back to its default setting, type:

`ok set-default auto-boot?`

Verify the setting by typing:

`ok printenv auto-boot?`

The system will respond with:

`auto-boot?     true     true`

To reset all variables to their default settings, type:

`ok set-defaults`

It's also possible to set these variables from the UNIX command line by issuing the `eeprom` command. You must be logged in as root to issue these commands. For example, to set the auto-boot? variable to true, type the following at the UNIX prompt:

`eeprom auto-boot?=true`

You can also view the OpenBoot configuration variables from a UNIX prompt by typing

`/usr/sbin/eeprom`

With no parameters, the system will display all the OpenBoot configuration settings, similar to the OpenBoot `printenv` command.

NOTE. *If you change an NVRAM setting on a SPARC system and the system will no longer start up, it is possible to reset the NVRAM variables to their default settings by holding down the Stop and N keys while the machine is powering up. When issuing this command, hold down Stop+N immediately after turning on the power to the SPARC system; keep it pressed for a few seconds or until you see the banner, if the display is available. This is a good technique to force a system's NVRAM variables to a known condition.*

The following NVRAM commands can be used to modify devaliases so that they remain permanent, even after a restart:

`nvalias alias device-path`	Store the command devalias *alias device-path* in NVRAMRC. (The alias persists until the nvunalias or set-defaults commands are executed.) Turns on use-nvramrc?
`nvunalias alias`	Delete the corresponding alias from NVRAMRC.

For example, to permanently create a devalias named disk3, which will represent a SCSI disk with a target ID of 3 on a sparc10 system, type the following:

`nvalias disk3 /iommu/sbus/espdma@f,400000/esp@f,800000/sd@3,0`

OpenBoot Security

Anyone that has access to the computer keyboard can access OpenBoot unless you set up your security variables. These variables are:

security-mode	security-mode can restrict the set of operations that users are allowed to perform at the OpenBoot prompt.
security-password	Firmware security password (never displayed). Do not set this variable directly. This variable is set using `password`.
security-#badlogins	Number of incorrect security password attempts.

CAUTION! *It is important to remember your security password and to set the security password before setting the security mode. If you forget this password, you cannot use your system; you must call your vendor's customer support service to make your machine bootable again.*

To set the security-password, type the following at the `ok` prompt:

```
ok password
ok New password (only first 8 chars are used): <enter password>
ok Retype new password: <enter passwd>
```

The security password you assign must be between zero and eight characters. Any characters after the eighth are ignored. You do not have to reset the system; the security feature takes effect as soon as you type the command.

After assigning a password, you can set the security variables that best fit your environment.

security-mode is used to restrict the use of OpenBoot commands. By assigning one of the following three values, access to commands is protected by a password. The syntax for setting security-mode is:

```
setenv security-mode <value>
```

The *value* that you enter for security-mode is one of three values:

full	All OpenBoot commands except go require a password. This security mode is the most restrictive.
command	All OpenBoot commands except boot and go require the password.
none	No password required (default).

The following example sets the OpenBoot environment so that all commands, except `boot` and `go`, require a password:

```
setenv security-mode command
```

With security-mode set to command, a password is not required if you type the `boot` command by itself or the `go` command. Any other command will require a password, including the use of the `boot` command with an argument.

Here are examples of when a password might be required when security-mode is set to command:

`ok boot`	(no password required)
`ok go`	(no password required)
`ok boot vmunix`	(password required)
`Password:`	(password is not echoed as it is typed)
`ok reset-all`	(password required)
`Password:`	(password is not echoed as it is typed)

If you enter an incorrect security password, there will be a delay of about 10 seconds before the next startup prompt appears. The number of times that an incorrect security password can be typed is stored in the security-#badlogins variable. The syntax is as follows:

```
security-#badlogins <variable>
```

For example, you can set the number of attempts to four with the following command:

```
security-#badlogins 4
```

OpenBoot Diagnostics

Various hardware diagnostics can be run in OpenBoot. These can be used to troubleshoot hardware and network problems. The diagnostic commands and a brief description are listed in Table 3-5.

Table 3-5   OpenBoot Diagnostics

Command	Description
probe-scsi	Identify devices attached to a SCSI bus.
test *device-specifier*	Execute the specified device's self-test method. For example: test floppy will test the floppy drive, if installed. test net will test the network connection.
test-all [*device-specifier*]	Test all devices that have a built-in self-test method below the specified device tree node. If *device-specifier* is absent, all devices beginning from the root node are tested.
watch-clock	Test the clock function.
watch-net	Monitor the network connection.

The following examples use some of the diagnostic features of OpenBoot. The first example uses probe-scsi to identify all the SCSI devices attached to a particular SCSI bus. This command is useful for identifying SCSI target ID's that are already in use, or to check to make sure all devices are connected and identified by the system.

```
ok probe-scsi
```

The system will respond with:

```
Target 1
        Unit 0    Disk    SEAGATE ST1120N 833400093849
                          Copyright ©     1992 Seagate
                          All rights reserved 0000
Target 3
        Unit 0    Disk    MAXTOR LXT-213S SUN2074.20
```

This next example will test the system video and perform various other tests.

```
ok test all
```

To test the diskette drive to determine whether or not it is functioning properly, put a formatted, high-density diskette in the drive and type:

```
ok test floppy
```

The system should respond:

```
Testing floppy disk system. A formatted disk should be in the drive.
Test succeeded.
```

Type `eject-floppy` to remove the diskette.

Table 3-6 describes other OpenBoot commands that you can use to gather information about the system.

Table 3-6   System Information Commands

Command	Description
banner	Display power-on banner.
show-sbus	Display list of installed and probed SBus devices.
.enet-addr	Display current Ethernet address.
.idprom	Display ID PROM contents, formatted.
.traps	Display a list of SPARC trap types.
.version	Display version and date of the startup PROM.
.speed	Display CPU and bus speeds.
show-devs	Display all installed and probed devices.

The following example uses the `banner` command to display the CPU type, the ethernet address, and the version and date of the startup PROM:

```
ok banner
```

The system responds with:

```
SPARCstation 10 (1 X 390Z50), No Keyboard
ROM Rev. 2.10, 64 MB memory installed, Serial #3151780
Ethernet address 8:0:20:1a:c7:e3, Host ID: 723017a4
```

This next example uses the .version command to display the version and date of the startup PROM.

Type:

`ok .version`

The system responds with:

`Release 2.15 Version 7 created 94/01/28 11:43:46`

The preceding example shows how to use the .enet-addr command to display the Ethernet address:

`0k .enet-addr`

The system responds with:

`8:0:20:1a:c7:e3`

Input and Output Control

The console is used as the primary means of communication between OpenBoot and the user. The console consists of an input device used for receiving information supplied by the user and an output device used for sending information to the user. Typically, the console is either the combination of a text/graphics display device and a keyboard or an ASCII terminal connected to a serial port.

The configuration variables related to the control of the console are:

input-device	Console input device (usually keyboard, ttya, or ttyb).
output-device	Console output device (usually screen, ttya, or ttyb).
screen-#columns	Number of on-screen columns (default=80 characters per line).
screen-#rows	Number of on-screen rows (default = 34 lines).

You can use these variables to assign the power-on defaults for the console. These values do not take effect until after the next power cycle or system reset.

If you select keyboard for input-device, and the device is not plugged in, input is accepted from the ttya port as a fallback device. If the system is powered on and the keyboard is not detected, the system will look to ttya, the serial port, for the system console.

The communication parameters on the serial port can be defined by setting the configuration variables for that port. These variables are:

Variable	Current Value	Default Value
ttyb-rts-dtr-off	false	false
ttyb-ignore-cd	true	true

continues

Variable	Current Value	Default Value (continued)
ttya-rts-dtr-off	false	false
ttya-ignore-cd	true	true
ttyb-mode	9600,8,n,1,-	9600,8,n,1,-
ttya-mode	9600,8,n,1,-	9600,8,n,1,-

Values for ttya-mode from left to right are:

Baud rate: 110, 300, 1200, 4800, 9600, 19200

Data bits: 5, 6, 7, 8

Parity: n (none), e (even), o (odd), m (mark), s (space)

Stop bits: 1, 1.5, 2

Handshake: -(none), h (hardware:rts/cts), s (software:xon/xoff)

boot

The primary function of the OpenBoot firmware is to start up the system. Starting up is the process of loading and executing a stand-alone program. An example of a stand-alone program is the operating system or the diagnostic monitor. In this discussion, the stand-alone program is the operating system kernel. After the kernel is loaded, it starts the UNIX system, mounts the necessary file systems and runs /sbin/init to bring the system to the "initdefault" state specified in /etc/inittab. This process was discussed in Part I of *Solaris 2.6 Administrator Certification Training Guide*.

Starting up can be initiated either automatically or by typing a command at the user interface, and it is commonly referred to as the bootstrap procedure. On most SPARC-based systems, the bootstrap procedure consists of the following basic phases:

1. The system hardware is powered on.

2. The system firmware (the PROM) executes power-on self-test (POST). The form and scope of these tests depends on the version of the firmware in your system.

3. After the tests have been completed successfully, the firmware attempts to autoboot if the appropriate OpenBoot configuration variable (auto-boot?) has been set.

The OpenBoot startup process is outlined in Figure 3-2.

Figure 3-2
OpenBoot startup process.

[Flowchart: OpenBoot startup process]

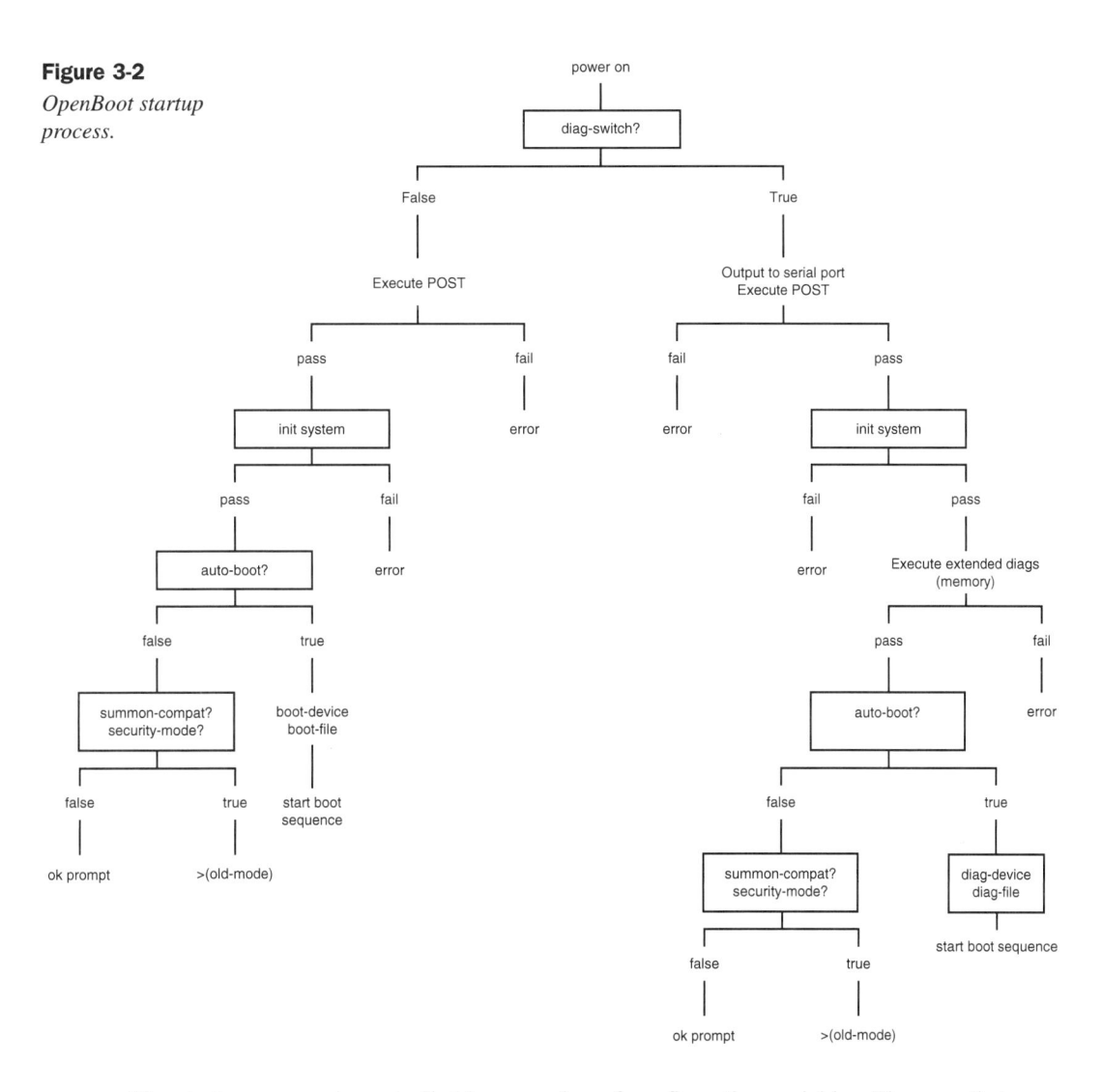

power on → diag-switch?

False branch:
- Execute POST
  - fail → error
  - pass → init system
    - fail → error
    - pass → auto-boot?
      - false → summon-compat? security-mode?
        - false → ok prompt
        - true → >(old-mode)
      - true → boot-device / boot-file → start boot sequence

True branch:
- Output to serial port, Execute POST
  - fail → error
  - pass → init system
    - fail → error
    - pass → Execute extended diags (memory)
      - fail → error
      - pass → auto-boot?
        - false → summon-compat? security-mode?
          - false → ok prompt
          - true → >(old-mode)
        - true → diag-device / diag-file → start boot sequence

The startup process is controlled by a number of configuration variables. The ones that affect the startup process are described in Table 3-7.

Table 3-7 Boot Configuration Variables

Variable	Description
auto-boot?	Controls whether the system automatically starts up after a system reset or when the power is turned on. The default for this variable is true. When the system is powered on, the system automatically starts up to the default run level.
boot-command	Specifies the command to be executed when auto-boot? is true. The default value of boot-command is boot with no command-line arguments.
diag-switch?	If the value is true, run in the diagnostic mode. This variable is false by default.
boot-device	Contains the name of the default startup device that is used when OpenBoot is not in diagnostic mode.
boot-file	Contains the default startup arguments that are used when OpenBoot is not in diagnostic mode. The default is no arguments. See Table 3-8 for details on when this variable is used.
diag-device	Contains the name of the default diagnostic mode startup device. The default is "net". See Table 3-8 for details on when this variable is used.
diag-file	Contains the default diagnostic mode startup arguments. The default is no arguments. See Table 3-8 for details on when this variable is used.

Typically, auto-boot? will be true, boot-command will be boot, and OpenBoot will not be in diagnostic mode. Consequently, the system will automatically load and execute the program and arguments described by boot-file from the device described by boot-device when the system is first turned on or following a system reset. The boot command and its options are described in Table 3-8.

boot has the following syntax:

```
boot [OBP name] [filename] [options] [flags]
```

[OBP name], [filename], [options], and [flags] are optional.

Table 3-8 boot Command

Option	Description
OBP name	Specify the OpenBoot PROM designations. For example, on Desktop SPARC-based systems, the designation /sbus/esp@0,800000/sd@3,0:a indicates a SCSI disk (sd) at target 3, lun0 on the SCSI bus, with the esp host adapter plugged into slot 0. This OBP name can be a devalias, such as disk0 (floppy 3-1/2" diskette drive), net (Ethernet), or tape (SCSI tape). If OBP name is not specified and if diagnostic-mode? returns true, then boot uses the device specified by the diag-device configuration variable.

Option	Description
filename	The name of the standalone program to be started up (for example, kernel/unix). The default is to start up /platform/platform-name/kernel/unix from the root partition. If specified, *filename* is relative to the root of the selected device and partition. If not, the boot program uses the value of the boot-file or diag-file based on the diag-switch? parameter.
options	-a
	The startup program interprets this flag to mean ask me, and so it prompts for the name of the standalone program to load.
	-f
	When starting an Autoclient system, this option forces the boot program to bypass the client's local cache and read all files over the network from the client's file server. This option is ignored for all non-Autoclient systems. The -f option is then passed to the standalone program.
	-r
	Triggers device reconfiguration during startup. This option is covered in Chapter 4, "Device Configuration and Naming."
flags	The boot program passes all startup *flags* to *filename*. They are not interpreted by boot. See the kernel section of this chapter for information on the options available with the default stand-alone program, kernel/unix.

If you want to start up the default program when auto-boot? is false, a few options are available for starting up the system from the ok prompt:

Type: `boot`

The machine will start up from the default startup device using no startup arguments. This is set in the boot-device variable.

Type: `boot [OBP name]`

By specifying an explicit *OBP name*, such as disk3, the machine will start up from the specified startup device using no startup arguments.

Example:

`boot disk3`

The system will boot to the disk drive defined by the devalias named disk3. It will then load kernel/unix as the default standalone startup program.

Type: `boot [options]`

By specifying explicit *options* with the `boot` command, the machine will use the specified arguments to start up from the default startup device.

Example:

`boot -a`

The system will then ask for the name of the standalone program to load. If you specify kernel/unix, which is the default, you will be prompted to enter the directory that contains the kernel modules. (See the kernel section for details on kernel modules.)

Type: `boot [OBP name] [options]`

By specifying the `boot` command with an explicit startup device and with explicit arguments, the machine will start up from the specified device with the specified arguments.

`boot disk3 -a`

This example will give the same prompts as the previous example except that I'm now specifying a different startup device. The system will start up the bootblock from the disk drive defined by the devalias named disk3.

During the startup process, OpenBoot performs the following steps:

1. The firmware can reset the machine if a client program has been executed since the last reset. The client program is normally an operating system or an operating system's loader program, but `boot` can also be used to load and execute other kinds of programs, such as diagnostics. For example, if you have just issued the `test net` command, when you next type `boot`, the system will reset before starting up.

2. The boot program is loaded into memory using a protocol that depends on the type of the selected device. You can start up from disk, tape, floppy, or the network. A disk startup might read a fixed number of blocks from the beginning of the disk, whereas a tape startup might read a particular tape file.

3. The loaded boot program is executed. The behavior of the boot program can be further controlled by the *argument* string, if any one was passed to the `boot` command on the command line.

The program loaded and executed by the startup process is a secondary boot program the purpose of which is to load the standalone program. The second-level program is either ufsboot, when starting up from a disk, or inetboot, when starting up across the network.

If starting up from disk, the bootstrap process consists of two conceptually distinct phases, primary startup and secondary startup. The PROM assumes that the program for the primary startup (bootblk) is in the primary bootblock, which resides in blocks 1 to 15 of the startup device. The bootblock is created using the `installboot` command. The software installation process typically installs the bootblock for you, so you won't normally need to issue this command unless you're recovering a corrupted bootblock.

To install a bootblock on disk c0t3d0s0, type the following:

`installboot /usr/platform/'uname -i'/lib/fs/ufs/bootblk /dev/rdsk/c0t3d0s0`

You cannot see the bootblock. It resides in a protected area of the disk that is not viewable. The program in the bootblock area will load the secondary startup program named ufsboot.

If when executing the `boot` command a *filename* was specified, then this *filename* is the name of the standalone startup program to be loaded. If the pathname is relative (does not begin with a slash), ufsboot will look for the standalone startup program in a platform-dependent search path. In other words, the relative path to the standalone program, will be prefixed with */platform/platform-name. platform-name* will be specific to your hardware.

NOTE. *Use the command* `uname -i` *to determine the platform-name of your system. For example, on a sparc10, the path will be /platform/SUNW,SPARCstation-10. Use the command* `uname -m` *to find the hardware-class-name of a system; for a sparc10, the hardware-class-name will be sun4m. If you look in the /platform directory, you'll see that /platform/SUNW,SPARCstation-10 is merely a link to /platform/sun4m.*

If, on the other hand, the path to *filename* is absolute, `boot` will use the specified path. The startup program then loads the standalone program, and then transfers control to it.

The following example describes how to specify the standalone startup program from the OpenBoot `ok` prompt:

```
ok boot disk5 kernel/unix -s
```

In the example, the PROM will look for the primary boot program (bootblk) on disk5 (/iommu/sbus/espdma@f,400000/esp@f,800000/sd@0,0). The primary startup program will then load ufsboot. This will load the standalone startup program named /platform/SUNW,SPARCstation-10/kernel/unix using the –s flag. Typical secondary startup programs, that is `kernel/unix`, accept arguments of the form: *filename –flags* where *filename* is the path to the standalone program and *-flags* is a list of options to be passed to the stand-alone program. The example will start up the operating system kernel, which is described in the next section. The –s flag will instruct the kernel to start up into single user mode.

kernel

The secondary startup program, ufsboot, which was described in the preceding section, loads the operating system kernel. The platform-specific kernel used by ufsboot is named /platform/`uname -m`/kernel/unix.

The kernel initializes itself and begins loading modules, using ufsboot to read the files. After the kernel has loaded enough modules to mount the root file system, it un-maps the ufsboot program and continues, using its own resources. The kernel creates a user process and starts the /sbin/init process, which starts other processes by reading the /etc/inittab file. The /sbin/init process is described in Part I of the *Solaris 2.6 Administrator Certification Training Guide*.

The kernel is dynamically configured in Solaris 2.6. It consists of a small static core and many dynamically loadable kernel modules. A kernel module is a hardware or software component that is used to perform a specific task on the system. An example of a loadable kernel module is a device driver that is loaded when the device is accessed. Drivers, file systems, STREAMS modules, and other modules are loaded automatically as they are needed, either at startup time or at runtime. After these modules are no longer in use, they can be unloaded. Modules are kept in memory until that memory is needed. The `modinfo` command provides information about the modules currently loaded on a system.

When the kernel is loading, it reads the /etc/system file where system configuration information is stored. This file modifies the kernel's treatment of loadable modules.

The following is an example of the default /etc/system file:

```
*ident    "@(#)system      1.18    97/06/27 SMI" /* SVR4 1.5 */
*
* SYSTEM SPECIFICATION FILE
*
* moddir:
*
*Set the search path for modules. This has a format similar to the
*csh path variable. If the module isn't found in the first directory
*it tries the second and so on. The default is /kernel /usr/kernel
*
*Example:
*moddir: /kernel /usr/kernel /other/modules
* root device and root filesystem configuration:
*
*The following may be used to override the defaults provided by
*the boot program:
*
*rootfs:               Set the filesystem type of the root.
*
*rootdev:      Set the root device. This should be a fully
*       expanded physical pathname. The default is the
*       physical pathname of the device where the boot
*       program resides. The physical pathname is
*       highly platform and configuration dependent.
*
*Example:
*       rootfs:ufs
*       rootdev:/sbus@1,f8000000/esp@0,800000/sd@3,0:a
*
*(Swap device configuration should be specified in /etc/vfstab.)
* exclude:
*
*Modules appearing in the moddir path which are NOT to be loaded,
*even if referenced. Note that `exclude' accepts either a module name,
*or a filename which includes the directory.
*
```

```
*Examples:
*        exclude: win
*        exclude: sys/shmsys
* forceload:
*
*Cause these modules to be loaded at boot time, (just before mounting
*the root filesystem) rather than at first reference. Note that
*forceload expects a filename which includes the directory. Also
*note that loading a module does not necessarily imply that it will
*be installed.
*
*Example:
*        forceload: drv/foo
* set:
*
*Set an integer variable in the kernel or a module to a new value.
*This facility should be used with caution. See system(4).
*
*Examples:
*
*To set variables in 'unix':
*
*        set nautopush=32
* set maxusers=40
*
*To set a variable named 'debug' in the module named 'test_module'
*
*        set test_module:debug = 0x13
```

The /etc/system file contains commands of the form:

```
set parameter=value
```

For example, the setting for the kernel parameter MAXUSERS is set in the /etc/system file with the following line:

```
set maxusers = 40
```

Commands that affect loadable modules are of the form:

```
set module:variable=value
```

If a system administrator finds the need to change a tunable parameter in the /etc/systems file, the sysdef command can be used to verify the change. sysdef lists all hardware devices, system devices, loadable modules, and the values of selected kernel-tunable parameters. The following is output from the sysdef command:

```
*
* Hostid
*
```

continues

continued

```
    723017a4
*
* sun4m Configuration
*
*
* Devices
*
packages (driver not attached)
        disk-label (driver not attached)
        deblocker (driver not attached)
        obp-tftp (driver not attached)
options, instance #0
aliases (driver not attached)
openprom (driver not attached)
iommu, instance #0
        sbus, instance #0
                espdma, instance #0
                        esp, instance #0
                                sd (driver not attached)
                                st (driver not attached)
                                sd, instance #0
                                sd, instance #1
                                sd, instance #2 (driver not attached)
                                sd, instance #3 (driver not attached)
                                sd, instance #4 (driver not attached)
                                sd, instance #5 (driver not attached)
                                sd, instance #6 (driver not attached)
                ledma, instance #0
                        le, instance #0
                SUNW,bpp (driver not attached)
                SUNW,DBRIe (driver not attached)
                        mmcodec (driver not attached)
                cgsix, instance #0
obio, instance #0
        zs, instance #0
        zs, instance #1
        eeprom (driver not attached)
        counter (driver not attached)
        interrupt (driver not attached)
        SUNW,fdtwo, instance #0
        auxio (driver not attached)
        power (driver not attached)
memory (driver not attached)
virtual-memory (driver not attached)
eccmemctl (driver not attached)
TI,TMS390Z50 (driver not attached)
pseudo, instance #0
        clone, instance #0
        ip, instance #0
        tcp, instance #0
```

```
            udp, instance #0
            icmp, instance #0
            arp, instance #0
            sad, instance #0
            consms, instance #0
            conskbd, instance #0
            wc, instance #0
            iwscn, instance #0
            ptsl, instance #0
            tl, instance #0
            cn, instance #0
            mm, instance #0
            md, instance #0
            openeepr, instance #0
            kstat, instance #0
            log, instance #0
            sy, instance #0
            pm, instance #0
            vol, instance #0
            llc1, instance #0
            ptm, instance #0
            pts, instance #0
            logindmux, instance #0
            ksyms, instance #0
*
* Loadable Objects
*
exec/aoutexec
exec/elfexec
exec/intpexec
fs/cachefs
fs/fifofs
fs/hsfs
fs/lofs
fs/nfs
        hard link: sys/nfs
fs/procfs
fs/sockfs
fs/specfs
fs/tmpfs
fs/ufs
fs/autofs
misc/consconfig
misc/des
misc/ipc
misc/klmmod
misc/klmops
misc/krtld
misc/nfs_dlboot
misc/nfssrv
misc/rpcsec
```

continues

continued

```
        misc/rpcsec_gss
        misc/scsi
        misc/seg_drv
        misc/seg_mapdev
        misc/strplumb
        misc/swapgeneric
        misc/tlimod
        misc/cis
        misc/cs
        misc/pcalloc
        misc/pcmcia
        misc/md_hotspares
        misc/md_mirror
        misc/md_notify
        misc/md_raid
        misc/md_stripe
        misc/md_trans
        sched/TS
        sched/TS_DPTBL
        strmod/bufmod
        strmod/connld
        strmod/dedump
        strmod/ldterm
        strmod/ms
        strmod/pckt
        strmod/pfmod
        strmod/pipemod
        strmod/ptem
        strmod/redirmod
        strmod/rpcmod
                hard link: sys/rpcmod
        strmod/timod
        strmod/tirdwr
        strmod/ttcompat
        strmod/hwc
        strmod/bd
        sys/c2audit
        sys/doorfs
        sys/inst_sync
        sys/kaio
        sys/msgsys
        sys/pipe
        sys/pset
        sys/semsys
        sys/shmsys
        genunix
        drv/arp
                hard link: strmod/arp
        drv/arp
        drv/be
```

```
drv/bpp
drv/clone
drv/clone
drv/cn
drv/cn
drv/conskbd
drv/conskbd
drv/consms
drv/consms
drv/esp
drv/icmp
drv/icmp
drv/ip
drv/ip
drv/isp
drv/iwscn
drv/iwscn
drv/le
drv/lebuffer
drv/llc1
drv/llc1
drv/log
drv/log
drv/mm
drv/mm
drv/openeepr
drv/openeepr
drv/options
drv/options
drv/pci_pci
drv/profile
drv/pseudo
drv/pseudo
drv/ptc
drv/ptc
drv/ptsl
drv/ptsl
drv/qe
drv/qec
drv/rts
drv/rts
drv/sad
drv/sad
drv/sd
drv/sd
drv/sp
drv/sp
drv/st
drv/st
drv/sy
```

continues

continued

```
                drv/sy
                drv/tcp
                drv/tcp
                drv/tl
                drv/tl
                drv/udp
                drv/udp
                drv/wc
                drv/wc
                drv/xbox
                drv/fas
                drv/hme
                drv/socal
                drv/pcic
                drv/pcic
                drv/pcs
                drv/pem
                drv/pem
                drv/stp4020
                drv/pcelx
                drv/pcmem
                drv/pcram
                drv/pcram
                drv/pcser
                drv/pcata
                drv/rtvc
                drv/ses
                drv/ses
                drv/pln
                drv/pln
                drv/soc
                drv/ssd
                drv/ssd
                drv/md
                drv/md
*
* System Configuration
*
swap files
swapfile              dev    swaplo blocks    free
/dev/dsk/c0t0d0s3     32,3        8 205016 205016
*
* Tunable Parameters
*
    1298432     maximum memory allowed in buffer cache (bufhwm)
         986    maximum number of processes (v.v_proc)
          99    maximum global priority in sys class (MAXCLSYSPRI)
         981    maximum processes per user id (v.v_maxup)
          30    auto update time limit in seconds (NAUTOUP)
          25    page stealing low water mark (GPGSLO)
```

```
        5       fsflush run rate (FSFLUSHR)
       25       minimum resident memory for avoiding deadlock (MINARMEM)
       25       minimum swapable memory for avoiding deadlock (MINASMEM)
*
* Utsname Tunables
*
5.6   release (REL)
sparc4   node name (NODE)
SunOS   system name (SYS)
Generic_105181-03   version (VER)
*
* Process Resource Limit Tunables (Current:Maximum)
*
ffffffff:ffffffffd       cpu time
ffffffff:ffffffffd       file size
ffffffff:ffffffffd       heap size
ffffffff:ffffffffd       stack size
       0:7ffff000        core file size
ffffffff:ffffffffd       file descriptors
       0:  800000        mapped memory
*
* Streams Tunables
*
    9   maximum number of pushes allowed (NSTRPUSH)
65536   maximum stream message size (STRMSGSZ)
 1024   max size of ctl part of message (STRCTLSZ)
*
* IPC Messages
*
    0   entries in msg map (MSGMAP)
    0   max message size (MSGMAX)
    0   max bytes on queue (MSGMNB)
    0   message queue identifiers (MSGMNI)
    0   message segment size (MSGSSZ)
    0   system message headers (MSGTQL)
    0   message segments (MSGSEG)
*
* IPC Semaphores
*
   10   entries in semaphore map (SEMMAP)
   10   semaphore identifiers (SEMMNI)
   60   semaphores in system (SEMMNS)
   30   undo structures in system (SEMMNU)
   25   max semaphores per id (SEMMSL)
   10   max operations per semop call (SEMOPM)
   10   max undo entries per process (SEMUME)
32767   semaphore maximum value (SEMVMX)
16384   adjust on exit max value (SEMAEM)
*
* IPC Shared Memory
*
```

continues

continued

```
     1048576     max shared memory segment size (SHMMAX)
           1     min shared memory segment size (SHMMIN)
         100     shared memory identifiers (SHMMNI)
           6     max attached shm segments per process (SHMSEG)
*
* Time Sharing Scheduler Tunables
*
    60      maximum time sharing user priority (TSMAXUPRI)
    SYS     system class name (SYS_NAME)
```

The `adb` (absolute debugger) command can also be used to verify that the change was actually made after the system has been started up, but be careful using it.

CAUTION! *`adb` can change kernel parameters on a running system and could potentially crash your system if used improperly. Undertake the following procedures with caution. Improper entries in the /etc/system file or improper use of `adb` can result in a corrupted system, causing the system to crash or be unable to restart.*

If the kernel parameter you're looking for is not displayed with `sysdef`, for example MAXUSERS, use `adb`. At the UNIX command prompt and logged in as root, execute the following command:

`adb -k /dev/ksyms /dev/mem`

/dev/ksyms is a special driver that provides an image of the kernel's symbol table. This can be used to examine the information in memory. `adb` will reply with the amount of physical memory (hex, in 4k pages) as follows:

`physmem 3dec`

A prompt will not be received after this, but `adb` is running and is ready for a command. To check a tunable parameter while in `adb`, use the following syntax:

    <parameter>/D   (displays the integer parameter in decimal)

    <parameter>/X   (displays the integer parameter in hexadecimal)

<parameter> is replaced with the kernel symbol being examined. For example:

```
maxusers/D
```

will display the MAXUSERS parameter in decimal notation as follows:

```
maxusers:      40
```

Type `shminfo_shmmax/D` to display the max shared memory segment size. The system responds with:

```
shminfo_shmmax: 1048576
```

Exit `adb` by typing `$q` followed by a <return>.

After the kernel has started, several other system configuration files are read and the startup process continues. The remaining startup processes are covered in Part I of the *Solaris 2.6 Administrator Certification Training Guide*, so I won't repeat them here. Also in Part I, I describe the proper system shutdown procedures to follow before turning off your system to avoid corrupting the file systems. In the next chapter, I'll describe how devices, such as disks, tape drives, and CD-ROMs, are configured and managed on a Sun system.

CHAPTER

4

Device Configuration and Naming

The following test objectives are covered in this chapter:

- Device and driver naming and configurations
- Displaying device and driver configuration information
- Meta devices

Device management in the Solaris 2.6 environment includes adding and removing peripheral devices, such as tape drives, disk drives, printers, and modems, from a system. It might also involve adding a third-party device driver to support a device. System administrators need to know how to specify device names if using commands to manage disks, file systems, and other devices. This chapter supplements chapters 2 and 12 of the *Solaris 2.6 Administrator Certification Training Guide, Part I* by describing disk device management in detail. In this chapter, I describe disk device naming conventions as well as adding, configuring, and displaying information about disk devices that are attached to your system.

Device Drivers

A Sun computer typically uses a wide range of peripheral and mass-storage devices, such as a SCSI disk drive, a keyboard and a mouse, and some kind of magnetic backup medium. Other commonly used devices include CD-ROM drives, printers, and plotters. Solaris communicates with peripheral devices through files called device files or drivers. A device driver is a low-level program that enables the kernel to communicate with a specific piece of hardware. The driver serves as the operating system's "interpreter" for that piece of hardware. Before Solaris can communicate with a device, the device must have a device driver.

If a system is started for the first time, the kernel creates a device hierarchy to represent all the devices connected to the system. This is the auto-configuration process, which is described later in this chapter. If a driver is not loaded for a particular peripheral, that device is not functional. In Solaris, each disk device is described in three ways, using three distinct naming conventions:

- **Physical device name**—Represents the full device pathname in the device information hierarchy.

- **Instance name**—Represents the kernel's abbreviation name for every possible device on the system.

- **Logical device name**—Used by system administrators with most file system commands to refer to devices.

System administrators need to understand these device names when using commands to manage disks and file systems.

Physical Device Name

Before the operating system (OS) is loaded, the system locates a particular device through the full device pathname. Full device pathnames are described in Chapter 2 of *Solaris 2.6 Administrator Certification Training Guide, Part I*. However, after the kernel is loaded, a device is located by its physical device pathname. Physical device names represent the full device pathname for a device. Notice that the two names are the same in structure. For example, let's view the full device pathname for a SCSI disk at target 0 by typing show-devs at the OpenBoot prompt. The full device pathname is displayed as:

```
/iommu@f,e0000000/sbus@f,e0001000/espdma@f,400000/esp@f,800000/sd
```

Now, let's look at the corresponding physical device name from the OS level. Use the dmesg command described later in this section to obtain information about devices connected to your system. By typing dmesg from the command prompt, you'll receive the following information about SCSI disk 0:

```
iommu0 at root: obio 0xe0000000
sbus0 at iommu0: obio 0xe0001000
espdma0 at sbus0: SBus slot f 0x400000
esp0:        esp-options=0x46
esp0 at espdma0: SBus slot f 0x800000 sparc ipl 4
sd0 at esp0: target 0 lun 0
sd0 is /iommu@f,e0000000/sbus@f,e0001000/espdma@f,400000/esp@f,800000/sd@0,0
    <SEAGATE-ST32550N-0014 cyl 3495 alt 2 hd 11 sec 109>
```

NOTE. *This same information is also available in the /var/adm/messages file.*

The physical device pathname for disk 0 is:

```
/iommu@f,e0000000/sbus@f,e0001000/espdma@f,400000/esp@f,800000/sd@0,0
```

As you can see, the physical device name and the full device name is the same. The difference is that full device pathname is simply a path to a particular device. The physical device is the actual driver used by Solaris to access that device from the OS.

Physical device files are found in the /devices directory; therefore, the physical device file for SCSI disk 0 would be:

```
/devices//iommu@f,e0000000/sbus@f,e0001000/espdma@f,400000/esp@f,800000/sd@0,0:<#>
```

Where <#> is a letter representing the disk slice.

The system commands used to provide information about physical devices are described as follows.

prtconf	Displays system configuration information, including the total amount of memory and the device configuration, as described by the system's hierarchy. This useful tool verifies whether a device has been seen by the system.
sysdef	Displays device configuration information, including system hardware, pseudo devices, loadable modules, and selected kernel parameters.
dmesg	Displays system diagnostic messages, as well as a list of devices attached to the system since the most recent restart.

The following is an example of the output presented by the prtconf command:

```
# prtconf
System Configuration:  Sun Microsystems   sun4m
Memory size: 64 Megabytes
System Peripherals (Software Nodes):

SUNW,SPARCstation-10
    packages (driver not attached)
        disk-label (driver not attached)
        deblocker (driver not attached)
        obp-tftp (driver not attached)
    options, instance #0
    aliases (driver not attached)
    openprom (driver not attached)
    iommu, instance #0
        sbus, instance #0
            espdma, instance #0
                esp, instance #0
                    sd (driver not attached)
                    st (driver not attached)
                    sd, instance #0
                    sd, instance #1
                    sd, instance #2 (driver not attached)
                    sd, instance #3 (driver not attached)
                    sd, instance #4 (driver not attached)
                    sd, instance #5 (driver not attached)
                    sd, instance #6
            ledma, instance #0
                le, instance #0
            SUNW,bpp (driver not attached)
            SUNW,DBRIe (driver not attached)
                mmcodec (driver not attached)
            cgsix, instance #0
        obio, instance #0
```

continues

continued

```
                zs, instance #0
                zs, instance #1
                eeprom (driver not attached)
                counter (driver not attached)
                interrupt (driver not attached)
                SUNW,fdtwo, instance #0
                    auxio (driver not attached)
                    power (driver not attached)
        memory (driver not attached)
        virtual-memory (driver not attached)
        eccmemctl (driver not attached)
        TI,TMS390Z50 (driver not attached)
        pseudo, instance #0
```

Next is an example of the output displayed by the `sysdef` command:

```
# sysdef
*
* Hostid
*
    723017a4
*
* sun4m Configuration
*
* Devices
*
packages (driver not attached)
        disk-label (driver not attached)
        deblocker (driver not attached)
        obp-tftp (driver not attached)
options, instance #0
aliases (driver not attached)
openprom (driver not attached)
iommu, instance #0
        sbus, instance #0
                espdma, instance #0
                        esp, instance #0
                                sd (driver not attached)
                                st (driver not attached)
                                sd, instance #0
                                sd, instance #1
                                sd, instance #2 (driver not attached)
                                sd, instance #3 (driver not attached)
                                sd, instance #4 (driver not attached)
                                sd, instance #5 (driver not attached)
                                sd, instance #6
```

```
                        ledma, instance #0
                                le, instance #0
                        SUNW,bpp (driver not attached)
                        SUNW,DBRIe (driver not attached)
                                mmcodec (driver not attached)
                        cgsix, instance #0
obio, instance #0
        zs, instance #0
        zs, instance #1
        eeprom (driver not attached)
        counter (driver not attached)
        interrupt (driver not attached)
        SUNW,fdtwo, instance #0
        auxio (driver not attached)
        power (driver not attached)
memory (driver not attached)
virtual-memory (driver not attached)
eccmemctl (driver not attached)
TI,TMS390Z50 (driver not attached)
pseudo, instance #0
        clone, instance #0
        ip, instance #0
        tcp, instance #0
        udp, instance #0
        icmp, instance #0
…….
…….
        vol, instance #0
        llc1, instance #0
        ptm, instance #0
        pts, instance #0
        logindmux, instance #0
        ksyms, instance #0
*
* Loadable Objects
*
exec/aoutexec
exec/elfexec
exec/intpexec
fs/cachefs
fs/fifofs
fs/hsfs
…..
….
….
```

continues

continued

```
                drv/ses
                drv/pln
                drv/pln
                drv/soc
                drv/ssd
                drv/ssd
                drv/md
                drv/md
                *
                * System Configuration
                *
                swap files
                swapfile              dev   swaplo blocks    free
                /dev/dsk/c0t0d0s3    32,3       8 205016 151128
                *
                * Tunable Parameters
                *
                1298432         maximum memory allowed in buffer cache (bufhwm)
                      986       maximum number of processes (v.v_proc)
                       99       maximum global priority in sys class (MAXCLSYSPRI)
                      981       maximum processes per user id (v.v_maxup)
                       30       auto update time limit in seconds (NAUTOUP)
                       25       page stealing low water mark (GPGSLO)
                        5        fsflush run rate (FSFLUSHR)
                       25       minimum resident memory for avoiding deadlock (MINARMEM)
                       25       minimum swapable memory for avoiding deadlock (MINASMEM)
                *
                * Utsname Tunables
                *
                5.6   release (REL)
                sparc4   node name (NODE)
                SunOS    system name (SYS)
                Generic_105181-03   version (VER)
                *
                * Process Resource Limit Tunables (Current:Maximum)
                *
                ffffffff:ffffffffd        cpu time
                ffffffff:ffffffffd        file size
                ffffffff:ffffffffd        heap size
                ffffffff:ffffffffd        stack size
                       0:7ffff000         core file size
                ffffffff:ffffffffd        file descriptors
                       0: 800000          mapped memory
                *
                * Streams Tunables
                *
                        9  maximum number of pushes allowed (NSTRPUSH)
                    65536  maximum stream message size (STRMSGSZ)
                     1024  max size of ctl part of message (STRCTLSZ)
                *
                * IPC Messages
                *
```

```
      0   entries in msg map (MSGMAP)
      0   max message size (MSGMAX)
      0   max bytes on queue (MSGMNB)
      0   message queue identifiers (MSGMNI)
      0   message segment size (MSGSSZ)
      0   system message headers (MSGTQL)
      0   message segments (MSGSEG)
*
* IPC Semaphores
*
     10   entries in semaphore map (SEMMAP)
     10   semaphore identifiers (SEMMNI)
     60   semaphores in system (SEMMNS)
     30   undo structures in system (SEMMNU)
     25   max semaphores per id (SEMMSL)
     10   max operations per semop call (SEMOPM)
     10   max undo entries per process (SEMUME)
  32767   semaphore maximum value (SEMVMX)
  16384   adjust on exit max value (SEMAEM)
*
* IPC Shared Memory
*
1048576     max shared memory segment size (SHMMAX)
      1     min shared memory segment size (SHMMIN)
    100     shared memory identifiers (SHMMNI)
      6     max attached shm segments per process (SHMSEG)
*
* Time Sharing Scheduler Tunables
*
60        maximum time sharing user priority (TSMAXUPRI)
SYS       system class name (SYS_NAME)
```

Finally, here's an example of the device information displayed using the `dmesg` command:

```
#dmesg
Sep 22 07:07

SunOS Release 5.6 Version Generic_105181-05 [UNIX(R) System V Release 4.0]
Copyright (c) 1983-1997, Sun Microsystems, Inc.
pac: enabled - SuperSPARC/SuperCache
cpu0: TI,TMS390Z55 (mid 8 impl 0x0 ver 0x0 clock 40 MHz)

mem = 65536K (0x4000000)
avail mem = 61095936
Ethernet address = 8:0:20:18:13:b1
root nexus = SUNW,SPARCstation-10
iommu0 at root: obio 0xe0000000
sbus0 at iommu0: obio 0xe0001000
espdma0 at sbus0: SBus slot f 0x400000
esp0:     esp-options=0x46
```

continues

continued

```
esp0 at espdma0: SBus slot f 0x800000 sparc ipl 4
esp0 is /iommu@f,e0000000/sbus@f,e0001000/espdma@f,400000/esp@f,800000
sd3 at esp0: target 3 lun 0
sd3 is /iommu@f,e0000000/sbus@f,e0001000/espdma@f,400000/esp@f,800000/sd@3,0
      <SEAGATE-ST31055N-0316 cyl 4104 alt 2 hd 4 sec 126>

root on /iommu@f,e0000000/sbus@f,e0001000/espdma@f,400000/esp@f,800000/sd@3,0:a fstype
➥ufs
obio0 at root
zs0 at obio0: obio 0x100000 sparc ipl 12
zs0 is /obio/zs@0,100000
zs1 at obio0: obio 0x0 sparc ipl 12
zs1 is /obio/zs@0,0
SUNW,leo0 at sbus0: SBus slot 3 0x0 SBus level 5 sparc ipl 9
SUNW,leo0 is /iommu@f,e0000000/sbus@f,e0001000/SUNW,leo@3,0
cpu 0 initialization complete - online
ledma0 at sbus0: SBus slot f 0x400010
le0 at ledma0: SBus slot f 0xc00000 sparc ipl 6
le0 is /iommu@f,e0000000/sbus@f,e0001000/ledma@f,400010/le@f,c00000
dump on /dev/dsk/c0t3d0s1 size 96500K
```

Use the output of `prtconf` and `sysdef` commands to identify which disk, tape, and CD-ROM devices are connected to the system. As shown in the previous examples, some devices display the `driver not attached` message next to the device instance. This message does not always mean that a driver is unavailable for this device. It means that no driver is currently attached to the device instance because there is no device at this node or the device is not in use. The OS automatically loads drivers when the device is accessed, and it unloads them when it is not in use.

The system determines what devices are attached to it at startup time. This is why it is important to have all peripherals powered on at startup, even if they are not currently being used. During startup, the kernel configures itself dynamically, loading needed modules into memory. Device drivers are loaded when devices, such as disk and tape devices, are accessed for the first time. This process is called auto configuration, because all kernel modules are loaded automatically if needed. As described in Chapter 3, "The Boot Process," the system administrator can customize the way in which kernel modules are loaded by modifying the /etc/system file.

Device Auto-Configuration

Auto-configuration offers many advantages over the manual configuration method used in earlier versions of Unix in which device drivers were manually added into the kernel, the kernel was recompiled, and the system had to be restarted. Now, with auto-configuration, the administrator simply connects the new device to the system and performs a reconfiguration startup as follows:

1. Create the /reconfigure file with the following command:

   ```
   touch /reconfigure
   ```

   The /reconfigure file causes the Solaris software to check for the presence of any newly installed devices the next time you turn on or start up your system.

2. Shut down the system using the shutdown procedure described in the *Solaris 2.6 Administrator Certification Training Guide, Part I.*

   If you need to connect the device, turn off power to the system and all peripherals, after Solaris has been properly shut down.

3. After the new device is connected, restore power to the peripherals first and then to the system. Verify that the peripheral device has been added by attempting to access it.

An optional method of performing a reconfiguration startup is to interrupt the start process and type `boot -r` at the OpenBoot prompt. I like the first method described, because the system administrator can instruct the system to perform the reconfiguration startup at any time by creating the /reconfigure file. Now, at the next restart, whether the administrator is there or not, the system performs the reconfiguration start up. This could happen at 3 a.m. if you like.

During a reconfiguration restart, a device hierarchy is created in the /devices directories to represent the devices connected to the system. The kernel uses this to associate drivers with their appropriate devices. Also, any kernel parameter changes that were made to the /etc/system file are parsed by the kernel at this time.

Auto-configuration offers the following benefits:

- Main memory is used more efficiently because modules are loaded as needed.
- There is no need to reconfigure the kernel if new devices are added to the system.
- Drivers can be loaded and tested without having to rebuild the kernel and restart the system.

Occasionally, you might install a new device and Solaris does not have a supporting device driver for it. Always check with the manufacturer to make sure that any device you plan to add to your system has a supported device driver. If a driver is not included with the standard Solaris release, the manufacturer should provide the software needed for the device to be properly installed, maintained, and administered. Third-part device drivers are installed as software packages using the `pkgadd` command. At a minimum, this software includes a device driver and its associated configuration (.conf) file. The .conf files reside in the /kernel/drv directories. Table 4-1 describes the contents of the sub-directories located in the /kernel directory.

Table 4-1 The /kernel Directory

Directory	Description
drv	Contains loadable device drivers and pseudo-device drivers.
exec	Contains modules used to run different types of executable files or shell scripts.
fs	Contains file system modules, such as ufs, nfs, proc, and so on.
misc	Contains miscellaneous system-related modules, such as swapgeneric and ipc.
sched	Contains OS schedulers.
strmod	Contains System V STREAMS loadable modules.
sys	Contains loadable system calls, such as system semaphore and system accounting operations.

Instance Name

The instance name represents the kernel's abbreviation name for every possible device on the system. For example, sd0 and sd1 represent the instance names of two SCSI disk devices. Instance names are mapped to a physical device name in the /etc/path_to_inst file. The following shows the contents of a path_to_inst file:

```
more /etc/path_to_inst

#       Caution! This file contains critical kernel state
#
"/iommu@f,e0000000" 0 "iommu"
"/iommu@f,e0000000/sbus@f,e0001000" 0 "sbus"
"/iommu@f,e0000000/sbus@f,e0001000/espdma@f,400000" 0 "dma"
"/iommu@f,e0000000/sbus@f,e0001000/espdma@f,400000/esp@f,800000" 0 "esp"
"/iommu@f,e0000000/sbus@f,e0001000/espdma@f,400000/esp@f,800000/st@5,0" 5 "st"
"/iommu@f,e0000000/sbus@f,e0001000/espdma@f,400000/esp@f,800000/st@4,0" 4 "st"
"/iommu@f,e0000000/sbus@f,e0001000/espdma@f,400000/esp@f,800000/st@6,0" 6 "st"
"/iommu@f,e0000000/sbus@f,e0001000/espdma@f,400000/esp@f,800000/st@1,0" 1 "st"
"/iommu@f,e0000000/sbus@f,e0001000/espdma@f,400000/esp@f,800000/st@0,0" 0 "st"
"/iommu@f,e0000000/sbus@f,e0001000/espdma@f,400000/esp@f,800000/st@3,0" 3 "st"
"/iommu@f,e0000000/sbus@f,e0001000/espdma@f,400000/esp@f,800000/st@2,0" 2 "st"
"/iommu@f,e0000000/sbus@f,e0001000/espdma@f,400000/esp@f,800000/sd@5,0" 5 "sd"
"/iommu@f,e0000000/sbus@f,e0001000/espdma@f,400000/esp@f,800000/sd@4,0" 4 "sd"
"/iommu@f,e0000000/sbus@f,e0001000/espdma@f,400000/esp@f,800000/sd@6,0" 6 "sd"
"/iommu@f,e0000000/sbus@f,e0001000/espdma@f,400000/esp@f,800000/sd@1,0" 1 "sd"
```

```
"/iommu@f,e0000000/sbus@f,e0001000/espdma@f,400000/esp@f,800000/sd@0,0" 0 "sd"
"/iommu@f,e0000000/sbus@f,e0001000/espdma@f,400000/esp@f,800000/sd@3,0" 3 "sd"
"/iommu@f,e0000000/sbus@f,e0001000/espdma@f,400000/esp@f,800000/sd@2,0" 2 "sd"
"/iommu@f,e0000000/sbus@f,e0001000/cgsix@2,0" 0 "cgsix"
"/iommu@f,e0000000/sbus@f,e0001000/sbusmem@f,0" 15 "sbusmem"
"/iommu@f,e0000000/sbus@f,e0001000/sbusmem@0,0" 0 "sbusmem"
"/iommu@f,e0000000/sbus@f,e0001000/sbusmem@1,0" 1 "sbusmem"
"/iommu@f,e0000000/sbus@f,e0001000/sbusmem@2,0" 2 "sbusmem"
"/iommu@f,e0000000/sbus@f,e0001000/sbusmem@3,0" 3 "sbusmem"
"/iommu@f,e0000000/sbus@f,e0001000/ledma@f,400010" 0 "ledma"
"/iommu@f,e0000000/sbus@f,e0001000/ledma@f,400010/le@f,c00000" 0 "le"
"/iommu@f,e0000000/sbus@f,e0001000/SUNW,bpp@f,4800000" 0 "bpp"
"/iommu@f,e0000000/sbus@f,e0001000/SUNW,DBRIe@f,8010000" 0 "dbri"
"/obio" 0 "obio"
"/obio/SUNW,fdtwo@0,700000" 0 "fd"
"/obio/zs@0,100000" 0 "zs"
"/obio/profile" 0 "profile"
"/obio/zs@0,0" 1 "zs"
"/options" 0 "options"
"/pseudo" 0 "pseudo"
```

Instance names can also be displayed by using the commands `dmesg`, `sysdef`, and `prtconf` described earlier in this section. For example, you can determine the mapping of an instance name to a physical device name by looking at the `dmesg` output, as shown in the following example.

```
sd3 at esp0: target 3 lun 0
sd3 is /iommu@f,e0000000/sbus@f,e0001000/espdma@f,400000/esp@f,800000/sd@3,0
```

In the example, sd3 is the instance name and /iommu@f,e0000000/sbus@f,e0001000/espdma@f,400000/esp@f,800000/sd@3,0 is the physical device name. After the instance name has been assigned to a device, it remains mapped to that device. To keep instance numbers persistent across restarts, the system records them in the /etc/path_to_inst file. This file is read only at startup time, and it is updated by the `add_drv` and `drvconfig` commands described later in this section. Devices already existing on a system are not rearranged when new devices are added, even if new devices are added to sbus slots numerically lower than those that are occupied by existing devices. In other words, the /etc/path_to_inst file, is appended to, not rewritten, when new devices are added.

CAUTION! *Do not remove the path_to_inst file; the system cannot start up without it. The system relies on information found in this file to find the root, usr, or swap device. Only make changes to this file after careful consideration.*

It is generally not necessary for the system administrator to change the path_to_inst file, because the system maintains it. The system administrator can however, change the assignment of instance numbers by editing this file and doing a reconfiguration start up. However, any changes made in this file are lost if `add_drv` or `drvconfig` is run before the system is restarted.

NOTE. *If there is ever an issue in which you cannot start up off the startup disk because of a problem with /etc/path_to_inst file, you should start up off from the CD-ROM* (`boot -sw cdrom`) *and copy the /etc/path_to_inst file contained on the CD-ROM to the /etc/path_to_inst on the startup disk. To do this, start up off the cdrom using* `boot -sw cdrom` *at the OpenBoot prompt. Then mount the startup disk on /a. Copy the /etc/path_to_inst file to /a/etc/path_to_inst. If this does not enable you to start up, the problem is deeper than just with the /etc/path_to_inst file.*

The `add_drv` command adds a new device driver to the system. The command syntax is as follows:

```
add_drv [ -b basedir ] [ -c class_name ] [ -i 'identify_name' ]
[ -m 'permission','...' ] [ -n ] [ -f ] [ -v ] device_driver
```

Option	Description
-b *basedir*	Sets the path to the root directory of the diskless client. It is used on the server to execute `add_drv` for a diskless client. The client machine must be restarted to install the driver.
-c *class_name*	Exports the class *class_name* for the driver being added to the system.
-i '*identify_name*'	Specify a white-space separated list of aliases for the driver *device_driver*.
-m '*permission*'	Specify the file system permissions for device nodes created by the system on behalf of *device_driver*.
-n	Do not try to load and attach *device_driver*; just modify the system configuration files for the *device_driver*.
-f	Forces `add_drv` to add the driver even if a reconfiguration start up is required. See the –v flag. Normally, if a reconfiguration start up is required to complete the configuration of the driver into the system, `add_drv` does not add the driver.
-v	Provides additional information regarding the success or failure of a driver's configuration into the system.

The following example adds the SUNW,test driver to the system, with an alias name of SUNW,alias. It assumes the driver has already been copied to the /usr/kernel/drv directory:

```
add_drv -m '* 0666 bin bin','a 0644 root sys' -i 'SUNW,alias' SUNW,test
```

Every minor node created by the system for the SUNW,test driver has the permission 0666, and is owned by a user bin in the group bin, except for the minor device a, which is owned by root, the group sys, and has a permission of 0644.

The add_drv command is used to inform the system about newly installed device drivers. Specifically, it updates the following files:

/etc/name_to_major	This file contains driver name to major number mapping. Every driver has a major number; the instances of the devices it manages each have their own unique minor number.
/etc/minor_perm	This file contains permission, owner, and group information used by drivers when creating new /devices entries (as when a device is accessed for the first time).
/etc/driver_aliases	This file contains alternative names for device drivers.
/etc/driver_classes	This file contains classes for device drivers (SBUS, VME, SCSI, and so on).

add_drv invokes the drvconfig command to configure the driver and then calls devlinks to make any device links from the /dev directory.

Syntax: drvconfig [options]

Option	Description
-d	Prints debugging information.
-i	Configures the driver for the specified driver file name only.
-r	Builds the device tree under the specified directory instead of the /devices directory, which is the default.

The drvconfig utility is responsible for configuring the /devices directory to reflect the dev_info tree held in the kernel. This utility is run automatically by the /etc/rcS script, which executes the drvconfig utility during a reconfiguration start up. If necessary, the command can also be run from the command line.

An example of when to use the drvconfig command would be if the system has been started up but the power to the CD-ROM was not turned on. During startup, the system did not detect the CD-ROM; therefore, its drivers were not installed. This can be verified by issuing the sysdef command and examining the output for sd6, the SCSI target ID for the CD-ROM.

```
sd, instance #6 (driver not attached)
```

To gain access to the CD-ROM, you could halt the system, turn on power to the CD-ROM, and start the system back up, or you could issue the following command at the command prompt:

```
drvconfig cdrom
```

Now if you issue the `sysdef` command, you'll see the following output for the CD-ROM:

```
sd, instance #6
```

Major and Minor Device Numbers

Each device has a major and minor device number assigned. These numbers serve to identify the proper device location and device driver to the kernel. This number is used by the operating system to key into the proper device driver whenever a physical device file corresponding to one of the devices it manages is opened. The major device number indicates the general device class, such as disk, tape, or serial line. The minor device number indicates the specific member within that class. All devices managed by a given device driver contain a unique minor number. Some drivers of pseudo-devices (software entities set up to look like devices) create new minor devices on demand. Together, the major and minor numbers uniquely define a device and its device driver.

Physical device files have a unique output when listed with the `ls -l` command, as seen in the following example:

```
cd /devices/iommu@f,e0000000/sbus@f,e0001000/espdma@f,400000/esp@f,800000
ls -l sd@0
```

The system responds with:

```
brw-r-----   1 root     sys       32,   0 Jul 21 07:44 sd@0,0:a
crw-r-----   1 root     sys       32,   0 Jul 21 07:44 sd@0,0:a,raw
brw-r-----   1 root     sys       32,   1 Jul 21 07:44 sd@0,0:b
crw-r-----   1 root     sys       32,   1 Aug 16 06:15 sd@0,0:b,raw
brw-r-----   1 root     sys       32,   2 Jul 21 07:44 sd@0,0:c
crw-r-----   1 root     sys       32,   2 Jul 21 07:44 sd@0,0:c,raw
brw-r-----   1 root     sys       32,   3 Jul 21 07:44 sd@0,0:d
crw-r-----   1 root     sys       32,   3 Jul 21 07:44 sd@0,0:d,raw
brw-r-----   1 root     sys       32,   4 Jul 21 07:44 sd@0,0:e
crw-r-----   1 root     sys       32,   4 Jul 21 07:44 sd@0,0:e,raw
brw-r-----   1 root     sys       32,   5 Jul 21 07:44 sd@0,0:f
crw-r-----   1 root     sys       32,   5 Jul 21 07:44 sd@0,0:f,raw
brw-r-----   1 root     sys       32,   6 Jul 21 07:44 sd@0,0:g
crw-r-----   1 root     sys       32,   6 Aug 16 06:13 sd@0,0:g,raw
brw-r-----   1 root     sys       32,   7 Jul 21 07:44 sd@0,0:h
crw-r-----   1 root     sys       32,   7 Jul 21 07:44 sd@0,0:h,raw
```

The long listing includes columns showing major and minor numbers for each device. All the devices listed in the previous example are managed by the sd driver, which is major number 32 in this example. Minor numbers are listed after the comma.

During the process of building the /devices directory, the `drvconfig` utility assigns each device a major device number by using the name-to-number mappings held in the /etc/name_to_major file. This file is maintained by the system and is undocumented. The following is a sample of the /etc/name_to_major file:

```
more /etc/name_to_major
cn 0
rootnex 1
pseudo 2
ip 3
logindmux 4
icmp 5
fas 6
hme 7
p9000 8
p9100 9
sp 10
clone 11
sad 12
mm 13
iwscn 14
wc 15
conskbd 16
consms 17
ipdcm 18
dump 19
se 20
log 21
sy 22
ptm 23
pts 24
ptc 25
ptsl 26
bwtwo 27
audio 28
zs 29
cgthree 30
cgtwo 31
sd 32
st 33
…... . .
…..… .
```

continues

continued

```
envctrl    131
cvc        132
cvcredir   133
eide       134
hd         135
tadbat     136
ts102      137
simba      138
uata       139
dad        140
atapicd    141
```

To create the minor device entries, the `drvconfig` utility uses the information placed in the dev_info node by the device driver. Permissions and ownership information are kept in the /etc/minor_perm file.

Logical Device Name

The final stage of the auto-configuration process involves the creation of the logical device name to reflect the new set of devices on the system. The logical device name is a link from the /dev directory to the physical device name located in the /devices directory. To see a list of logical device names for the disks connected to your system, execute a long listing on the /dev/dsk directory as follows:

```
ls -l /dev/dsk
total 48
lrwxrwxrwx   1 root     root          84 Jul 21 07:45 c0t0d0s0 ->
../../devices/iommu@f,e0000000/sbus @f,e0001000/espdma@f,400000/esp@f,800000/sd@0,0:a
lrwxrwxrwx   1 root     root          84 Jul 21 07:45 c0t0d0s1 ->
../../devices/iommu@f,e0000000/sbus @f,e0001000/espdma@f,400000/esp@f,800000/sd@0,0:b
lrwxrwxrwx   1 root     root          84 Jul 21 07:45 c0t0d0s2 ->
../../devices/iommu@f,e0000000/sbus @f,e0001000/espdma@f,400000/esp@f,800000/sd@0,0:c
lrwxrwxrwx   1 root     root          84 Jul 21 07:45 c0t0d0s3 ->
../../devices/iommu@f,e0000000/sbus @f,e0001000/espdma@f,400000/esp@f,800000/sd@0,0:d
lrwxrwxrwx   1 root     root          84 Jul 21 07:45 c0t0d0s4 ->
../../devices/iommu@f,e0000000/sbus @f,e0001000/espdma@f,400000/esp@f,800000/sd@0,0:e
lrwxrwxrwx   1 root     root          84 Jul 21 07:45 c0t0d0s5 ->
../../devices/iommu@f,e0000000/sbus @f,e0001000/espdma@f,400000/esp@f,800000/sd@0,0:f
.......
.......
```

On the second line of output from the `ls -l` command in the previous example, notice that the logical device name c0t0d0s0 is linked to the physical device name

`../../devices/iommu@f,e0000000/sbus @f,e0001000/espdma@f,400000/esp@f,800000/sd@0,0:a.`

The logical device name is the name that the system administrator uses to refer to a particular device if running various Solaris file system commands. For example, if running the `mount` command, use the logical device name /dev/dsk/c0t0d0s7 to mount the file system /home:

mount /dev/dsk/c0t0d0s7 /home

Logical device files in the /dev directory are symbolically linked to physical device files in the /devices directory. Logical device names are used to access disk devices if you

- Add a new disk to the system.
- Move a disk from one system to another.
- Access (or mount) a file system residing on a local disk.
- Back up a local file system.
- Repair a file system.

Logical devices are organized in subdirectories under the /dev directory by their device types:

/dev/dsk	Block interface to disk devices
/dev/rdsk	Raw or character interface to disk devices
/dev/rmt	Tapes devices
/dev/term	Serial line devices
/dev/cua	Dial out modems
/dev/pts	Pseudo terminals
/dev/fbs	Frame buffers
/dev/sad	STREAMS administrative driver

The `disks` command creates entries in the /dev directory for disk drives attached to the system. Similarly, the `tapes` command creates entries for tape drives attached to a system, the `ports` command creates entries for the serial ports, and `esp` creates entries for SCSI host adapters. All these commands create the symbolic links found in the /dev directories. In the context of this chapter, the `disks` command uses the following syntax:

/usr/sbin/disks [-r *rootdir*]

Where [-r *rootdir*] is an optional parameter that looks for the /dev/dsk, /dev/rdsk, and /devices directory under *rootdir*, not directly under /.

The `disks` command creates symbolic links in the /dev/dsk and /dev/rdsk directories pointing to the actual physical device files found under the /devices directory tree. It performs the following steps:

1. `disks` searches the kernel device tree to see what hard drives are attached to the system. It notes the /devices pathnames for the slices on the drive and determines the physical component of the corresponding /dev/dsk or /dev/rdsk name.

2. The /dev/dsk and /dev/rdsk directories are checked for disk entries, that is symbolic links with names of the form cN[tN]dNsN, where N represents a decimal number. cN is the logical controller number, an arbitrary number assigned by this program to designate a particular disk controller. The first controller found on a system, is assigned number 0. tN is the SCSI target ID of the disk attached to the SCSI bus. dN refers to the disk number attached to the controller. This number is always 0 except on storage arrays. sN is the slice number on the disk. Here are a few examples of logical device file names for disk drives:

    dev/dsk/c0t0d0s0—refers to slice 0 on a SCSI disk drive with a target ID of 0 on SCSI controller 0—buffered device.

    dev/rdsk/c0t0d0s0—refers to slice 0 on a SCSI disk drive with a target ID of 0 on SCSI controller 0—raw device.

3. If all the disk entries are not found in the /dev/dsk for a disk that has been found under the /devices directory tree, `disks` creates the missing symbolic links. If none of the entries for a particular disk are found in /dev/dsk, `disks` checks to see if any entries exist for other disks attached to the same controller, and if so, it creates new entries using the same controller number that is used for other disks on the same controller. If no other /dev/dsk entries are found for slices of disks belonging to the same physical controller as the current disk, `disks` assigns the lowest-unused controller number and creates entries for the disk slices using this newly-assigned controller number.

Disk drives have an entry under both the /dev/dsk directory and the /dev/rdsk directory. The *dsk* directory refers to the block or buffered device file, and the /rdsk directory refers to the character or raw device file. The "r" in rdsk stands for "raw." If you are not familiar with these devices, refer to Chapter 12 of the *Solaris 2.6 Administrator Certification Guide, Part I* in which block and character devices are described.

The /dev/dsk directory contains the disk entries to the block device nodes in /devices, as seen in the following command:

```
ls -l /dev/dsk
total 48
lrwxrwxrwx   1 root     root           84 Jul 21 07:45 c0t0d0s0 ->
/devices/iommu@f,e0000000/sbus@f,e0001000/espdma@f,400000/esp@f,800000/sd@0,0:a
lrwxrwxrwx   1 root     root           84 Jul 21 07:45 c0t0d0s1 ->
/devices/iommu@f,e0000000/sbus@f,e0001000/espdma@f,400000/esp@f,800000/sd@0,0:b
lrwxrwxrwx   1 root     root           84 Jul 21 07:45 c0t0d0s2 ->
/devices/iommu@f,e0000000/sbus@f,e0001000/espdma@f,400000/esp@f,800000/sd@0,0:c
......
......
```

The /dev/rdsk directory contains the disk entries for the character device nodes in /devices, as seen in the following command:

```
ls -l /dev/rdsk
lrwxrwxrwx   1 root     root           88 Jul 21 07:45 c0t0d0s0 ->
/devices/iommu@f,e0000000/sbus@f,e0001000/espdma@f,400000/esp@f,800000/sd@0,0:a,raw
lrwxrwxrwx   1 root     root           88 Jul 21 07:45 c0t0d0s1 ->
/devices/iommu@f,e0000000/sbus@f,e0001000/espdma@f,400000/esp@f,800000/sd@0,0:b,raw
lrwxrwxrwx   1 root     root           88 Jul 21 07:45 c0t0d0s2 ->
/devices/iommu@f,e0000000/sbus@f,e0001000/espdma@f,400000/esp@f,800000/sd@0,0:c,raw
......
......
```

The `disks` command is run automatically each time a reconfiguration start up is performed or if `add_drv` is executed. If invoking `disks` manually, first run `drvconfig` to ensure /devices is consistent with the current device configuration.

If executing a reconfigure start up, a number of utilities are run to build the logical device names. They are

1. The /devices directory is built by the `drvconfig` utility.

2. The links from the /dev/directory to the /devices directory are built by a number of Solaris utilities:

    a. `disks`   Installs /dev links for disk

    b. `tapes`   Installs /dev links for tape

    c. `ports`   Installs /dev links for serial lines

    d. `devlinks` Installs /dev links for miscellaneous and pseudo devices

3. The `devlinks` command builds the /dev directory links according to specifications found in the /etc/devlink.tab file.

Meta Devices

With standard disk devices, each disk slice has its own physical and logical device. Remember from Chapter 3 of the *Solaris 2.6 Administrator Certification Guide, Part I*, a file system cannot span more than one disk slice. In other words, a file system is limited to the size of a single disk. On a large server with many disk drives, standard methods of disk slicing are inadequate and inefficient. Sun has addressed these issues with two unbundled Sun packages: Solstice DiskSuite and Sun's Enterprise Volume Manager. Both packages allow disks slices to be grouped together to form a logical device that is referred to as a meta device. A meta device driver is a logical device that represents several disks or disk slices. Typically, DiskSuite is used on smaller Sun systems, those using multi-packs. The Enterprise Volume Manager package is much more robust, and it is used on larger servers that use SparcStorage arrays.

Meta devices are the basic functional unit of the meta disk driver. After you create meta devices, you can use them like physical disk partitions. These logical devices can be made up of one of the following components:

- A single partition or disk.

- A concatenated partition called a concatenated stripe. Concatenated stripes work much the way the UNIX `cat` command program is used to concatenate two or more files together to create one larger file. If partitions are concatenated, the addressing of the component blocks is done on the components sequentially. The file system can use the entire concatenation.

- A stripe is similar to concatenation, except the addressing of the component blocks is interlaced on the slices rather than sequentially. Striping is used to gain performance. By striping data across disks, multiple controllers can access data simultaneously.

- A mirror replicates all writes to a single logical device (the mirror) then to multiple devices (the sub-mirrors), while distributing read operations. This provides redundancy of data in the event of a disk or hardware failure.

Meta devices can provide increased capacity, higher availability, and better performance. To gain increased capacity, the system administrator creates meta devices that are either concatenations or stripes. Mirroring and UFS logging provide higher availability and striping can help performance. Furthermore, meta devices are transparent to applications software and to component and controller hardware.

The meta device driver is implemented as a set of loadable, pseudo device drivers. It uses other physical device drivers to pass I/O requests to and from the underlying devices. The meta device driver resides between the file system interface and the device driver interface, and it interprets information between the two. After passing through the meta device driver, information is received in the expected form by both the file system and by the device drivers. The meta device is a loadable device driver, and it has all the same characteristics as any other disk device driver.

The standard meta device name begins with "d," and it is followed by a number. By default, there are 128 unique meta devices in the range 0–127. Additional meta devices can be added. The meta block device accesses the disk using the system's normal buffering mechanism. There is also a character, or raw, device that provides for direct transmission between the disk and the user's read or write buffer. The names of the block devices are found in the /dev/md/dsk directory, and the names of the raw devices are found in the /dev/md/rdsk directory.

This concludes the discussion on device drivers and device names. In Chapter 5, "The Solaris File Systems," we will use these device names when initializing and managing file systems.

CHAPTER 5

The Solaris File Systems

The following test objectives are covered in this chapter:

- Constructing file systems
- Configuration files
- Tuning file systems
- Using large file systems
- Mounting and unmounting file systems
- Volume manager
- Displaying file system information

In Chapter 3 of the *Solaris 2.6 Administrator Certification Guide, Part I*, I described how to create, check, mount, and display file systems with Solaris 2.6. I explained file system structure, disk geometry, disk slices, and the format utility. You are tested on these topics again on the second exam, so I recommend that you review that chapter if any of these topics are unclear to you. In this chapter, I continue the discussion of file systems and specifically cover the following topics:

- Constructing a file system
- Tuning a file system
- Using large file systems
- Using additional options when mounting and un-mounting file systems
- Working with removable media and with Volume Manager
- Getting information on file systems

Constructing a File System

In Part I of the *Solaris 2.6 Administrator Certification Training Guide*, I described how newfs is the friendly front end to the mkfs command. The newfs command automatically determines all the necessary parameters to pass to mkfs to construct new file systems. newfs was added in Solaris to make the creation of new file systems easier. It's highly recommended that the newfs command be used to create file systems, but it's also important to see what is happening "behind the scenes" with the mkfs utility. The syntax for mkfs is /usr/sbin/mkfs [options] <character device name>; the options are described in Table 5-1.

Table 5-1 *mkfs* **Command**

Option	Description
-F	File system type. This option can be used to specify the file system type. If this option is omitted, the /etc/vfstab and /etc/default/fs files are checked to determine a file system type.
-m	Show the command line that was used to create the specified file system. No changes are made to the file system.
-V	Verbose. Show the command line, but do not execute anything.
-o <specific options>	A list of options specific to the type of file system. The list must have the following format: -o followed by a space, followed by a series of keyword [=value] pairs, separated by commas, with no intervening spaces.

continues

Table 5-1 *mkfs* Command (continued)

keyword=value	Description
apc=<*n*>	Reserved space for bad block replacement on SCSI devices. The default is 0.
N	Print out the file system parameters without actually creating the file system.
nsect=<*n*>	The number of sectors per track on the disk. The default is 32.
ntrack=<*n*>	The number of tracks per cylinder on the disk. The default is 16.
bsize=<*n*>	Logical block size, either 4096 (4KB) or 8192 (8KB). The default is 8192. The sun4u architecture does not support the 4096 block size.
fragsize=<*bytes*>	The smallest amount of disk space, in bytes, to allocate to a file. The value must be a power of 2 selected from the range 512 to the logical block size. If logical block size is 4096, legal values are 512, 1024, 2048, and 4096. If the logical block size is 8192, 8192 is also a legal value. The default is 1024.
cgsize=<*cyls*>	The number of cylinders per cylinder group. The default is 16.
free=<*n*>	The minimum percentage of free space to maintain in the file system. This space is off limits to normal users. After the file system is filled to this threshold, only the superuser can continue writing to the file system. This parameter can be subsequently changed using the `tunefs` command. The default is 10 percent.
rps=<*rps*>	The rotational speed of the disk, specified in revolutions per second. The default is 60.
nbpi=<*value*>	The *value* specified is the number of bytes per inode, which specifies the density of inodes in the file system. The number is divided into the total size of the file system to determine the fixed number of inodes to create. It should reflect the expected average size of files in the file system. If fewer inodes are desired, a larger number should be used. To create more inodes, a smaller number should be given. The default is 2048.
opt=<*value*>	Space or time optimization preference. The *value* can be s or t. Specify s to optimize for disk space. Specify t to optimize for speed (time). The default is t. Generally, you should optimize for time unless the file system is over 90 percent full.
gap=<*milliseconds*>	Rotational delay, specified in milliseconds. Indicates the expected time (in milliseconds) required to service a transfer completion interrupt and to initiate a new transfer on the same disk. The *value* is used to decide how much rotational spacing to place between successive blocks in a file. The default is determined by the actual disk used.
nrpos=<*n*>	The number of different rotational positions in which to divide a cylinder group. The default is 8.
maxcontig=<blocks>	The maximum number of blocks, belonging to one file, that is allocated contiguously before inserting a rotational delay. For a 4KB file system, the default is 14; for an 8KB file system it is 7. This parameter can subsequently be changed using the `tunefs` command.

mkfs constructs a file system on the character, or raw, device found in the /dev/rdsk directory. Again, it is highly recommended that you do not run the mkfs command directly but instead use the friendlier newfs command, which automatically determines all the necessary parameters required by mkfs to construct the file system. In the following example, I'm specifying the -v option to the newfs command to output all the parameters passed to the mkfs utility. If you need more information on newfs, the command is described in detail in Chapter 3 of the *Solaris 2.6 Administrator Certification Guide, Part I*.

```
newfs -v /dev/rdsk/c0t0d0s0
```

The system outputs the following information and creates a new file system on /dev/rdsk/c0t0d0s0:

```
newfs: construct a new file system /dev/rdsk/c0t0d0s0: (y/n)? y
mkfs -F ufs /dev/rdsk/c0t0d0s0 2097576 117 9 8192 1024 32 6 90 4096 t 0 -1 8 15
/dev/rdsk/c0t0d0s0:     2097576 sectors in 1992 cylinders of 9 tracks, 117 sectors
1024.2MB in 63 cyl groups (32 c/g, 16.45MB/g, 4096 i/g)
super-block backups (for fsck -F ufs -o b=#) at:
32, 33856, 67680, 101504, 135328, 169152, 202976, 236800, 270624, 304448,
338272, 372096, 405920, 439744, 473568, 507392, 539168, 572992, 606816,
640640, 674464, 708288, 742112, 775936, 809760, 843584, 877408, 911232,
945056, 978880, 1012704, 1046528, 1078304, 1112128, 1145952, 1179776, 1213600,
1247424, 1281248, 1315072, 1348896, 1382720, 1416544, 1450368, 1484192,
1518016, 1551840, 1585664, 1617440, 1651264, 1685088, 1718912, 1752736,
1786560, 1820384, 1854208, 1888032, 1921856, 1955680, 1989504, 2023328,
2057152, 2090976,
```

After creating the file system with newfs, the labelit utility can be used to write or display labels on un-mounted disk file systems. The syntax for labelit is labelit -F ufs <special> [fsname volume]. Labeling a file system is optional, and is only required if using programs, such as volcopy, which is covered later in this section. The labelit command is described in Table 5-2.

Table 5-2 *labelit* **Command**

Parameter	Description
special	Name should be the physical disk section (for example, /dev/dsk/c0t0d0s6).
fsname	Represents the mount point (for example, root (/), /home, and so on) of the file system.
volume	Can be used to represent the physical volume name.

Option	Description
-F	Specify the file system type on which to operate. The file system type should either be specified here or be determinable from /etc/vfstab entry. If no matching entry is found, the default file system type specified in /etc/default/fs is used.
-V	Print the command line, but do not perform any action.

If *fsname* and *volume* are not specified, labelit prints the current values of these labels. Both *fsname* and *volume* are limited to six or fewer characters.

The following is an example of how to label a disk partition using the labelit command. Type:

labelit -F ufs /dev/rdsk/c0t0d0s6 disk1 vol1

The system responds with:

fsname: disk1
volume: vol1

The volcopy command can be used by the administrator (root) to make a copy of a labeled file system. This command works with ufs file systems, but the file system must be labeled with the labelit utility before issuing the volcopy command. To determine if a file system is a ufs file system, issue this command

fstyp   /dev/rdsk/c0t0d0s6

The system reports:

ufs

The volcopy command can be used to copy a file system from one disk to another.

The syntax for volcopy is volcopy [options] <fsname> <srcdevice> <volname1> <destdevice> <volname2>. volcopy is described in Table 5-3.

Table 5-3 *volcopy* Command

Option	Description
-F	Specify the file system type on which to operate. This should either be specified here or be determinable from /etc/vfstab entry. If no matching entry is found, the default file system type specified in /etc/default/fs is used.
-V	Print the command line, but do not perform any action.
-a	Require the operator to respond "yes" or "no." If the -a option is not specified, volcopy pauses ten seconds before the copy is made.
-o <options>	A list of options specific to the type of file system. The list must have the following format: -o followed by a space, followed by a series of *keyword [=value]* pairs, separated by commas, with no intervening spaces.
fsname	Represents the mount point (for example, root, u1, and so on) of the file system being copied.
srcdevice/destdevice	The disk partition specified using the raw device (for example, /dev/rdsk/c1t0d0s7, /dev/rdsk/c1t0d1s7, and so on).

Option	Description
srcdevice/volname1	The device and physical volume from which the copy of the file system is being extracted.
destdevice/volname2	The target device and physical volume.

fsname and *volname* are limited to six or fewer characters and recorded in the superblock. *volname* might be '-' to use the existing volume name.

The following example copies the contents of /home1 to /home2. Type:

```
volcopy -F ufs disk1 /dev/rdsk/c0t0d0s6 vol1 /dev/rdsk/c0t1d0s6 vol2
```

NOTE. *In Solaris 2.6, this command returned the following error:* Bus Error - core dumped. *As of this writing, a patch has not been provided to fix the problem.*

Other commands can also be used to copy file systems, ufsdump, cpio, tar, and dd to name a few. These commands were discussed in Part I of the *Solaris 2.6 Administrator Certification Training Guide*.

Tuning File Systems

A situation might arise where you might want to change some of the parameters that were set when you originally created the file system. Perhaps you want to change the *minfree* value to free up some additional disk space on a large disk drive. Using the tunefs command, you can modify the following file system parameters:

maxcontig

rotdelay

maxbpg

minfree

optimization

See Table 5-1, the mkfs Command, for a description of these options.

CAUTION! tunefs *is one of those commands that can destroy a file system in seconds. Always backup the entire file system before using* tunefs.

The syntax for tunefs is tunefs [-a <maxcontig>] [-d <rotdelay>] [-e <maxbpg>] [-m <minfree>] [-o [<value>] special/filesystem. The tunefs command is described in Table 5-4.

Table 5-4   *tunefs* Command

Option	Description
-a *<maxcontig>*	Specify the maximum number of contiguous blocks that are laid out before forcing a rotational delay (see the -d option). The default value is 1, because most device drivers require an interrupt per disk transfer. Device drivers that can chain several buffers together in a single transfer should set this to the maximum chain length.
-d *<rotdelay>*	Specify the expected time (in milliseconds) to service a transfer completion interrupt and to initiate a new transfer on the same disk. It is used to decide how much rotational spacing to place between successive blocks in a file.
-e *<maxbpg>*	Sets the maximum number of blocks any single file can allocate out of a cylinder group before it is forced to begin allocating blocks from another cylinder group. Typically, this value is set to approximately one quarter of the total blocks in a cylinder group. The intent is to prevent any single file from using up all the blocks in a single cylinder group. The affect of this limit is to cause big files to do long seeks more frequently than if they were enabled to allocate all the blocks in a cylinder group before seeking elsewhere. For file systems with exclusively large files, this parameter should be set higher.
-m *<minfree>*	Specify the percentage of space held back from normal users; the minimum free space threshold. The default value used is 10 percent.
-o *<value>*	Change optimization strategy for the file system. The *value* is either space or time. Use: space—to conserve space. time—to attempt to organize file layout to minimize access time. Generally, optimize a file system for time, unless it is over 90 percent full.
<special>/*<filesystem>*	Enter either the *special* device name (that is /dev/rdsk/c0t0d0s6) or the *filesystem* name (that is, /home).

The file system must be un-mounted before using tunefs.

To change the minimum free space (minfree) on a file system from 10 percent to 5 percent, type the following:

```
tunefs -m5 /dev/rdsk/c0t0d0s6
minimum percentage of free space changes from 10% to 5%
```

The man page of tunefs recommends that the minfree be set at 10 percent, and that if you set the value under that, you would lose performance. This means that 10 percent of the disk is unusable. This might not have been too bad in the days when disks were a couple hundred megabytes in size, but on a 9GB disk, you're losing 900MB of disk space. The mention of loss of performance in the main page is misleading. With such large disk drives, one can afford to have minfree as low as 1 percent. This has been found to be a practical and affordable limit. In addition, performance does not become an issue here because locating free blocks even within a 90MB area is efficient. A rule of thumb is to use the default 10 percent minfree value for file systems up to 1GB, and then adjust the minfree value so that your minfree area is no larger than 100MB. As for the performance, applications do not complain about the lower minfree value. The one exception would be the root (/) file system, in which the system administrator can use his or her judgment to allow more free space just to be conservative, in case root (/) ever becomes 100 percent full.

Later, if you want to see what parameters were used when creating a file system, issue the mkfs command. Type:

```
mkfs -m /dev/rdsk/c0t0d0s6
```

The system responds with:

```
mkfs -F ufs -o nsect=117,ntrack=9,bsize=8192,fragsize=1024,cgsize=16,free=5,rps=
90,nbpi=2062,opt=t,apc=0,gap=0,nrpos=8,maxcontig=15 /dev/rdsk/c0t0d0s6 205334
```

Another good command to view file system parameters is the fstyp command. Use the -v option to obtain a full listing of a file system's parameters as follows. Type:

```
fstyp -v /dev/rdsk/c0t0d0s6
```

The system responds with:

```
ufs
magic       11954    format    dynamic   time      Sat Oct  2 10:11:06 1999
sblkno      16       cblkno    24        iblkno    32        dblkno      528
sbsize      3072     cgsize    2048      cgoffset  64        cgmask      0xfffffff0
ncg         13       size      102667    blocks    95994
bsize       8192     shift     13        mask      0xffffe000
fsize       1024     shift     10        mask      0xfffffc00
frag        8        shift     3         fsbtodb   1
minfree     5%       maxbpg    2048      optim     time
maxcontig   15       rotdelay  0ms       rps       90
csaddr      528      cssize    1024      shift     9         mask        0xfffffe00
ntrak       9        nsect     117       spc       1053      ncyl        195
cpg         16       bpg       1053      fpg       8424      ipg         3968
nindir      2048     inopb     64        nspf      2
nbfree      11995    ndir      2         nifree    51577     nffree      1
cgrotor     0        fmod      0         ronly     0
fs_reclaim is not set
file system state is valid, fsclean is 1
blocks available in each rotational position
cylinder number 0:
    position 0:    0    8   15   22   30   37   44   52   59
    position 1:    1    9   16   23   31   38   45   53   60
    position 2:    2   10   17   24   39   46   61
    position 3:    3   18   25   32   40   47   54   62
    position 4:    4   11   19   26   33   41   48   55   63
    position 5:    5   12   20   27   34   42   49   56
    position 6:    6   13   21   28   35   50   57   64
    position 7:    7   14   29   36   43   51   58   65
```

```
cylinder number 1:
    position 0:     66    74    81    88    103   110   117   125
    position 1:     67    82    89    96    104   111   118   126
    position 2:     68    75    83    90    97    105   112   119   127
    position 3:     69    76    84    91    98    106   113   120
    position 4:     70    77    85    92    99    114   121   128
    position 5:     71    78    93    100   107   115   122   129
    position 6:     72    79    86    94    101   108   116   123   130
    position 7:     73    80    87    95    102   109   124   131
......
......
```

NOTE. *It's always a good idea to print out the* `mkfs` *options used on a file system along with information provided by the* `prtvtoc` *command. Put the printout in your system log. If you ever need to rebuild a file system because of a hard drive failure, you can recreate it exactly as it was before.*

Large Versus Small Files

On a 32-bit system, a large file is a regular file whose size is greater than or equal to 2.31GB. A small file is a regular file whose size is less than 2GB. Some utilities can handle large files, others cannot. A utility is called *large file aware* if it can process large files in the same manner as it does small files. A utility that is large file aware is able to handle large files as input and to generate large files as output. The `newfs`, `mkfs`, `mount`, `umount`, `tunefs`, `labelit`, and `quota` utilities discussed in this chapter are all large file aware for `ufs` file systems.

On the other hand, a utility is called *large file safe* if it causes no data loss or corruption if it encounters a large file. A utility that is large file safe is unable to properly process a large file, but returns an appropriate error. An example of some utilities that are not large file aware but are large file safe include `vi` editor, `mailx`, and `lp` commands.

I discuss large files further in the next section, describing mounting a file system.

Mounting a File System

In Chapter 3 of the *Solaris 2.6 Administrator Certification Training Guide, Part I*, I described the basics of how to mount file systems. I purposely did not bring up all the many options available in the `mount` command to avoid confusion. The syntax for `mount` is `mount -F <fstype> [generic_options] [ -o specific_options ] [ -O ]`. Table 5-5 describes these options.

Table 5-5 *mount* Command

Option	Description
-F <fstype>	Used to specify the FSType on which to operate. The FSType must be specified or must be determined from the /etc/vfstab file or by consulting /etc/default/fs or /etc/dfs/fstypes.
generic_options	
-m	Mount the file system without making an entry in /etc/mnttab.
-r	Mount the file system read-only.
-O	Overlay mount. Enable the file system to be mounted over an existing mount point, making the underlying file system inaccessible. If a mount is attempted on a pre-existing mount point without setting this flag, the mount fails, producing the error "device busy."
-p	Print the list of mounted file systems in the /etc/vfstab format. This must be the only option specified.
-v	Print the list of mounted file systems in verbose format. This must be the only option specified.
-V	Echo the complete command line, but do not execute the command. umount generates a command line by using the options and arguments provided by the user and adding to them information derived from /etc/mnttab. This option should be used to verify and validate the command line.
-o	Specify FSType-specific options. See the "-o specific options" in the following list.
-o specific options	Options that can be specified with the -o option. If you specify multiple options, separate them with commas (no spaces). For example, -o ro,nosuid.
-rw|ro	Specifies read/write or read-only. The default is read/write.
-nosuid	Disallows setuid execution and prevents devices on the file system from being opened. The default is to enable setuid execution and enable devices to be opened.
-remount	With rw, remounts a file system with read/write access.
-f	Fakes an entry in /etc/mnttab, but doesn't really mount any file systems.
-n	Mounts the file system without making an entry in /etc/mnttab.
-largefiles	This option specifies that a file system might contain one or more files larger than 2GB. It is not required that a file system mounted with this option contain files larger than 2GB, but the option enables such files within the file system.
-nolargefiles	This option provides total compatibility with previous file system behavior, enforcing the 2GB maximum file size limit.

The following examples illustrate the options described in table 5-5.

A file system has been created on disk c0t0d0 on slice s6. The directory to be mounted on this disk slice is /home2. To mount the file system, first create the directory called /home2, and type:

```
mount /dev/dsk/c0t0d0s0 /home2
```

If the file system has been mounted, you return to a command prompt. No other message is displayed.

In this example, the -v option is used with the mount command to display a list of mounted file systems:

```
mount -v
```

The system responds with:

```
/dev/dsk/c0t3d0s0 on / type ufs read/write/setuid/largefiles on Fri Oct  1 13:04:06
➥1999
/dev/dsk/c0t3d0s6 on /usr type ufs read/write/setuid/largefiles on Fri Oct  1 13:04:06
➥1999
/proc on /proc type proc read/write/setuid on Fri Oct  1 13:04:06 1999
fd on /dev/fd type fd read/write/setuid on Fri Oct  1 13:04:06 1999
/dev/dsk/c0t3d0s1 on /var type ufs read/write/setuid/largefiles on Fri Oct  1 13:04:06
➥1999
/dev/dsk/c0t3d0s3 on /export type ufs setuid/read/write/largefiles on Fri Oct  1
13:04:08 1999
/dev/dsk/c0t3d0s5 on /opt type ufs setuid/read/write/largefiles on Fri Oct  1 13:04:08
➥1999
swap on /tmp type tmpfs read/write on Fri Oct  1 13:04:08 1999
sparc4:/usr on /net/sparc4/usr type nfs nosuid/remote on Fri Oct  1 13:39:00 1999
/dev/dsk/c0t0d0s0 on /h
```

Type the mount command with the -p option to display a list of mounted file systems in /etc/vfstab format as follows:

```
mount -p
```

The system responds with:

```
/dev/dsk/c0t3d0s0 - / ufs - no rw,suid,largefiles
/dev/dsk/c0t3d0s6 - /usr ufs - no rw,suid,largefiles
/proc - /proc proc - no rw,suid
fd - /dev/fd fd - no rw,suid
/dev/dsk/c0t3d0s1 - /var ufs - no rw,suid,largefiles
/dev/dsk/c0t3d0s3 - /export ufs - no suid,rw,largefiles
/dev/dsk/c0t3d0s5 - /opt ufs - no suid,rw,largefiles
swap - /tmp tmpfs - no
sparc4:/usr - /net/sparc4/usr nfs - no nosuid
/dev/dsk/c0t0d0s0 - /home2 ufs - no suid,rw,largefiles
```

The -p option is useful to obtain the correct settings if making an entry in the /etc/vfstab file.

The following example mounts a file system as read only:

```
mount -o ro /dev/dsk/c0t0d0s0 /home2
```

The following example uses the mount command to map a directory to a file system as read/writeable, it disallows setuid execution, and enables the creation of large files:

```
mount -o rw,nosuid,largefiles /dev/dsk/c0t0d0s0 /home2
```

Type mount with no options to verify that the file system has been mounted and to review the mount options that were used:

```
mount
```

The system responds with information about all mounted file systems including /home2 as shown:

```
/home2 on /dev/dsk/c0t0d0s0 read/write/nosuid/largefiles on Tue Oct 5 06:56:33 1999
```

NOTE. *After you mount a file system with the default* largefiles *mount option and large files have been created, you cannot remount the file system with the* nolargefiles *option until you remove any large files and run* fsck *to reset the state to nolargefiles.*

/etc/mnttab

When a file system is mounted, an entry is maintained in the mounted file system table called /etc/mnttab. This file contains information about devices that are currently mounted. The mount command adds entries to this file, and umount removes entries from this file. Do not manually edit this file. Each entry is a line of fields separated by spaces in the form:

<special> <mount_point> <fstype> <options> <time>

Where:

special	This is the resource to be mounted (that is, /dev/dsk/c0t0d0s0).
mount_point	This is the pathname of the directory on which the file system is mounted.
fstype	This is the file system type.
options	This is the list of mount options used to mount the file system.
time	This is the time at which the file system was mounted.

An example /etc/mnttab file is as follows:

```
more /etc/mnttab
/dev/dsk/c0t3d0s0    /     ufs   rw,suid,dev=800018,largefiles    938797446
/dev/dsk/c0t3d0s6    /usr  ufs   rw,suid,dev=80001e,largefiles    938797446
/proc    /proc   proc   rw,suid,dev=2900000   938797446
fd       /dev/fd fd     rw,suid,dev=29c0000   938797446
/dev/dsk/c0t3d0s1    /var  ufs   rw,suid,dev=800019,largefiles    938797446
/dev/dsk/c0t3d0s3    /export ufs   suid,rw,largefiles,dev=80001b   938797448
/dev/dsk/c0t3d0s5    /opt  ufs   suid,rw,largefiles,dev=80001d    938797448
swap     /tmp    tmpfs  dev=1   938797448
-hosts   /net    autofs  ignore,indirect,nosuid,nobrowse,dev=2b40001   938799233
-xfn     /xfn    autofs  ignore,indirect,dev=2b40003   938799234
sparc48:vold(pid362)   /vol   nfs   ignore,noquota,dev=2b00001    938799248
-hosts   /net/sparc4/usr autofs   nosuid,nobrowse,ignore,nest,dev=2b40004 938799536
sparc4:/usr    /net/sparc4/usr nfs   nosuid,dev=2b00002    938799540
/dev/dsk/c0t0d0s0    /home2  ufs  rw,nosuid,largefiles,dev=800000 939120993
```

Unmounting a File System

To unmount a file system, use the `umount` command as follows:

`umount <mount-point>`

In the preceding code, `mount-point` is the name of the file system that you want to unmount. This can be either the directory name in which the file system is mounted or the device name path of the file system. For example, to unmount the /home2 file system, type:

`umount /home2`

Alternatively, you can specify the device name path for the file system as follows:

`umount /dev/dsk/c0t0d0s6`

Unmounting a file system removes it from the file system mount point, and deletes the entry from the /etc/mnttab file. Some file system administration tasks cannot be performed on mounted file systems, such as `labelit`, `fsck`, and `tunefs`. You should unmount a file system if:

- It is no longer needed or has been replaced by a file system that contains software that is more current.
- You need to check and repair it using the `fsck` command.
- It is a good idea to unmount a file system before doing a complete backup.

NOTE. *File systems are automatically unmounted as part of the system shutdown procedure.*

Before you can unmount a file system, you must be logged in as the administrator (root), and the file system must not be busy. A file system is considered busy if a user is in a directory in the file system or if a program has a file open in that file system. You can make a file system available for unmounting, by changing to a directory in a different file system or logging out of the system. If something is causing the file system to be busy, you can use the `fuser` command described in Table 5-6 to list all the processes accessing the file system and to stop them if necessary. Always notify users however, before unmounting a file system. The syntax for `fuser` is `/usr/sbin/fuser [options] file|filesystem`.

Table 5-6 *fuser* **Command**

Argument	Description
file|*filesystem*	This argument specifies the file or file system you are checking.

Option	Description
-c	Report on files that are mount points for file systems and on any files within that mounted file system.
-f	Print a report for the named file but not for files within a mounted file system.
-k	Send the SIGKILL signal to each process. Because this option spawns kills for each process, the kill messages might not show up immediately.
-u	Display the user login name in parentheses following the process ID.

The following example uses the `fuser` command to find out why /home2 is busy:

`fuser -u /home2`

The system displays each process and user login name that is using this file system:

`/home2:      8448c(root)      8396c(root)`

The following command stops all processes that are using the /home2 file system by sending a SIGKILL to each one. Don't use it without first warning the users.

`fuser -c -k /home2`

Volume Manager

Volume manager, with the `vold` daemon, is the mechanism that manages removable media, such as the CD-ROM and disk drives. Mounting and unmounting a file system requires root privileges. How then do you enable users to insert, mount, and unmount CD-ROMs and disks without being the administrator (root)? Volume manager solves this problem. Another problem with removable media is that after a file system has been mounted and then you remove the media, what happens to the mount? Usually when you disconnect a disk drive while it is mounted, the system begins displaying errors and messages. The same happens if you remove a disk or CD-ROM while it is mounted. Volume manager, with its `vold` daemon, provides some assistance to overcome these problems. The `vold` daemon takes care of all the interfacing to the device, mounting and unmounting removable media, and merging it as transparently as possible within the normal Solaris file system. Volume manager provides three major benefits:

- By automatically mounting disks and CDs, it simplifies their use.
- It enables the user to access disks and CDs without having to be logged in as the root.
- It enables the administrator (root) to give other systems on the network automatic access to any disks and CDs the users insert into your system.

To begin, let's look at the two devices the systems administrator needs to manage: the disk drive and the CD-ROM. Volume manager provides access to both devices through the /vol/dev directory. In addition, you see that volume manager creates links to the disk and CD-ROM devices through various directories as follows:

Link	Description
/vol/dev/diskette0	Directory providing block device access for the media in floppy drive 0.
/vol/dev/rdiskette0	Directory providing character device access for the media in floppy drive 0.
/vol/dev/aliases/floppy0	Symbolic link to the character device for the media in floppy drive 0.
/dev/rdiskette	Directory providing character device access for the media in the primary floppy drive, usually drive 0.
/vol/dev/aliases/cdrom0	Directory providing character device access for the media in the primary CD-ROM drive.
/vol/dev/dsk/	Directory providing access to the CDROM buffered, or block, device.
/vol/dev/rdsk/	Directory providing access to the CDROM character, or raw, device.
/cdrom/cdrom0	Symbolic link to the buffered device for the media in CD-ROM drive 0.
/floppy/floppy0	Symbolic link to the buffered device for the media in floppy drive 0.

Volume Manager automatically mounts CD and disk file systems when removable media containing recognizable file systems are inserted into the devices. The CD or disk file system is automatically mounted in the /vol/dev directories described earlier.

The `vold` daemon is the workhorse behind volume manager and is automatically started at startup by the /etc/init.d/volmgt script. `vold` reads the /etc/vold.conf configuration file at startup. The vold.conf file contains the volume management configuration information used by `vold`. This information includes the database to use, labels that are supported, devices to use, actions to take if certain media events occur, and the list of file systems that are unsafe to eject without unmounting. The vold.conf file looks like this:

```
# @(#)vold.conf 1.21       96/05/10 SMI
#
# Volume Daemon Configuration file
#

# Database to use (must be first)
db db_mem.so

# Labels supported
label dos label_dos.so floppy rmscsi pcmem
label cdrom label_cdrom.so cdrom
label sun label_sun.so floppy rmscsi pcmem

# Devices to use
use cdrom drive /dev/rdsk/c*s2 dev_cdrom.so cdrom%d
use floppy drive /dev/rdiskette[0-9] dev_floppy.so floppy%d
use pcmem drive /dev/rdsk/c*s2 dev_pcmem.so pcmem%d forceload=true
# use rmscsi drive /dev/rdsk/c*s2 dev_rmscsi.so rmscsi%d

# Actions
insert dev/diskette[0-9]/* user=root /usr/sbin/rmmount
insert dev/dsk/* user=root /usr/sbin/rmmount
eject dev/diskette[0-9]/* user=root /usr/sbin/rmmount
eject dev/dsk/* user=root /usr/sbin/rmmount
notify rdsk/* group=tty user=root /usr/lib/vold/volmissing -p

# List of file system types unsafe to eject
unsafe ufs hsfs pcfs
```

Each section in the vold.conf file is labeled as to its function. Of these sections, you can safely modify the Devices to Use, which are described in Table 5-7 and Actions, which are described in Table 5-8.

The "Devices to Use" section describes the devices to be managed by `vold` and has the following syntax: use <device> <type> <special> <shared_object> <symname> [options].

Table 5-7 vold.conf—Devices to Use

Parameter Fields	Description
device	The type of removable media device to be used. Legal values are cdrom and floppy.
type	The specific capabilities of the device. Legal value is drive.
special	This parameter specifies the device or devices to be used. Path usually begins with /dev.
shared_object	The name of the program that manages this device. vold expects to find this program in /usr/lib/vold.
symname	The symbolic name that refers to this device. The symname is placed in the device directory.
options	The user, group, and mode permissions for the media inserted (optional).

The *special* and *symname* parameters are related. If *special* contains any shell wildcard characters (that is, has one or more asterisks or question marks in it), then the *symname* must have a %d at its end. In this case, the devices that are found to match the regular expression are sorted, and then numbered. The first device has a zero filled in for the %d, the second device found has a one, and so on.

If the special specification does not have any shell wildcard characters then the *symname* parameter must explicitly specify a number at its end.

The Actions section specifies which program should be called if a particular event (action) occurs. The syntax for the Actions field is as follows:

```
insert regex [ options ] <program> <program_args>

eject regex [ options ] <program> <program_args>

notify regex [ options ] <program> <program_args>
```

Table 5-8 vold.conf—Actions

Parameters	Description
insert|eject|notify	The media event prompting the event
regex	This sh regular expression is matched against each entry in the /vol file system that is being affected by this event.
options	You can specify which user or group name this event is to run (optional).

Parameters	Description
program	The full pathname of an executable program to be run if *regex* is matched.
program_args	Arguments to the program.

In the default vold.conf file, you see the following entries under the Devices to Use and Actions sections:

```
# Devices to use
use cdrom drive /dev/rdsk/c*s2 dev_cdrom.so cdrom%d
use floppy drive /dev/rdiskette[0-9] dev_floppy.so floppy%d
use pcmem drive /dev/rdsk/c*s2 dev_pcmem.so pcmem%d forceload=true
# use rmscsi drive /dev/rdsk/c*s2 dev_rmscsi.so rmscsi%d

# Actions
insert dev/diskette[0-9]/* user=root /usr/sbin/rmmount
insert dev/dsk/* user=root /usr/sbin/rmmount
eject dev/diskette[0-9]/* user=root /usr/sbin/rmmount
eject dev/dsk/* user=root /usr/sbin/rmmount
notify rdsk/* group=tty user=root /usr/lib/vold/volmissing -p
```

When a CD is inserted into the CD-ROM named /dev/dsk/c0t6d0, the following happens:

1. vold detects that the CD has been inserted and runs the /usr/sbin/rmmount command. rmmount is the utility that automatically mounts a file system on a CD-ROM and floppy. It determines what type of file system, if any, is on the media. If a file system is present, rmmount mounts the file system (for a CD-ROM, in /cdrom0).

   If the media is read-only (either a CD-ROM or a floppy with write-protect tab set), the file system is mounted read-only. If a file system is not identified, rmmount does not mount a file system.

2. After the mount is complete, Actions associated with the media type are executed. The Actions enable the notification of other programs that new media is available. For example, the default action for mounting a CD-ROM or a floppy is to start the File Manager.

   These actions are described in the configuration file, /etc/rmmount.conf. Here's an example of the default /etc/rmmount.conf file:

```
# @(#)rmmount.conf 1.3    96/05/10 SMI
#
# Removable Media Mounter configuration file.
#
# File system identification
ident hsfs ident_hsfs.so cdrom
ident ufs ident_ufs.so cdrom floppy rmscsi pcmem
ident pcfs ident_pcfs.so floppy rmscsi pcmem
```

```
# Actions
action cdrom  action_filemgr.so
action floppy action_filemgr.so
action rmscsi action_filemgr.so
```

3. If the user issues the `eject` command, `vold` sees the media event and executes the action associated with that event. In this case, it runs /usr/sbin/rmmount. rmmount unmounts mounted file systems and executes actions associated with the media type called out in the /etc/rmmount.conf file. If a file system is "busy" (that is, it contains the current working directory of a live process), the eject action fails.

The System Administrator can modify vold.conf to specify which program should be called if media events happen, such as eject or insert. If the vold.conf configuration file is modified, `vold` must be told to reread the /etc/vold.conf file. Do this by stopping and starting `vold` as follows. Type:

`/etc/init.d/volmgt stop`

Then type:

`/etc/init.d/volmgt start`

There are several other commands to help you administer volume manager on your system, and they are described in Table 5-9.

Command	Description
`rmmount`	Removable media mounter. Used by `vold` to automatically mount /cdrom and /floppy if a CD or disk is installed.
`volcancel`	Cancels a user's request to access a particular CD-ROM or floppy file system. This command, issued by the System Administrator, is useful if the removable media containing the file system is not currently in the drive.
`volcheck`	The System Administrator issues this command to check the drive for installed media. By default, checks the drive pointed to by /dev/diskette.
`volmissing`	This action, which is specified in the vold.conf file, notifies the user if an attempt is made to access a CD or disk that is no longer in the drive.
`vold`	Volume Management daemon, controlled by /etc/vold.conf.

To some, volume management might seem more trouble than it's worth. To disable volume management, remove (or rename) the file named /etc/rc2.d/S92volmgt. Then, run the command: `/etc/init.d/volmgt stop`. If you want to have volume management on the CD but not the floppy, comment out the entries in the Devices to Use and Actions section of the vold.conf file with a # as follows:

```
# Devices to use
use cdrom drive /dev/rdsk/c*s2 dev_cdrom.so cdrom%d
#use floppy drive /dev/rdiskette[0-9] dev_floppy.so floppy%d
use pcmem drive /dev/rdsk/c*s2 dev_pcmem.so pcmem%d forceload=true
# use rmscsi drive /dev/rdsk/c*s2 dev_rmscsi.so rmscsi%d

# Actions
#insert dev/diskette[0-9]/* user=root /usr/sbin/rmmount
insert dev/dsk/* user=root /usr/sbin/rmmount
#eject dev/diskette[0-9]/* user=root /usr/sbin/rmmount
eject dev/dsk/* user=root /usr/sbin/rmmount
notify rdsk/* group=tty user=root /usr/lib/vold/volmissing -p
```

With the changes made to /etc/vold.conf, when the vold daemon starts up, it manages only the CD-ROM and not the floppy.

vold is picky. Knowing this is the key to not making vold crash or not work for some reason. With other computers, such as PCs, you can eject CD-ROM's with no problems. With Solaris, vold isn't that robust, and therefore, the Systems Administrator needs to follow a few ground rules when using volume manager, which are

- Always use vold commands for everything to do with CD-ROM's and floppy disks. Use the commands listed in Table 5-9 to accomplish your task.

- Before pressing the button on the outside of the box to eject a CD-ROM disk, be sure to type eject cdrom. This is to ensure you don't already have a CD in the reader.

- Never press the button to eject a CD when there is a CD already in the machine. This could cause vold to stop working. Again, use the eject cdrom command instead.

- Never kill the vold daemon. Instead, use the /etc/init.d/volmgt stop command. This is a good recommendation for all daemons that have scripts to stop and start in /etc/init.d directory. Killing the vold daemon often causes it to not restart or stop correctly.

- If you can't stop or start vold using the /etc/init.d/volmgt script, you need to restart the system to get vold working properly.

Troubleshooting Volume Manager

From time to time, there are problems with mounting a floppy or a CD-ROM. First, check to see if volume management knows about the device. The best way to do this is to look in /vol/dev/rdiskette0 and see if there is something there. If not, the volcheck command has not been run or there is some hardware problem. If references to /vol lock up the system, it means that the daemon has died, and you need to restart the vold daemon as described earlier.

If `vold` is working properly, here's what you see after inserting a formatted disk and typing:

```
ls -l /vol/dev/rdiskette0
```

System responds:

```
total 0
crw-rw-rw-   1 nobody   nobody    91,  7 Oct 13 14:56 unlabeled
```

NOTE. *The volume is unlabeled; therefore, the file in /vol/dev/rdiskette0 is called unlabeled.*

Check to make sure there is a link in /floppy to the character device in /vol/dev/rdiskette0 as shown next. Type:

```
ls -l /floppy
```

The system responds with:

```
total 18
lrwxrwxrwx   1 root     nobody    11 Oct 13 14:56 floppy0 -> ./unlabeled
```

If there's a name in /vol/dev/rdiskette0 as previously described and there's nothing mounted in /floppy/<*name_of_media*>, it's likely that data on the media is not a file system that is recognized. For example, maybe it's a `tar` archive, a `cpio` backup, or a Macintosh file system. Don't use volume manager to get to these file types. Instead, access them through the block or character devices found in /vol/dev/rdiskette0 or /vol/dev/diskette0, with user tools to interpret the data on them, such as `tar`, `dd`, or `cpio`. For example, if you're trying to access a `tar` archive on a disk, use this command:

```
tar tvf /vol/dev/rdiskette0/unlabeled
```

All `tar` files on the floppy disk be listed.

To create a `tar` file on a floppy disk, the disk must contain a SunOS volume label. Use the `fdformat` command described in Table 5-9 to format a disk and add a volume label.

Table 5-9   fdformat Command

Syntax: *fdformat [options] [<devname>]*

Option	Description
-b *label*	Label the media with a volume label. A SunOS volume label is restricted to eight characters. A DOS volume label is restricted to all uppercase characters.
-B *filename*	Install a special startup loader in filename on an MS-DOS disk. This option is only meaningful when the -d option (or -t dos) is also specified.

Option	Description
-d	Format MS-DOS media.
-D	Format a 720KB (3.5") or 360KB (5.25") double-density disk. This is the default for double-density type drives. It is needed if the drive is a high or extendeddensity type.
-e	Eject the disk when done.
-E	Format a 2.88MB (3.5") extended-density disk. This is the default for extended-density type drives.
-f	Force. Do not ask for confirmation before starting format.
-H	Format a 1.44MB (3.5") or 1.2MB (5.25") high-density disk. This is the default for high-density type drives; it is needed if the drive is the extended-density type.
-l	Format 720KB (3.5") or 360KB (5.25") double-density disk.
-L	Format 720KB (3.5") or 360KB (5.25") double-density disk.
-m	Format 1.2MB (3.5") medium-density disk.
-M	Write a 1.2MB (3.5" medium-density format on a high-density disk (use only with the -t nec option).
-U	umount any file systems and then format.
-q	Quiet; do not print status messages.
-v	Verify each block of the disk after the format.
-x	Skip the format, and only write a SunOS label or an MS-DOS file system.
-t dos	Install an MS-DOS file system and startup sector formatting. This is equivalent to the DOS format command or the –d option.
-t nec	Install an NEC-DOS file system and startup sector on the disk after formatting. This should be used only with the –M option.

In Table 5-9, the device specified for *devname* depends on whether you're using volume management or not. On systems using volume manager, replace *devname* with floppy0. If not using volume manager, replace *devname* with rdiskette0.

If *devname* is omitted, the default disk drive (/vol/dev/rdiskette0/unlabeled), if one exists, is used.

By default, fdformat uses the configured capacity of the drive to format the disk. For example, a 3.5 inch high-density drive uses disks with a formatted capacity of 1.44MBs. After formatting and verifying, fdformat writes an operating-system label on block 0. Use the -t dos option (same as the -d option) to put an MS-DOS file system on the disk after the format is done. Otherwise, fdformat writes a SunOS label in block 0.

To format the default disk device with a SunOS label so that it can be used to create a `tar` archive, insert the floppy disk and issue the following command:

`fdformat <cr>`

The system responds:

```
Formatting 1.44 MB in /vol/dev/rdiskette0/unlabeled
Press return to start formatting floppy
```

Press the Enter key and the system displays a series of dots, as follows, until formatting is complete:

```
...................................
```

You can then create a `tar` archive on the disk as follows. Type:

`tar cvf /vol/dev/rdiskette0/unlabeled /etc/hosts`

The /etc/hosts file is written to the disk in `tar` format.

If you're still having problems with volume manager, one way to gather debugging information is to run the `rmmount` command with the debug flag. To do this, edit /etc/vold.conf and change the lines that have `/usr/sbin/rmmount` to include the `-D` flag. For example:

`insert /vol*/dev/diskette[0-9]/* user=root /usr/sbin/rmmount -D`

This causes various debugging messages to appear on the console.

To see debugging messages from the volume manager daemon, run the daemon, /usr/sbin/vold, with the `-v` `-L 10` flags and it logs data to /var/adm/vold.log. This file might contain information that could be useful in troubleshooting.

You might also want to mount the CD-ROM on a different mount point using volume management. `vold`, by default, mounts the CD-ROM on the mount point /cdrom/cdrom0, but the user can mount it on a different mount point by following these instructions:

1. If the volume manager is running, bring up the file manager and eject the CD-ROM by issuing the following command:

   `eject cdrom`

2. Stop the volume management daemon by issuing:

   `/etc/init.d/volmgt stop`

3. Make the directory called /test as follows:

   `mkdir /test`

4. Insert the CD-ROM in the CD drive and issue the command:

   /usr/sbin/vold -d /test &

Now instead of using the /vol directory, `vold` will use /test as the starting directory.

Information on File Systems

In Part I of the *Solaris 2.6 Administrator Certification Training Guide*, I described the `df` and `fsck` commands. The `df` command gives us capacity information on each mounted file system. The output of `df` and `fsck` is often misunderstood. This section goes into more detail on these two commands and describes the output so that you can better understand the information displayed. I begin with the `fsck` command. Remember, only run `fsck` on umounted file systems as shown in the following example. Type:

```
umount /home2
fsck /dev/rdsk/c0t0d0s6
```

The system responds with:

```
** /dev/rdsk/c0t0d0s6
** Last Mounted on /home2
** Phase 1 - Check Blocks and Sizes
** Phase 2 - Check Pathnames
** Phase 3 - Check Connectivity
** Phase 4 - Check Reference Counts
** Phase 5 - Check Cyl groups
5 files, 19 used, 95975 free (15 frags, 11995 blocks,  0.0% fragmentation)
```

`fsck` first reports some things related to usage.

files	Number of files in the file system
used	Number of data blocks used
free	Number of data blocks free (fragments and whole blocks)

NOTE. *A fragment is one data block in size and a block consists of a number of data blocks, typically eight.*

Then `fsck` reports more details of the free space.

frags	Number of free fragments (from fragmented blocks)
blocks	Number of *blocks* free (whole un-fragmented blocks)
% frag	Free fragments as a percentage of the whole disk size

Fragmentation does not refer to fragmentation in the sense of a file's disk blocks being inefficiently scattered across the whole file system, as you see in a DOS file system.

In Solaris, a high percentage fragmentation implies that much of the free space is tied up in fragments. In the previous example, fragmentation was 0 percent. High fragmentation affects creating new files and especially those larger than a few data blocks. Typically, high fragmentation would be caused by creating large numbers of small files. The solution is to either create a larger file system or decrease the block size (finer granularity). For example, in a file system that creates predominantly 5KB files on an 8KB block size, there are many 3KB frags free and never used. In the extreme case, this would result in a file system that is effectively full, despite only 5/8 of the file system being used. If the block size is decreased to 4KB, which is the smallest block size available in Solaris 2.6, there is some improvement. The solution can be summarized as follows:

Block size	Typical pattern
8KB blocks	Many 5KB frag blocks and 3KB frags wasted
4KB blocks	Many full blocks plus 1 full frag block per 4 full blocks, which is much better

Now, let's review the output from the `df` command:

```
mount /dev/dsk/c0t0d0s6 /home2
df   -k /home2
```

The system responds with:

```
Filesystem          Kbytes    used    avail    capacity    Mounted on
/dev/dsk/c0t0d0s6   95994     19      91176    1%          /home2
```

The information presented is:

95994KBs	The file system size. This value includes the 5 percent `minfree`.
19KBs used	The amount of space used in the file system.
91176KBs avail	Space available in the file system. This value is equal to the file system size less the `minfree%` less the space used (95994-5%-19).
1 percent capacity	Space used as a percentage calculated as follows: kilobytes used/(kilobytes available less `minfree%`)

This concludes the discussion of local file systems. In the next chapter, I discuss how to connect systems over the network. I also describe how to share file systems with other hosts on the network using NFS (Networked File Systems).

CHAPTER 6

The NFS Environment

The following test objectives are covered in this chapter:

- NFS servers and clients
- Configuring and managing the NFS environment
- Sharing and accessing remote resources
- WebNFS
- Using Automount

The Network File System (NFS) service enables computers of different architectures, running different operating systems (OSs), to share file systems across a network. Just as the `mount` command enables you to mount a file system on a local disk, NFS enables you to mount a file system that is located on another system anywhere on the network. Furthermore, NFS support has been implemented on many platforms ranging from MS-DOS on personal computers to mainframe OSs, such as MVS. Each OS applies the NFS model to its file system semantics. For example, a Sun system can mount the file system from a Windows NT or Linux system located miles away. File system operations, such as reading and writing, function as though they were accessing a local file. Response time might be slower because of network traffic, but the connection is transparent to the user regardless of the hardware or OS. The NFS service provides the following benefits:

- Enable multiple computers to use the same files so that everyone on the network can access the same data. This eliminates the need to have redundant data on several systems.

- Reduces storage costs, by having computers share applications and data.

- Provides data consistency and reliability, because all users can read the same set of files.

- Makes mounting of file systems transparent to users.

- Makes accessing remote files transparent to users.

- Supports heterogeneous environments.

- Reduces system administration overhead.

The NFS service makes the physical location of the file system irrelevant to the user. You can use NFS to enable users to see all the data, regardless of location. Instead of placing copies of commonly used files on every system, the NFS service enables the system administrator to place one copy on one computer's disk and have all other systems access it across the network. Under NFS operation, remote file systems are almost indistinguishable from local ones.

Servers and Clients

With NFS, systems have a client-server relationship. The NFS server is where the file system resides. Any system with a local file system can be a NFS server. As I will describe later in this chapter, the system administrator configures the NFS server to make file systems available to other systems and users. The system administrator has complete control over which file systems can be mounted and who can mount them.

A NFS client is a system that mounts a remote file system from a NFS server. I'll describe later in this chapter how the system administrator creates a local directory and mounts the file system. As you will see, a system can be both a NFS server and a client.

NFS on Solaris

NFS was developed by Sun Microsystems, and it has been ported to most popular OSs. The implementation of NFS is large, and it varies from system to system. As the NFS service evolved, it went through a few version levels. Therefore, if using NFS to connect to another system, you need to be aware of the different versions of NFS.

NFS Version 2 was the first version of the NFS protocol in wide use. It continues to be available on a large variety of platforms. SunOS releases previous to Solaris 2.5 support Version 2 of the NFS protocol. NFS 2.0 suffers many shortcomings. For example, Unix-based servers are moving to 64-bit implementations, and the 8KB data packet size used by NFS Version 2 is a bottleneck for transferring data. Sun, Digital, IBM, Hewlett-Packard, and Data General toiled with these and other problems and together they released NFS 3.0 in 1995 as RFC 1813.

NFS 3.0 was introduced with Solaris 2.5. Several changes have been made to improve inter-operability and performance. However, to take advantage of these improvements, the Version 3 protocol must be running on both the NFS server and the NFS clients. NFS 3.0 introduced the following enhancements over Version 2:

- NFS 3.0 enables safe asynchronous writes onto the server, which improves performance by enabling the server to cache client write requests in memory. The client does not need to wait for the server to commit the changes to disk; therefore, the response time is faster.

- The server can batch requests, which improves the response time on the server.

- All NFS operations return the file attributes, which are stored in the local cache. Because the cache is updated more often, the need to do a separate operation to update this data arises less often. Therefore, the number of remote procedure calls to the server is reduced, improving performance.

- The process for verifying file access permissions has been improved. In particular, Version 2 would generate a message reporting a "write error" or a "read error" if users tried to copy a remote file to which they did not have permissions. In Version 3, the permissions are checked before the file is opened, so the error is reported as an "open error."

- Version 3 removes the 8KB transfer size limit and enables the client and server to negotiate a maximum transfer size.

- Access control list (ACL) support was added to the Version 3 release. ACLs provide a finer-grained mechanism to set file access permissions than is available through standard UNIX file permissions.

- The default transport protocol for the NFS protocol was changed from User Datagram Protocol (UDP) to the Transport Control Protocol (TCP), which helps performance on slow networks and wide-area networks (WANs). UDP was preferred initially because it performed well on local-area networks (LANs) and was faster than TCP. Although UDP benefited from the high bandwidth and low latency typical of LANs, it performed poorly when subjected to the low bandwidth and high latency of WANs, such as the Internet. In recent years, improvements in hardware and TCP implementations have narrowed this advantage enough that TCP implementations can now outperform UDP. A growing number of NFS implementations now support TCP. TCP provides congestion control and error recovery.

- Version 3 improved the network lock manager, which provides UNIX record locking and PC file sharing for NFS files. The locking mechanism is now more reliable for NFS files; therefore, commands like `ksh` and `mail`, which use locking, are less likely to hang.

With Solaris 2.6, the NFS 3.0 protocol went through yet more enhancements. These include:

- The Solaris 2.6 release of the NFS 3.0 protocol can correctly manipulate files larger than 2GBs, which was not formerly possible.

- The Solaris 2.6 implementation defaults to a 32KB transfer size. The effect of larger transfer sizes is to reduce the number of NFS requests required to move a given quantity of data, providing a better use of network bandwidth and I/O resources on clients and servers. If the server supports it, a client can issue a read request that downloads a file in a single operation.

- The Solaris 2.6 release supports dynamic failover of read-only file systems. This provides a high level of availability. With failover, multiple replicas are specified in case a NFS server goes down, and another mount point on an alternative server can be specified.

- The Solaris 2.6 release provides WebNFS the capability to make a file system on the Internet accessible through firewalls using an extension to the NFS protocol. WebNFS provides greater throughput, under a heavy load, than does Hypertext Transfer Protocol (HTTP) access to a Web server. In addition, it provides the capability to share files over the Internet without the administrative overhead of an anonymous File Transfer Protocol (FTP) site. WebNFS is described later in this chapter.

NOTE. *When using NFS, make sure that the systems you'll be connecting to are all at the same version of NFS. You might experience problems if your system is at NFS Version 2 and the system to which you are trying to connect is at NFS 3.0.*

NFS Daemons

NFS uses a number of daemons to handle its services. These services are initialized at start up from the /etc/init.d/nfs.server and /etc/init.d/nfs.clients startup scripts. The most important daemons are outlined in the following table.

nfsd	Handles file system exporting and file access requests from remote systems. A NFS server runs multiple instances of this daemon. This daemon is usually invoked at run level 3 and started by the /etc/init.d/nfs.server startup script.
mountd	Handles mount requests from NFS clients. This daemon also provides information about which file systems are mounted by which clients. Use the showmount command described later in this chapter to view this information.
lockd	Manages file locking on both the NFS server and the NFS client systems.
statd	Interacts with lockd to provide the crash and recovery functions for the locking services on NFS.
rpcbind	Facilitates the initial connection between the client and the server.

Setting Up NFS

Servers enable other systems to access their file systems by sharing them over the NFS environment. We refer to a shared file system as a shared resource. You specify which file systems are to be shared by entering the information in a file called /etc/dfs/dfstab. Entries in this file are shared automatically whenever you start the NFS server operation. You should set up automatic sharing if you need to share the same set of file systems on a regular basis. Most file system sharing should be done automatically; the only time that manual sharing should occur is during testing or troubleshooting.

The /etc/dfs/dfstab file lists all the file systems that your NFS server shares with its NFS clients. It also controls which clients can mount a file system. If you want to modify /etc/dfs/dfstab to add or delete a file system or to modify the way sharing is done, edit the file with a text editor, such as vi or textedit. The next time the computer enters run level 3, the system reads the updated /etc/dfs/dfstab to determine which file systems should be shared automatically.

Each line in the dfstab file consists of a share command as shown in the following example:

```
more /etc/dfs/dfstab
```

The system displays the contents of /etc/dfs/dfstab:

```
#       Place share(1M) commands here for automatic execution
#       on entering init state 3.
#
#       Issue the command '/etc/init.d/nfs.server start' to run the NFS
#       daemon processes and the share commands, after adding the very
#       first entry to this file.
#
#       share [-F fstype] [ -o options] [-d "<text>"] <pathname> [resource]
#       .e.g,
#       share  -F nfs  -o rw=engineering  -d "home dirs"  /export/home2
share -F nfs /export
share -F nfs /cdrom/solaris_srvr_intranet_ext_1_0
```

The /usr/sbin/share command exports a resource, or makes a resource available for mounting. If invoked with no arguments, share displays all shared file systems. The share command, described in Table 6-1, can be run at the command line to achieve the same results as the /etc/dfs/dfstab file, but use this method only when testing.

The syntax for the share command is

share -F <FSType> -o <options> -d <description> <pathname>

In the previous code example, *pathname* is the name of the file system to be shared.

Table 6-1 *share* **Command**

Option	Description
-F <FSType>	Specify the files system type, such as nfs. If the –F option is omitted, the first file system type listed in /etc/dfs/fstypes is used as the default.
-o <options>	Select from the following options:
	rw — pathname is shared read/write to all clients. This is also the default behavior.
	rw=client[:client]... — pathname is shared read/write but only to the listed clients. No other systems can access pathname.
	ro — pathname is shared read-only to all clients.
	ro=client[:client]... — pathname is shared read-only but only to the listed clients. No other systems can access pathname.
anon=<uid>	Set *uid* to be the effective user ID of unknown users. By default, unknown users are given the effective *uid* nobody. If *uid* is set to –1, access is denied.
index=<file>	Load a *file* rather than a listing of the directory containing this specific file when the directory is referenced by a NFS Uniform Resource Locator (URL). See the WebNFS section later in this chapter.

continues

Table 6-1 *share* **Command (continued)**

Option	Description
nosub	Prevents clients from mounting subdirectories of shared directories.
nosuid	The server file system silently ignores any attempt to enable the setuid or setgid mode bits. By default, clients are enabled to create files on the shared file system if the setuid or setgid mode is enabled. See Part I of the *System Administrator Certification Training Guide* for a description of setuid and setgid.
public	Enables NFS browsing of the file system by a WebNFS enabled browser. Only one file system per server can use this option. The -ro=list and -rw=list options can be included with this option.
root=host[: host]...	Only root users from the specified hosts have root access. By default, no host has root access; so, root users are mapped to an anonymous user ID (see the anon=uid option previously described).
-d <description>	Provide a description of the resource being shared.

To share a file system as read-only every time the system is started up, add this line to the /etc/dfs/dfstab file:

```
share -F nfs -o ro /data
```

After editing the /etc/dfs/dfstab file, restart the NFS server by either restarting it or by typing:

```
/etc/init.d/nfs.server start
```

You only need to start the nfs.server script after you make the first entry in the /etc/dfs/dfstab file. This is because at start up, when the system enters run level 3, mountd and nfsd are not started if the /etc/dfs/dfstab file is empty. After you have made an initial entry and have executed the nfs.server script, modifications can be made to /etc/dfs/dfstab without restarting the daemons. You simply execute the shareall command, and any new entries in the /etc/dfs/dfstab file are shared.

NOTE. *Even if you share a file system from the command line by typing the* share *command, mountd and nfsd are still not running until you make an entry into /etc/dfs/dfstab and run the nfs.server script.*

After you have at least one entry in the /etc/dfs/dfstab file and after both mountd and nfsd are running, you can share additional file systems by typing the share command directly from the command line. Be aware however, that if you don't add the entry to the /etc/dfs/dfstab file, the file system is not automatically shared the next time the system is restarted.

The `dfshares` command displays information about the shared resources available to the host from a NFS server. The syntax for `dfshares` is:

```
dfshares <servername>
```

You can view the shared file systems on a remote NFS server by using the `dfshares` command as follows:

```
dfshares apollo
```

If no *servername* is specified, all resources currently being shared on the local host are displayed. Another place to find information on shared resources is in the server's /etc/dfs/sharetab file. This file contains a list of the resources currently being shared.

NFS Security

With NFS, you need to be concerned about security. When issuing the previous share command, any system can access the file system through your network. It's a good idea to be more specific about who can mount the file system. The following examples illustrate how to setup a share with restrictions as to which hosts can mount the shared resource:

```
share -F nfs -o ro=apollo:neptune:zeus /data
```

The file system named /data is shared read-only to the listed clients only. No other systems can access /data. Another method is to share a file system read-only to some hosts and read-write to others. Use the following command to accomplish this:

```
share -F nfs -o ro=apollo rw=neptune:zeus /data
```

In the example, apollo has read-only access; neptune and zeus have read-write access.

The next example specifies that root access be granted to the client named zeus. A root user coming from any other system is recognized only as nobody and has limited access rights:

```
share -F nfs -o root=zeus /data
```

CAUTION! *Root permissions should not be enabled on a NFS file system. Administrators might find this annoying if trying to modify a file through a NFS mount, but disastrous mistakes can be eliminated. For example, if a root user wants to purge a file system called /data on one host, a* `rm -rf *` *would be disastrous if there is a NFS mounted file system with root permission mounted under /data. If /data/thor is a mounted file system under /data, the files located on the NFS server would be wiped out.*

To remove a shared file system, issue the `unshare` command on the server as follows:

unshare /data

The /data file system is no longer shared. You can verify this by issuing the `share` command with no options:

share

The system responds:

-           /home   ro,anon=0   " "

Only the file system named /home is returned as shared.

NOTE. *If* `share` *commands are invoked multiple times on the same file system, the last* `share` *invocation supersedes the previous. The options set by the last* `share` *command replace the old options.*

Mounting a Remote File System

In Part I of the *Solaris Administrator Certification Training Guide*, I described how to mount a local file system using the `mount` command. We'll use the same `mount` command to mount a shared file system on a remote host using NFS. The syntax for mounting NFS file systems is:

mount -F nfs <options> <-o specific_options > <-O> <server>:<filesystem>   <mount_point>

In the previous code example, `server` is the name of the NFS server in which the file system is located, `filesystem` is the name of the shared file system on the NFS server, and `mount_point` is the name of the local directory which serves as the mount point.

As you can see, it is similar to mounting a local file system. The options are described in Table 6-2.

Table 6-2   NFS *mount* Command

Option	Description
-r	Mount the specified file system as read-only.
-m	Do not append an entry to the /etc/mnttab table of mounted file systems.

Option	Description
-o <specific_options>	specific_options is any of the following options separated by a comma.
rw | ro	The resource is mounted read-write or read-only. The default is rw.
suid | nosuid	Setuid execution is enabled or disabled. The default is suid.
remount	If a file system is mounted as read-only, this option remounts the file system as read-write.
bg | fg	If the first attempt to mount the remote file system fails, retry in the background (bg), or in the foreground (fg). The default is fg.
quota	Enables quota to check whether the user is over quota on this file system; if the file system has quotas enabled on the server, quotas will still be checked for operations on this file system.
noquota	Prevents quota from checking whether the user exceeded the quota on this file system; if the file system has quotas enabled on the server, quotas will still be checked for operations on this file system.
retry=n	The number of times to retry the mount operation. The default is 10000.
vers= <NFS version number>	By default, the version of NFS protocol used between the client and the server is the highest one available on both systems. If the NFS server does not support NFS 3.0 protocol, then the NFS mount uses NFS Version 2 protocol.
port=n	The server IP port number. The default is NFS_PORT.
rsize=<n>	Set the read buffer size to <n> bytes. The default value is 32768 if using Version 3 of the NFS protocol. The default can be negotiated down if the server prefers a smaller transfer size. If using Version 2, then the default value is 8192.
wsize=<n>	Set the write buffer size to <n> bytes. The default value is 32768 if using Version 3 of the NFS protocol. The default can be negotiated down if the server prefers a smaller transfer size. If using Version 2, then the default value is 8192.
timeo=<n>	Set the NFS timeout to <n> tenths of a second. The default value is 11 tenths of a second for connectionless transports and 600 tenths of a second for connection-oriented transports.
retrans=<n>	Set the number of NFS retransmissions to <n>; the default value is 5. For connection-oriented transports, this option has no effect, because it is assumed that the transport will perform retransmissions on behalf of NFS.
soft | hard	Returns an error if the server does not respond (soft), or continues the retry request until the server responds (hard). If using hard, the system appears to hang until the NFS server responds. The default value is hard.
intr | nointr	Enable (do not enable) keyboard interrupts to kill a process that is hung while waiting for a response on a hard-mounted file system. The default is intr, which makes it possible for clients to interrupt applications that might be waiting for a NFS server to respond.
-O	The overlay mount enables the file system to be mounted over an existing mount point, making the underlying file system inaccessible. If a mount is attempted on a pre-existing mount point without setting this flag, the mount fails, producing the error "device busy."

A note regarding foreground (fg) and background (bg) mounts. File systems mounted with the bg option indicate that mount is to retry in the background if the server's mount daemon (mountd) does not respond when, for example, the NFS server is restarted. From the NFS client, mount retries the request up to the count specified in the retry=<n> option. After the file system is mounted, each NFS request made in the kernel waits a specified number of seconds for a response (specified with the timeo=<n> option). If no response arrives, the time-out is multiplied by two and the request is retransmitted. If the number of retransmissions has reached the number specified in the retrans=<n> option, a file system mounted with the soft option returns an error and the file system mounted with the hard option prints a warning message and continues to retry the request. Sun recommends that file systems mounted as read-write, or containing executable files, should always be mounted with the hard option. If using soft mounted file systems, unexpected I/O errors can occur. Take, for example, a write request. If the NFS server goes down, the pending write request would simply give up, resulting in a corrupted file on the remote file system. A read-write file system should always be mounted with the hard and intr options specified. This enables users to make their own decisions about killing hung processes.

If a file system is mounted hard and the intr option is not specified, then, the process hangs until the remote file system reappears if the NFS server goes down. For a terminal process, this can be annoying. If intr is specified, then sending an interrupt signal to the process kills it. For a terminal process, this can be done by typing Ctrl-C. For a background process, sending an INT or QUIT signal as follows usually works:

```
kill -QUIT 3421
```

NOTE. *Sending a KILL signal (-9) does not kill a hung NFS process.*

To mount a file system called /data, which is located on a NFS server called thor, issue the following command, as root, from the NFS client:

```
mount -F nfs -o ro thor:/data /thor_data
```

In this case, the /data file system from the server thor is mounted read-only on /thor_data on the local system. Mounting from the command line enables temporary viewing of the file system. If the umount command is issued or the system is restarted, the mount is lost. If you would like this file system to be mounted automatically at every start up, add the following line to the /etc/vfstab file:

```
thor:/data - /thor_data nfs - yes ro
```

NOTE. *The* mount *and* umount *commands require root access. The* umount *command and /etc/vfstab file are described in Part I of the Solaris Administrator Certification Training Guide.*

To view resources that can be mounted on the local or remote system, use the dfmounts command as follows:

```
dfmounts sparcserver
```

The system responds with a list of file systems currently mounted on sparcserver:

```
RESOURCE     SERVER          PATHNAME                                       CLIENTS
   -         sparcserver     /cdrom/sol_2_6_hw2_sparc_smcc_dt/s0             pyramid2
   -         sparcserver     /cdrom/solaris_srvr_intranet_ext_1_0 (anon)     ntserver
   -         sparcserver     /jumpstart                                      pyramid2
   -         sparcserver     /usr/local/boot/Solaris_2.6/Tools/Boot          pyramid2
```

Sometimes you rely on NFS mount points for critical information. If the NFS server were to go down unexpectedly, you would lose the information contained at that mount point. You can address this issue by using client-side failover. With client-side failover, you specify an alternative file system to use in case the primary file system fails. These file systems should contain equivalent directory structures and identical files. This option is available only on read-only file systems. To set up client-side failover, follow this procedure:

On the NFS client, mount the file system using the -ro option. You can do this from the command line, or by adding an entry to the /etc/vfstab file that looks like the following:

```
zeus,thor:/data   -   /remote_data   nfs   -   no   -o ro
```

If multiple file systems are named and the first server in the list is down, then failover uses the next alternative server to access files. To mount a replicated set of NFS file systems, which might have different paths to the file system, use the following mount command:

```
mount -F nfs -o ro zeus:/usr/local/data,thor:/home/data /usr/local/data
```

Replication is discussed again in the section that describes autofs.

WebNFS

WebNFS is a product and proposed standard protocol from Sun Microsystems that extends its NFS to the Internet. Sun believes WebNFS offers considerable performance advantages over the current Internet protocols, the HTTP and the FTP. Netscape, Oracle, IBM, Apple, and Novell have announced support for WebNFS.

The World Wide Web has become the people's choice for information distribution and sharing across the Internet. The Web's ease of use and widespread availability has enabled it to outshine similar technologies. Unfortunately, the protocol for the Web, HTTP, leaves much to be desired in terms of performance. HTTP is a one-way protocol that transfers multiple data formats inefficiently. Entire pages and all their contents must be transferred at the same time to the requesting browser. On the other hand, NFS works with only portions of files at a time, usually only the sections that are in use. It is possible to update sections of a file with NFS, a task that is virtually impossible with HTTP. The following are the benefits of WebNFS over HTTP and FTP:

- **Connection Management**—A WebNFS client can download multiple files over a single, persistent TCP connection.

- **Concurrency**—WebNFS clients can issue multiple, concurrent requests to a NFS server. The effect is a better use of server and network resources and better performance for the end user.

- **Fault Tolerance**—WebNFS is well known for its fault tolerance in the face of network and server failures. If interrupted, other FTPs require the download to be resumed from the beginning, causing users to retrace steps and waste time in duplicating efforts. However, if a WebNFS client faces an interruption, it can resume a download from where it was previously left off.

- **Performance and Scalability**—NFS servers currently handle over 21,000 operations per second. They are highly integrated with the OS, tuned for maximum system performance, and easy to administer.

WebNFS makes remote file access simple and safe. In addition, it can work with and through firewalls, meaning system administrators can now specify which directories or files they want to "export," or make available over the Internet. After these files are exported and an application requests them, WebNFS can automatically locate them, negotiate file access privileges, and transparently "mount" the files from anywhere on the Internet. Users can then access that data as if it were local to their machine.

Unlike current file access protocols, such as FTP and HTTP, WebNFS is a complete file system, which supports in-place editing of a file, eliminating the need to download, edit, and upload the file. Instead, users can edit the original file right from their desktops. This saves time and preserves the integrity of shared files.

WebNFS can mount an entire file system at a time or it can communicate with individual files on the server. This feature is known as multi-component lookup (MCL), and it enables the client to look up a document based on a full given path to a file rather than having to look up individual components of that path until deriving the actual file location. For example, to look up a file like /books/solaris/test.txt in NFS, you have to look up the individual components (books and solaris) before you can find test.txt. With WebNFS, you simply pass the entire path to the server itself and have the server return the file handle directly; this improves performance by saving several steps of data transfers.

WebNFS also follows the improvements in NFS 3.0 by including larger data transfers than the 8KB limit imposed in NFS 2.0, a 64-bit data word size for files, and file systems larger than 4 gigabytes.

To use WebNFS, your Web browser needs a client and the Web or FTP server needs to have a WebNFS server. If requesting a file with WebNFS, your Internet address or URL would look something like one of the following:

```
nfs://computer.site.com/filedirectory/file
nfs://<server>:<port>/<path>
nfs://mymachine.javaworld.com:2049/home/rawn/webnfs.txt
nfs://mymachine.javaworld.com/pub/edit.doc
```

NOTE. *Notice the pathname for a NFS URL should not begin with a slash. A path that begins with a slash is evaluated relative to the server's root, rather than the public file handle directory.*

NFS replaces the HTTP or FTP schema and needs to be implemented directly into the browser. The default port number is 2049; if *port* is omitted, it defaults to 2049. This is the NFS port for TCP connections. The previously shown directory structure is actually a relative path from a base that the NFS server understands.

WebNFS has several advantages over HTTP and FTP. The WebNFS protocol does not require the opening and closing of a connection for each requested file. Very large file downloads are supported, and because they are downloaded in sections, they can be re-sent more quickly in case the download is interrupted. Sun Microsystems suggests that WebNFS might be a technology proposal to replace, or be part of, the next generation of HTTP, currently being worked on by members of the World Wide Web Consortium (W3C).

How to Enable WebNFS Access

Starting with Solaris 2.6, all file systems available for NFS mounting are automatically available for WebNFS access. To manually configure a file system for WebNFS access, follow these steps:

1. Edit the /etc/dfs/dfstab file. Add one entry to the /etc/dfs/dfstab file for the file system that you want shared automatically. The `index` tag is optional:

    ```
    share -F nfs -o ro,public,index=index.html /export/ftp
    ```

2. Check that the NFS service is running on the server. If this is the first `share` command, or set of `share` commands, that you have initiated, it is likely that the NFS daemons are not running. The following commands kill and restart the daemons.

    ```
    /etc/init.d/nfs.server stop
    /etc/init.d/nfs.server start
    ```

3. Share the file system. After the entry is in /etc/dfs/dfstab, the file system can be shared either by restarting the system or by using the `shareall` command. If the NFS daemons were restarted in Step 2, then this command does not need to be run because the init.d script runs the command.

    ```
    shareall
    ```

4. Verify that the information is correct. Execute the `share` command to check that the correct options are listed:

    ```
    share
    ```

    The system should respond with output that looks something like this:

    ```
    -         /export/share/man    ro                          ""
    -         /usr/src             rw=eng                      ""
    -         /export/ftp          ro,public,index=index.html  ""
    ```

Using a Browser to Access a NFS URL

Browsers capable of supporting WebNFS access should provide access using a NFS URL that looks something like:

```
nfs://<server>:<port>/<path>
```

In the previous code example, *server* is the name of the file server, *port* is the port number to use (the default value is 2049), and *path* is the path to the file or file system. The *path* can be either relative to the public file handle or relative to the root file system on the server.

NOTE. *Make sure your browser supports WebNFS, otherwise you'll get an error similar to the following: "NFS URLs are not supported." Currently, Sun's HotJava browser supports WebNFS and Netscape says that they will provide support on a future release. Microsoft's Internet Explorer does not support WebNFS.*

You can enable WebNFS access for clients that are not part of the local subnet by configuring the firewall to enable a TCP connection on port 2049. Just allowing access for httpd does not allow NFS URLs to be used.

Autofs

When a network contains even a moderate number of systems, all trying to mount file systems from each other, managing NFS can quickly become a nightmare. The Autofs facility, also called the automounter, is designed to handle such situations by providing a method in which remote directories are mounted only when they are being used. When a user or application accesses a NFS mount point, the mount is established. When the file system is no longer needed, or has not been accessed for a certain period, the file system is automatically unmounted. As a result, network overhead is lower, the system boots faster because NFS mounts are done later, and systems can be shut down with fewer ill effects and hung processes.

File systems shared through the NFS service can be mounted using Autofs. Autofs, a client-side service, is a file system structure that provides automatic mounting. The autofs file system is initialized by automount, which is run automatically when a system is started up. The automount daemon, named automountd, runs continuously, mounting and unmounting remote directories on an as-needed basis.

Mounting does not need to be done at system startup, and the user no longer has to know the superuser password to mount a directory. With Autofs, users do not use the `mount` and `umount` commands. The autofs service mounts file systems as the user accesses them and unmounts file systems when they are no longer required without any intervention on the part of the user.

Some file systems however, still need to be mounted using the `mount` command with root privileges. A diskless computer for example, must mount / (root), /usr, and /usr/kvm using the `mount` command and cannot take advantage of autofs.

Two programs support the autofs service: `automount` and `automountd`. Both are run when a system is started up by the /etc/init.d/autofs script.

The `automount` service sets up the autofs mount points and associates the information in the auto_master files with each mount point. The `automount` command, called at system startup time, reads the master map file named auto_master to create the initial set of autofs mounts.

These autofs mounts are not automatically mounted at startup time. They are trigger points, also called trigger nodes, under which file systems are mounted in the future. The syntax for `automount` is:

```
automount -t duration -v
```

In the previous code example:

-t	Duration sets the time, in seconds, which a file system is to remain mounted if it is not being used.
-v	Selects the verbose mode. Running this command in the verbose mode allows easier troubleshooting.

If not specifically set, the value for *duration* of an unused mount is set to five minutes. In most circumstances, this value is good; however, on systems that have many automounted file systems, you might need to increase the duration value. In particular, if a server has many users, active checking of the automounted file systems every five minutes can be inefficient. By unmounting the file systems every five minutes, it is possible that /etc/mnttab, which is checked by `df`, can get large. Checking the autofs file systems every 1800 seconds (or 30 minutes) could be more optimal. Edit the /etc/init.d/autofs script to change the default values.

If autofs receives a request to access a file system that is not currently mounted, autofs calls `automountd`, which actually mounts the requested file system under the trigger node.

The `automountd` daemon handles the mount and unmount requests from the autofs service. The syntax of the command is:

```
automountd  < -Tnv >  < -D name=value >
```

In the previous code example:

-T	Displays each Remote Procedure Call (RPC) to standard output. Use this option for troubleshooting.
-n	Disables browsing on all autofs nodes.
-v	Logs all status messages to the console.
-D	name=value substitutes value for the automount map variable indicated by name. The default value for the automount map is /etc/auto_master.

The `automountd` daemon is completely independent from the `automount` command. Because of this separation, it is possible to add, delete, or change map information without first having to stop and start the `automountd` daemon process.

To illustrate autofs in action, here is what happens:

automount and automountd initiate at startup time from the /etc/init.d/autofs script. If a request is made to access a file system at an autofs mount point, the system goes through the following steps:

1. Autofs intercepts the request.
2. Autofs sends a message to the automountd for the requested file system to be mounted.
3. automountd locates the file system information in a map and performs the mount.
4. Autofs enables the intercepted request to proceed.
5. Autofs unmounts the file system after a period of inactivity.

NOTE. *Mounts managed through the autofs service should not be manually mounted or unmounted. Even if the operation is successful, the autofs service does not check that the object has been unmounted, resulting in possible inconsistency. A restart clears all autofs mount points.*

To see who might be using a particular NFS mount, use the showmount command described in Table 6-3. The syntax for the showmount command is showmount <options>.

Table 6-3 *showmount* **Command**

Option	Description
-a	Print all the remote mounts in the format: *hostname* : *directory* *hostname* is the name of the client, and *directory* is the root of the file system that has been mounted.
-d	List directories that have been remotely mounted by clients.
-e	Print the list of shared file systems.

The following example illustrates the use of showmount to display file systems currently mounted from remote systems. On the NFS server named neptune, type the following command:

showmount -a

The system displays the following information:

apollo:/export/home/neil

`showmount` tells us that the remote host, apollo, is currently mounting to /export/home/neil on this server.

Autofs Maps

The behavior of the automounter is governed by its configuration files, called maps. Autofs searches through these maps to navigate its way through the network. Map files contain information, such as the password entries of all users on a network or the names of all host computers on a network.

Master Map

To start the navigation process, the `automount` command reads the master map at system startup. This master map is what tells the automounter about map files and mount points. The master map lists all direct and indirect maps and their associated directories.

The master map, which is specified in the /etc/auto_master file, associates a directory with a map. The master map is a list that specifies all the maps that autofs should check. The following example shows what an auto_master file could contain:

```
# Master map for automounter
#
 +auto_master
 /net      -hosts       -nosuid,nobrowse
 /home     auto_home           -nobrowse
 /xfn      -xfn
```

The previous example shows the default auto_master file. Each line in the master map, /etc/auto_master , has the following syntax:

```
<mount-point> <map-name> <mount-options>
```

---

mount-point	This is the full (absolute) pathname of a directory that is used as the mount point. If the directory does not exist, autofs creates it if possible. If the directory does exist and is not empty, mounting on it hides its contents. In this case, autofs issues a warning. Using the notation /- as a mount point indicates a direct map with no particular mount point is associated with the map.
map-name	This is the map that autofs uses to find directions to locations or mount information. If the name is preceded by a slash (/), autofs interprets the name as a local file. Otherwise, autofs searches for the mount information using the search specified in the name-service switch configuration file (/etc/nsswitch.conf). Name service switches are described in Chapter 7, "Name Services."

Master Map

mount-options This is an optional, comma-separated list of options that apply to the mounting of the entries specified in map-name, unless the entries in map-name list other options. Options for each specific type of file system are listed later in this chapter under the mount command syntax. For NFS specific mount points, the bg (background) and fg (foreground) options do not apply.

NOTE. *A line beginning with a number sign (#) is a comment, and everything that follows it until the end of the line is ignored. To split long lines into shorter ones, put a backslash (\\) at the end of the line. The maximum number of characters in an entry is 1024.*

Every Solaris installation comes with a master map, called /etc/auto_master, with the default entries as shown earlier. Without any changes to the generic system setup, clients should be able to access remote file systems through the /net mount point. The following entry in the /etc/auto_master enables this to happen:

```
/net    -hosts    -nosuid,nobrowse
```

For example, let's say you have a NFS server named apollo that has the /export file system exported. Another system exists on the network named zeus. This system has the default /etc/auto_master file, and by default, it has a directory named /net. If you type:

```
ls /net
```

The command comes back showing that the directory is empty: nothing is in this directory. Now type:

```
ls /net/apollo
```

The system responds with:

```
export
```

Why was it empty the first time I issued the `ls` command? Why when I issued `ls /net/apollo` did it find a subdirectory? This is the automounter in action. When I specified /net with a host name, `automountd` looked at the map file, in this case /etc/hosts, and found apollo and its IP address. It then went to apollo, found the exported file system, and created a local mount point for /net/apollo/export. It also added this entry to the /etc/mnttab file:

```
-hosts   /net/sparc48/export      autofs   nosuid,nobrowse,ignore,nest,dev=2b80005\
➥941812769
```

This entry in the /etc/mnttab file is referred to as a trigger node.

If I type mount, I don't see anything mounted at this point:

```
mount
/ on /dev/dsk/c0t3d0s0 read/write/setuid/largefiles on Mon Nov  1 06:05:46 1999
/usr on /dev/dsk/c0t3d0s6 read/write/setuid/largefiles on Mon Nov  1 06:05:46 1999
/proc on /proc read/write/setuid on Mon Nov  1 06:05:46 1999
/dev/fd on fd read/write/setuid on Mon Nov  1 06:05:46 1999
/export on /dev/dsk/c0t3d0s3 setuid/read/write/largefiles on Mon Nov  1 06:05:49 1999
/export/swap on /dev/dsk/c0t3d0s4 setuid/read/write/largefiles on Mon Nov  1 06:5:49
➥1999
/tmp on swap read/write on Mon Nov  1 06:05:49 1999
```

Now type:

```
ls /net/apollo/export
```

You'll notice a bit of a delay while automountd mounts the file system; the system then responds with:

```
files     lost+found
```

The files listed are files located on apollo in the /export directory. If I type mount, I'll see a file system mounted on apollo that wasn't listed before:

```
mount
/ on /dev/dsk/c0t3d0s0 read/write/setuid/largefiles on Mon Nov  1 06:05:46 1999
/usr on /dev/dsk/c0t3d0s6 read/write/setuid/largefiles on Mon Nov  1 06:05:46 1999
/proc on /proc read/write/setuid on Mon Nov  1 06:05:46 1999
/dev/fd on fd read/write/setuid on Mon Nov  1 06:05:46 1999
/export on /dev/dsk/c0t3d0s3 setuid/read/write/largefiles on Mon Nov  1 06:05:49 1999
/export/swap on /dev/dsk/c0t3d0s4 setuid/read/write/largefiles on Mon Nov  1 06:05:49
➥1999
/tmp on swap read/write on Mon Nov  1 06:05:49 1999
/net/apollo/export on apollo:/export nosuid/remote on Fri Nov  5 09:48:03 1999
```

Automounter automatically mounted the /export file system that was located on apollo. Now look at the /etc/mnttab file again, and you see additional entries:

```
more /etc/mnttab
/dev/dsk/c0t3d0s0         /           ufs    rw,suid,dev=800018,largefiles    941454346
/dev/dsk/c0t3d0s6         /usr        ufs    rw,suid,dev=80001e,largefiles    941454346
/proc       /proc    proc     rw,suid,dev=2940000        941454346
fd          /dev/fd  fd       rw,suid,dev=2a00000        941454346
/dev/dsk/c0t3d0s3         /export ufs       suid,rw,largefiles,dev=80001b    941454349
/dev/dsk/c0t3d0s4         /export/swap     ufs      suid,rw,largefiles,dev=80001c
➥941454349
swap        /tmp     tmpfs    dev=1    941454349
-hosts      /net     autofs   ignore,indirect,nosuid,nobrowse,dev=2b80001    941454394
auto_home            /home    autofs   ignore,indirect,nobrowse,dev=2b80002    941454394
-xfn        /xfn     autofs   ignore,indirect,dev=2b80003        941454394
sparcserver:vold(pid246)            /vol     nfs      ignore,noquota,dev=2b40001 941454409
```

```
-hosts    /net/apollo/export       autofs   nosuid,nobrowse,ignore,nest,dev=2b80005
➥941812769
apollo:/export /net/apollo/export    nfs     nosuid,dev=2b40003 941813283
```

If the /net/apollo/export directory is accessed, the autofs service completes the process with these steps:

1. pings the server's mount service to see if it's alive.

2. mounts the requested file system under /net/apollo/export. Now /etc/mnttab file contains the following entries:

```
-hosts    /net/apollo/export       autofs   nosuid,nobrowse,ignore,nest,dev=2b80005 941812769
apollo:/export /net/apollo/export    nfs     nosuid,dev=2b40003 941813283
```

Because the automounter enables all users to mount file systems, root access is not required. It also provides for automatic unmounting of file systems; so, there is no need to unmount file systems when you are done.

Direct Map

A direct map lists a set of unrelated mount points, which might be spread out across the file system. A complete path (that is, /usr/local/bin or /usr/man) is listed in the map as a mount point. The best example of where to use a direct mount point is for /usr/man. The /usr directory contains many other directories, such as /usr/bin and /usr/local; therefore, it cannot be an indirect mount point. If you were to use an indirect map for /usr/man, the local /usr file system would be the mount point, and you would cover up the local /usr/bin and /usr/etc directories when you establish the mount. A direct map enables automounter to complete mounts on a single directory entry like /usr/man, appearing as a link with the name of the direct mount point.

A direct map is specified in a configuration file called /etc/auto_direct. With a direct map, there is a direct association between a mount point on the client and a directory on the server. Direct maps have a full pathname and indicate the relationship explicitly. This is a typical /etc/auto_direct map:

```
/usr/local          -ro \
    /bin                ivy:/export/local/sun4 \
    /share              ivy:/export/local/share \
    /src                ivy:/export/local/src
/usr/man            -ro    oak:/usr/man \
                    rose:/usr/man \
                    willow:/usr/man
/usr/games          -ro    peach:/usr/games
/usr/spool/news         -ro    pine:/usr/spool/news \
                                willow:/var/spool/news
```

NOTE. *The backslash at the end of each splits long lines into shorter ones. The operating system sees it as one line.*

Lines in direct maps have the following syntax:

`<key> <mount-options> <location>`

The field in each line is described as follows.

key	This field indicates the pathname of the mount point in a direct map. This pathname specifies the local directory on which to mount the NFS file system.
mount-options	This field indicates the options you want to apply to this particular mount. They are required only if they differ from the map default options specified in the /etc/auto_master file. Options for each specific type of file system are listed later in this chapter under the `mount` command syntax. There is no concatenation of options between the automounter maps. Any options added to an automounter map override all the options listed in previously searched maps. For instance, options included in the auto_master map would be overwritten by corresponding entries in any other map.
location	This field indicates the remote location of the file system specified as server:pathname. More than one location can be specified. The pathname should not include an automounted mount point; it should be the actual absolute path to the file system. For instance, the location of a home directory should be listed as server:/export/home/username, not as server:/home/username.

In the previous example of the /etc/auto_direct map file, the mount points, /usr/man and /usr/spool/news, list more than one location:

```
/usr/man            -ro     apollo:/usr/man \
                            zeus:/usr/man \
                            neptune:/usr/man
/usr/spool/news             -ro     jupiter:/usr/spool/news \
                                    saturn:/var/spool/news
```

Multiple locations, like those previously shown, are used for replication, or failover. For the purposes of failover, a file system can be called a replica if each file is the same size and is of the same type of file system. Permissions, creation dates, and other file attributes are not a consideration. If the file size or the file system types are different, then the re-map fails and the process hangs until the old server becomes available.

Replication makes sense only if you mount a file system that is read-only, because you must have some control over the locations of files you write or modify. You don't want to modify one server's files on one occasion and, minutes later, modify the "same" file on another server. The benefit of replication is that the best available server is used automatically without any effort required by the user.

If the file systems are configured as replicas, the clients have the advantage of using failover. Not only is the best server automatically determined but, if that server becomes unavailable, the client automatically uses the next-best server.

An example of a good file system to configure as a replica is the manual (man) pages. In a large network, more than one server can export the current set of manual pages. Which server you mount them from does not matter, as long as the server is running and exporting its file systems. In the previous example, multiple mount locations are expressed as a list of mount locations in the map entry. With multiple mount locations specified, you can mount the man pages from the apollo, zeus, or neptune servers. The best server depends on a number of factors, including the number of servers supporting a particular NFS protocol level, the proximity of the server, and weighting. The process of selecting a server goes like this:

- During the sorting process, a count of the number of servers supporting the NFS Version 2 and NFS 3.0 protocols is made. The protocol supported on the most servers is the protocol supported by default. This provides the client with the maximum number of servers to depend on. If version 3 servers are more abundant, the sorting process becomes more complex. Normally servers on the local subnet are given preference over servers on a remote subnet. A version 2 server can complicate matters, because it could be closer than the nearest version 3 server. If there is a version 2 server on the local subnet and the closest version 3 server is on a remote subnet, the version 2 server is given preference. This is only checked if there are more version 3 servers than version 2 servers. If there are more version 2 servers, then only a version 2 server is selected.

- After the largest subset of servers that have the same protocol version is found, that server list is sorted by proximity. Servers on the local subnet are given preference over servers on a remote subnet. The closest server is given preference, which reduces latency and network traffic. If there are several servers supporting the same protocol on the local subnet, the time to connect to each server is determined and the fastest is used.

- You can also influence the selection of servers at the same proximity level by adding a numeric weighting value in parentheses after the server name in the autofs map. For example:

```
/usr/man -ro apollo,zeus(1),neptune(2):/usr/man
```

Servers without a weighting have a value of zero, which makes it the most likely server to be selected. The higher the weighting value, the lower the chance the server be selected. All other server selection factors are more important than weighting. Weighting is only considered when selecting between servers with the same network proximity.

With failover, the sorting is checked once at mount time, to select one server from which to mount, and again if the mounted server becomes unavailable. Failover is particularly useful in a large network with many subnets. Autofs chooses the nearest server and therefore confines NFS network traffic to a local network segment. In servers with multiple network interfaces, Autofs lists the host name associated with each network interface as if it were a separate server. It then selects the nearest interface to the client.

In this example, I'm going to set up a direct map for /usr/local on apollo. Currently, apollo has a directory called /usr/local with the following directories:

```
ls /usr/local
```

The following local directories are displayed:

```
bin     etc     files   programs
```

If you set up the automount direct map, you'll see how the /usr/local directory is overwritten by the NFS mount.

First, I need to add the following entry in the master map file called /etc/auto_master:

```
/-      /etc/auto_direct
```

Next, I'll create the direct map file called /etc/auto_direct with the following entry:

```
/usr/local      zeus:/usr/local
```

Because I'm modifying a direct map, I need to stop and restart automount as follows:

```
/etc/init.d/autofs stop
/etc/init.d/autofs start
```

Now, if you have access to the /usr/local directory, the NFS mount point is established using the direct map that you have set up. The contents of /usr/local have changed because the direct map has covered up the local copy of /usr/local:

```
ls /usr/local
```

You'll see the following directories listed:

```
fasttrack       answerbook
```

NOTE. *The local contents of /usr/local have not been overwritten. After the NFS mount point is unmounted, the original contents of /usr/local are redisplayed.*

By typing the `mount` command, you see that /usr/local is now mounted remotely from zeus:

```
mount
/ on /dev/dsk/c0t3d0s0 read/write/setuid/largefiles on Mon Nov 1 06:05:46 1999
/usr on /dev/dsk/c0t3d0s6 read/write/setuid/largefiles on Mon Nov 1 06:05:46 1999
/proc on /proc read/write/setuid on Mon Nov 1 06:05:46 1999
/dev/fd on fd read/write/setuid on Mon Nov 1 06:05:46 1999
/export on /dev/dsk/c0t3d0s3 setuid/read/write/largefiles on Mon Nov 1 06:05:49 1999
/export/swap on /dev/dsk/c0t3d0s4 setuid/read/write/largefiles on Mon Nov 1 06:05:49
➥1999
/tmp on swap read/write on Mon Nov 1 06:05:49 1999
/usr/local on zeus:/usr/local read/write/remote on Sat Nov 6 08:06:40 1999
```

Indirect Map

Indirect maps are the simplest and most useful automounter conventions. An indirect map uses a substitution value of a key to establish the association between a mount point on the client and a directory on the server. Indirect maps are useful for accessing specific file systems, like home directories from anywhere on the network. The following entry in the /etc/auto_master file is an example of an indirect map:

```
/share          /etc/auto_share
```

With this entry in the /etc/auto_master file, /etc/auto_share is the name of the indirect map file for the mount point /share. For this entry, you also need to create an indirect map file named /etc/auto_share, which would look like this:

```
# share directory map for automounter
#
ws              neptune:/export/share/ws
```

If the /share directory is accessed, the autofs service creates a trigger node for /share/ws and the following entry is made in the /etc/mnttab file:

```
-hosts   /share/ws      autofs   nosuid,nobrowse,ignore,nest,dev=###
```

If the /share/ws directory is accessed, the autofs service completes the process with these steps:

1. pings the server's mount service to see if it's alive.

2. mounts the requested file system under /share. Now /etc/mnttab file contains the following entries:

    ```
    -hosts   /share/ws      autofs   nosuid,nobrowse,ignore,nest,dev=###
    neptune:/export/share/ws /share/ws   nfs    nosuid,dev=####    #####
    ```

Lines in indirect maps have the following general syntax:

`<key>   <mount-options>   <location>`

The field in each line is described as follows.

key	*key* is a simple name (no slashes) in an indirect map.
mount-options	The *mount-options* are the options you want to apply to this particular mount, and they are described in Table 6-2. They are required only if they differ from the map default options specified in the /etc/auto_master file.
location	*location* is the remote location of the file system specified as server:pathname. More than one location can be specified. The pathname should not include an automounted mount point; it should be the actual absolute path to the file system. For instance, the location of a directory should be listed as server:/usr/local not as server:/net/server/usr/local.

An example of an indirect map would be for user home directories. As users log into several different systems, their home directory is not always local on the system. It's convenient to use automounter to access their home directory regardless of the system to which they log in. To accomplish this, the default /etc/auto_master map file needs to contains the following entry:

```
/home      /etc/auto_home        -nobrowse
```

/etc/auto_home is the name of the indirect map file that contains the entries to be mounted under /home. A typical /etc/auto_home map file might look like this:

```
more /etc/auto_home
   dean           willow:/export/home/dean
   william        cypress:/export/home/william
   nicole         poplar:/export/home/nicole
   glenda         pine:/export/home/glenda
   steve          apple:/export/home/steve
   burk           ivy:/export/home/burk
   neil    -rw,nosuid    peach:/export/home/neil
```

Now let's assume that the /etc/auto_home map is on the host oak. If user neil has an entry in the password database specifying his home directory as /home/neil, then whenever he logs in to computer oak, autofs mounts the directory /export/home/neil residing on the computer peach. His home directory is mounted read-write, nosuid. Anyone, including Neil, has access to this path from any computer set up with the master map referring to the /etc/auto_home map in the previous example.

Under these conditions, user neil can run `login`, or `rlogin`, on any computer that has the /etc/auto_home map setup, and his home directory is mounted in place for him.

Another example of when to use an indirect map is if you want to make all project-related files available under a directory called /data. This directory is to be common across all workstations at the site. Follow these steps to set up the indirect map:

1. Add an entry for the /data directory to the /etc/auto_master map file:

    ```
    /data      /etc/auto_data      -nosuid
    ```

    The auto_data map file, named /etc/auto_data, determines the contents of the /data directory.

2. Add the `-nosuid` option as a precaution.

    The `-nosuid` option prevents users from creating files with the setuid or setgid bit set. See Part I of the *Solaris 2.6 Administrator Certification Training Guide* if you're not familiar with setuid/setgid.

3. Create the /etc/auto_data file and add entries to the auto_data map.

    The auto_data map is organized so that each entry describes a sub-project. Edit /etc/auto_data to create a map that looks like the following:

    ```
    compiler     apollo:/export/data/&
    windows          apollo:/export/data/&
    files            zeus:/export/data/&
    drivers      apollo:/export/data/&
    man          zeus:/export/data/&
    tools        zeus:/export/data/&
    ```

NOTE. *The ampersand (&) at the end of each entry is just an abbreviation for the entry key. For instance, the first entry is equivalent to:* `compiler   apollo:/export/data/compiler`.

Because the servers apollo and zeus view the same autofs map, any users who log in to these computers find the /data file system as expected. These users are provided direct access to local files through loopback mounts instead of NFS mounts.

4. Because you changed the /etc/auto_master map, the final step is to stop autofs and restart it as follows:

    ```
    /etc/init.d/autofs stop
    /etc/init.d/autofs start
    ```

    Now, if a user changes to the /data/compiler directory, the mount point to apollo:/export/data/compiler is created:

    ```
    cd /data/compiler
    ```

Now type `mount` to see the mount point that was established:

```
mount
```

The system shows that /data/compiler is mapped to apollo:/export/data/compiler as follows:

```
/data/compiler on apollo:/export/data/compiler read/write/remote on Fri Nov  5
➥17:17:02 1999
```

If the user changes to /data/tools, the mount point to zeus:/export/data/tools is created under the mount point /data/tools.

NOTE. *There is no need to create the directory /data/compiler to be used as the mount point. Automounter creates all the necessary directories before establishing the mount.*

The system administrator can modify, delete, or add entries to maps to meet the needs of the environment. As applications, and other file systems that users require, change their location, the maps must reflect those changes. You can modify autofs maps at any time. However, changes do not take place until the file system is unmounted and remounted. If a change is made to the auto_master map, or to a direct map, those changes do not take place until the automounter is restarted as follows:

```
/etc/init.d/autofs stop
/etc/init.d/autofs start
```

Another method is to force auto_master and direct map changes to be recognized immediately by running `automount` from the command line as follows:

```
automount -v
```

When to Use Automount

The most common and most advantageous use of automount is for mounting infrequently-used file systems on a NFS client, such as online reference manual pages. Another common use is accessing user home directories anywhere on the network. This use works well for users that do not have a dedicated system and that tend to log in from different locations. In the past, to permit access, the system administrator had to create home directories on every system into which the user logged in. Data had to be duplicated everywhere and it was always out-of-sync. You certainly don't want to create permanent NFS mounts for all user home directories on each system; so this is an excellent use for automount.

Automount is also used if a read-only file system exists on more than one server. Using automount instead of conventional NFS mounting, you can configure the NFS client to query all the servers on which the file system exists and mount from the server that responds first.

Avoid using automount to mount frequently used file systems, such as those containing user commands or frequently-used applications; conventional NFS mounting is more efficient in this situation. It is quite practical and typical, therefore, to combine the use of automount with conventional NFS mounting on the same NFS client.

When managing NFS, and especially automounter, the system administrator can quickly become overwhelmed with all the configuration files that must be kept consistent across the many different systems. For example, the /etc/auto_master and the related direct and indirect map files must be updated whenever the name of a host or file system changes. This can be nearly impossible on a large network. Chapter 7, "Name Services," describes how NIS can be used to help manage all these configuration files, including /etc/passwd and /etc/hosts, from a single location.

CHAPTER 7

Name Services

The following test objectives are covered in this chapter:

- Overview of naming services
- Configuring and managing NIS servers and clients
- NIS, NIS+, and DNS
- NIS+ security

Name services store information in a central location that users, systems, and applications must have to communicate across the network. Information is stored in files, maps, or database tables. Without a central name service, each system would have to maintain its own copy of this information. Therefore, centrally locating this data makes it easier to administer large networks. The information handled by a name service includes:

- System (host) names and addresses
- User names
- Passwords
- Access permissions

The Solaris 2.6 release provides the following name services:

/etc files	The original UNIX naming system
NIS	The Network Information Service
NIS+	The Network Information Service Plus (see NIS+ described later in this chapter)
DNS	The Domain Name System (see DNS described later in this chapter)

A NIS enables centralized management of host files so that systems can be identified by common names instead of numerical addresses. This makes communication simpler because users do not have to remember and try to enter cumbersome numerical addresses like "129.44.3.1."

Addresses are not the only network information that systems need to store. They also need to store security information, email addresses, information about their Ethernet interfaces, network services, groups of users enabled to use the network, services offered on the network, and so on. As networks offer more services, the list grows. As a result, each system might need to keep an entire set of files similar to /etc/hosts.

As this information changes, without a name service, administrators must keep it current on every system in the network. In a small network, this is simply tedious, but on a medium or large network, the job becomes not only time-consuming but also nearly unmanageable.

A NIS solves this problem. It stores network information on servers and provides the information to any workstation that asks for it.

/etc Files

/etc files are the traditional UNIX way of maintaining information about hosts, users, passwords, groups, and automount maps, just to name a few. These files are text files that can be edited using the vi editor or Solstice AdminSuite, and they have been described throughout Parts 1 and 2 of this series.

NIS

The NIS, formerly called the "Yellow Pages (YP)," is a distributed database system that enables the system administrator to administer the configuration of many hosts from a central location. Common configuration information, which would have to be maintained separately on each host in a network without NIS, can be stored and maintained in a central location and then propagated to all the nodes in the network. NIS stores information about workstation names and addresses, users, the network itself, and network services. This collection of network information is referred to as the NIS namespace. This chapter explains how to configure and administer the servers and clients in a NIS domain.

NOTE. *The NIS was formerly known as Sun Yellow Pages (YP). The functionality of the two remains the same; only the name has changed. The name "Yellow Pages" is a registered trademark in the United Kingdom of British Telecommunications PLC, and it may not be used without permission.*

NIS is a huge topic, which could potentially span several volumes. The purpose of this chapter is to prepare you for questions regarding NIS that might appear on the exam. I also want to provide an overview of NIS, complete enough so that you are equipped to set up a basic NIS network and have a basic understanding of its use. Before I begin a discussion of the structure of NIS, you need to be aware that the NIS administration databases are called maps. A domain is a collection of systems that share a common set of NIS maps.

Structure of the NIS Network

The systems within a NIS network are configured in the following ways:

- Master server
- Slave servers
- Clients of NIS servers

The center of the NIS network is the NIS master server. The system designated as master server contains the set of maps that you, the NIS administrator, create and update as necessary. After the NIS network is set up, any changes to the maps must be made on the master server. Each NIS domain must have one, and only one, master server. The master server should be a system that can propagate NIS updates with minimal performance degradation.

In addition to the master server, you can create backup servers, called NIS slave servers, to take some of the load off the master server and to substitute for the master server if it is down. If you create a NIS slave server, the maps on the master server are transferred to the slave server. A slave server has a complete copy of the master set of NIS maps. If a change is made to a map on the master server, the updates are propagated among the slave servers. The existence of slave servers enables the system administrator to evenly distribute the load that results from answering NIS requests. It also minimizes the impact of a server becoming unavailable.

Typically, all the hosts in the network, including the master and slave servers, are NIS clients. If a process on a NIS client requests configuration information, it calls NIS instead of looking in its local configuration files. For group and password information and mail aliases, the /etc/files might be consulted first, then NIS might be consulted if the requested information is not found in the /etc/files.

Any system can be a NIS client, but only systems with disks should be NIS servers, whether master or slave. Servers are also clients of themselves.

As mentioned earlier, the set of maps shared by the servers and clients is called the NIS domain. The master copies of the maps are located on the NIS master server, in the directory /var/yp/<domainname>, in which *domainname* is a chosen name for your own domain. Under the *domainname* directory, each map is stored as two files: mapname.dir and mapname.pag. Each slave server has an identical directory containing the same set of maps.

When a client starts up, it broadcasts a request for a server that serves its domain. Any server that has the set of maps for the client's domain, whether it's a master or a slave server, can answer the request. The client "binds" to the first server that answers its request, and that server then answers all its NIS queries.

A host cannot be the master server for more than one NIS domain. However, a master server for one domain might be a slave server for another domain. A host can be a slave server for multiple domains. A client belongs to only one domain.

Determining the Number of NIS Servers You Need

The following guidelines can be used for determining the number of NIS servers that you need in your domain:

- You should put a server on each sub network in your domain. When a client starts up, it broadcasts a message to find the nearest server. Solaris 2.6 does not require the server to be on the same subnet; however, earlier implementations of NIS historically have required that a server exist on every subnet using NIS.

- In general, a server can serve about 30 NIS clients, if the clients and servers run at the same speed. If the clients are faster than the servers are, then you need more servers. If the clients are slower than the servers are, each server can serve 50 or more clients.

Determining Which Hosts Will Be NIS Servers

Determine which systems on your network will be NIS servers as follows:

- Choose servers that are reliable and highly available.

- Choose fast servers that are not used for CPU-intensive applications. Do not use gateways or terminal servers as NIS servers.

- Distribute servers appropriately among client networks. Because a NIS client can bind only to a server on its own subnet, each subnet must have enough servers to accommodate the clients on that subnet.

Information Managed by NIS

NIS stores information in a set of files called maps. NIS maps were designed to replace UNIX /etc files, as well as other configuration files.

NIS maps are two-column tables. One column is the key and the other column is the information value related to the key. NIS finds information for a client by searching through the keys. Some information is stored in several maps because each map uses a different key. For example, the names and addresses of systems are stored in two maps: hosts.byname and hosts.byaddr. If a server has a system's name and needs to find its address, it looks in the hosts.byname map. If it has the address and needs to find the name, it looks in the hosts.byaddr map.

Maps for a domain are located in each server's /var/yp/<domainname> directory. For example, the maps that belong to the domain pyramid.com are located in each server's /var/yp/pyramid.com directory.

A NIS Makefile is stored in the /var/yp directory of the NIS server at installation time. If you run the `/usr/ccs/bin/make` command in that directory, `makedbm` creates or modifies the default NIS maps from the input files. For example, an input file might be /etc/hosts. By now, you should be familiar with the content of this file. Issue the following command to create the NIS map files:

```
cd /var/yp
/usr/ccs/bin/make
```

NOTE. *Never* make *the maps on a slave server. Always run the* make *command on the master server.*

Creating NIS maps is described in more detail in the "Configuring a NIS Master Server" section.

Solaris provides a default set of NIS maps, described in Table 7-1. You might want to use all or only some of these maps. NIS can also use whatever maps you create or add if you install other software products.

Table 7-1   Default NIS Maps

Map Name	Corresponding	Description NIS Admin File
bootparams	bootparams	This map contains the path names that file's clients need during start up: root, swap, and possibly others.
ethers.byaddr	ethers	This map contains system names and Ethernet addresses. The Ethernet address is the key in the map.
ethers.byname	ethers	This map is the same as ethers.byaddr, except that the key is the system name instead of the Ethernet address.
group.bygid	group	This map contains group security information with GID (group ID) as the key.
group.byname	group	This map contains group security information with group name as the key.
hosts.byaddr	hosts	This map contains system name, and IP address, with IP address as the key.
hosts.byname	hosts	This map contains system name and IP address, with system (host) name as the key.
mail.aliases	aliases	This map contains aliases and mail addresses, with aliases as the key.
mail.byaddr	aliases	This map contains mail address and alias, with mail addresses as the key.

continues

Table 7-1   Default NIS Maps (continued)

Map Name	Corresponding	Description NIS Admin File
netgroup.byhost	netgroup	This map contains group name, user name, and system name, with the system name as the key.
netgroup.byuser	netgroup	This map is the same as netgroup.byhost, except that key is the user name.
netgroup	netgroup	This map is the same as netgroup.byhost, except that key is the group name.
netid.byname	passwd,	This map is used for UNIX-style hosts and group authentication. Contains system name and mail address (including domain name). If there is a netid file available, it is consulted, in addition to the data available through the other files.
netmasks.byaddr	netmasks	This map contains the network masks to be used with IP submitting, with the address as the key.
networks.byaddr	networks	This map contains names of networks known to your system and their IP addresses, with the address as the key.
networks.byname	networks	This map is the same as networks.byaddr, except the key is name of network.
passwd.adjunct.byname	passwd and	This map contains auditing shadow information and the hidden password information for C2 clients.
passwd.byname	passwd and	This map contains password shadow information with the user name as key.
passwd.byuid	passwd and	This map is the same as passwd.byname, shadow except that key is user ID.
protocols.byname	protocols	This map contains the network protocols known to your network with protocol as key.
protocols.bynumber	protocols	This map is the same as protocols.byname, except that the key is protocol number.
rpc.bynumber	rpc	This map contains program number and name of Remote Procedure Calls (RPCs) known to your system. The key is the RPC program number.
services.byname	services	This map lists Internet services known to your network. The key is the port or protocol.

Map Name	Corresponding	Description NIS Admin File
services.byservice	services	This map lists Internet services known to your network. The key is the service name.
ypservers	N/A	This map lists the NIS servers known to your network.

The information in these files is put into NIS databases automatically when you create a NIS master server. Other system files can also be managed by NIS, if you want to customize your configuration.

NIS makes updating network databases much simpler than with the /etc file system. You no longer have to change the administrative /etc files on every system each time you modify the network environment. For example, if you add a new system to a network running NIS, you only have to update the input file in the master server and run `/usr/ccs/bin/make`. This process automatically updates the hosts.byname and hosts.byaddr maps. These maps are then transferred to any slave servers and made available to all the domain's client systems and their programs.

Just as you use the `cat` command to display the contents of a text file, you can use the `ypcat` command to display the values in a map. The `ypcat` basic syntax is:

`ypcat <mapname>`

In this case, *mapname* is the name of the map you want to examine.

You can use the `ypwhich` command to determine which server is the master of a particular map. Type the following:

`ypwhich -m <mapname>`

In this case, *mapname* is the name of the map whose master you want to find. `ypwhich` responds by displaying the name of the master server.

Planning Your NIS Domain

Before you configure systems as NIS servers or clients, you must plan the NIS domain. Each domain has a domain name, and each system sharing the common set of maps belongs to that domain. Follow these steps to plan your domain:

1. Decide which systems will be in your NIS domain.

2. Choose a NIS domain name. A NIS domain name can be up to 256 characters long, although much shorter names are more practical. A good practice is to limit domain names to no more than 32 characters. Domain names are case-sensitive. For convenience, you can use your Internet domain name as the basis for your NIS domain name. For example, if your Internet domain name is pdesigninc.com, you can name your NIS domain pdesigninc.com.

3. Before a system can use NIS services, the correct NIS domain name and system name must be set. A system's name is set by the system's /etc/nodename file and the system's domain name is set by the system's /etc/defaultdomain file. These files are read at start up time and the contents are used by the `uname -s` and `domainname` commands, respectively. A sample /etc/nodename file would look like this:

```
more /etc/nodename
```

The system responds with:

```
sparcserver
```

A sample /etc/defaultdomain file would look like this:

```
more /etc/defaultdomain
```

The system responds with:

```
pdesigninc.com
```

You are now ready to configure your NIS master server.

Configuring a NIS Master Server

Before configuring a NIS master server, make sure the NIS package is installed. The package names are SUNWypu and SUNWypr. Use the `pkginfo` command to check for these packages. Both packages are part of the standard Solaris 2.6 release. The daemons that support the NIS service are described in Table 7-2.

Table 7-2 NIS Daemons

Daemon	Function
ypserv	This daemon is the NIS database lookup server. The ypserv daemon's primary function is to look up information in its local database of NIS maps. If the /var/yp/ypserv.log file exists when ypserv starts up, log information is written to it if error conditions arise. At least one ypserv daemon must be present on the network for the NIS service to function.
ypbind	This daemon is the NIS binding process that runs on all client systems that are set up to use NIS. The function of ypbind is to remember information that lets all NIS client processes on a node communicate with some NIS server process.
ypxfr	This daemon is the high-speed map transfer. ypxfr moves a NIS map in the default domain to the local host. It creates a temporary map in the directory /var/yp/ypdomain.
rpc.yppasswdd	This daemon handles password change requests from the yppasswd command. It changes a password entry in the passwd, shadow, and security/passwd.adjunct files.

Daemon	Function
rpc.ypupdated	This daemon updates NIS information. ypupdated consults the updaters file in the /var/yp directory to determine which NIS maps should be updated and how to change them.

The commands that you use to manage the NIS service are shown in Table 7-3. I'll describe some of these commands in more detail later as I show examples of setting up NIS.

Table 7-3   NIS Commands

Utility	Function
make	This command updates NIS maps by reading the Makefile (if run in the /var/yp directory). You can use make to update all maps based on the input files or to update individual maps.
makedbm	This command creates a dbm file for a NIS map. The makedbm command takes the infile and converts it to a pair of files in ndbm format. When you run make in the /var/yp directory makedbm creates or modifies the default NIS maps from the input files.
ypcat	This command lists data in a NIS map.
ypinit	This command builds and installs a NIS database and initializes NIS client's ypservers list. ypinit is used to set up a NIS client system. You must be the super-user to run this command.
yppoll	This command gets a map order number from a server. The yppoll command asks an ypserv process what the order number is and which host is the master NIS server for the named map.
yppush	This command propagates a new version of a NIS map from the NIS master server to NIS slave servers.
ypset	This command sets binding to a particular server. ypset is useful for binding a client node that is on a different broadcast network.
ypstart	This command is used to start the NIS. After the host has been configured using the ypinit command, ypstart automatically determines the NIS status of the machine and starts the appropriate daemons.
ypstop	This command is used to stop the NIS.
ypwhich	This command returns the name of the NIS server that supplies the NIS name services to a NIS client, or it returns the name of the master for a map.

A NIS master server holds the source files for all the NIS maps in the domain. Any changes to the NIS maps must be made on the NIS master server. The NIS master server delivers information to NIS clients and supplies the NIS slave servers with up-to-date maps. Before starting up the NIS master server, some of the NIS source files need to be created.

One of the primary uses of NIS is to manage user logins and host files in a large networked environment. In a large network of systems, with several hundred users, imagine trying to keep the /etc/hosts, /etc/passwd, and /etc/group files up to date. Without NIS, every time a new system is added or removed, the /etc/hosts file must be updated. It's important to keep your /etc/hosts files in sync on every system on the network. Furthermore, without NIS, if a user changes a password, then that user must notify the system administrator that his or her password has changed. The system administrator must then make sure that all the /etc/shadow files are updated across the network. If not, the user is not able to login to another system using the new password.

The system administrator can manage the system configuration files, such as /etc/hosts and /etc/passwd, using NIS. With NIS, the system administrator sets up the /etc/hosts, /etc/passwd, and /etc/group files on one server. Rather than keeping a copy of the configuration file on each system, all systems look to this server for configuration information.

Creating the Master passwd File

The first task in setting up a NIS master server is to prepare the source file for the passwd map. However, be careful with this source file. The source files can be located either in the /etc directory on the master server or in some other directory. Locating the source files in /etc is undesirable because the contents of the maps are then the same as the contents of the local files on the master server. This is a special problem for passwd and shadow files, because all users would have access to the master server maps and because the root password would be passed to all YP clients through the passwd map.

Sun recommends, that for security reasons, and to prevent unauthorized root access, the files used to build the NIS password maps should not contain an entry for root. Therefore, the password maps should not be built from the files located in the master server's /etc directory. The password files used to build the password maps should have the root entry removed from them and they should be located in a directory that can be protected from unauthorized access.

For this exercise, copy all the source files from the /etc directory into the /var/yp directory. Because the source files are located in a directory other than /etc, modify the Makefile in /var/yp by changing the DIR=/etc line to DIR=/var/yp. Also, modify the PWDIR password macro in the Makefile to refer to the directory, in which the passwd and shadow files reside, by changing the line PWDIR=/etc to PWDIR=/var/yp.

Now, to create the passwd source file, use a copy of the /etc/passwd file on the system that becomes the master NIS server. Create a passwd file that has all the logins in it. This file is used to create the NIS map. You can do this by following these steps:

1. Copy the /etc/passwd file from each host in your network to the /var/yp directory on the host that will be the master server. Name each copy /var/yp/passwd.<hostname>, in which hostname is the name of the host it came from.

2. Concatenate all the passwd files together into a temporary passwd file, as follows:

   ```
   cd /var/yp
   cat passwd passwd.hostname1 passwd.hostname2 ... > passwd.temp
   ```

3. Issue the `sort` command to sort the temporary passwd file by user name, and then pipe it to the `uniq` command to remove duplicate entries:

   ```
   sort -t : -k 1,1 /var/yp/passwd.temp | uniq > /var/yp/passwd.temp
   ```

   NIS does not require that the passwd file be sorted in any particular way. Sorting the passwd file simply makes it easier to find duplicate entries.

4. Examine /var/yp/passwd.temp for duplicate user names that were not caught by the previous `uniq` command. This could happen if a user login occurs twice but the lines are not exactly the same. If you find multiple entries for the same user, edit the file to remove redundant ones. Make sure each user in your network has a unique user name and UID (user ID).

5. Now, issue the following command to sort the temporary passwd file by UID:

   ```
   sort -o /var/yp/passwd.temp -t : -k 3n,3 /var/yp/passwd.temp
   ```

6. Examine /var/yp/passwd.temp for duplicate UIDs once more. If you find multiple entries with the same UID, edit the file to change the UIDs so that no two users have the same UID.

7. Remove the root login from the /var/yp/passwd file. If you notice that the root login occurs more than once, remove all entries.

8. After you have a complete passwd file with no duplicates, move /var/yp/passwd.temp (the sorted, edited file) to /var/yp/passwd. This file is used to generate the passwd map for your NIS domain. Remove all the /var/yp/passwd.<hostname> files from the master server.

Creating the Master group File

Just like creating a master /var/yp/passwd file, the next task is to prepare one master /var/yp/group file to be used to create a NIS map as follows:

1. Copy the /etc/group file from each host in your NIS domain to the /etc directory on the host that will be the master server. Name each copy /var/yp/group.<hostname>, in which *hostname* is the name of the host it came from.

2. Concatenate all the group files together, including the master server's group file, into a temporary group file, as follows:

   ```
   cd /var/yp
   cat group group.hostname1 group.hostname2 ... > group.temp
   ```

3. Issue the following command to sort the temporary group file by group name:

   ```
   sort -o /var/yp/group.temp -t: -k1,1 /var/yp/group.temp
   ```

   NIS does not require that the group file be sorted in any particular way. Sorting the group file simply makes it easier to find duplicate entries.

4. Examine /var/yp/group.temp for duplicate group names. If a group name appears more than once, merge the groups with the same name into one group and remove the duplicate entries.

5. Now, issue the following command to sort the temporary group file by GID:

   ```
   sort -o /var/yp/group.temp -t: -k 3n,3 /var/yp/group.temp
   ```

6. Examine /var/yp/group.temp for duplicate GIDs. If you find multiple entries with the same GID, edit the file to change the GIDs so that no two groups have the same GID.

7. Move /var/yp/group.temp (the sorted, edited file) to /var/yp/group. This file is used to generate the group map for your NIS domain.

8. Remove the /var/yp/group.<*hostname*> files from the master server.

Creating the Master hosts File

Now create the master /etc/hosts file the same way you created the master /var/yp/passwd and /var/yp/group files by following these steps:

1. Copy the /etc/hosts file from each host in your NIS domain to the /etc directory on the host that will be the master server. Name each copy /var/yp/hosts.<hostname>, in which hostname is the name of the host from which it came.

2. Concatenate all the hosts files together, including the master server's host file, into a temporary hosts file, as follows:

   ```
   cd /var/yp
   cat hosts hosts.hostname1 hosts.hostname2 ... > hosts.temp
   ```

3. Issue the following command to sort the temporary hosts file so that duplicate IP addresses are on adjacent lines:

   ```
   sort -o /var/yp/hosts.temp /var/yp/hosts.temp
   ```

4. Examine /var/yp/hosts.temp for duplicate IP addresses. If you need to map an IP address to multiple host names, include them as aliases in a single entry.

5. Issue the following command to sort the temporary hosts file by host name:

   ```
   sort -o /var/yp/hosts.temp -b -k 2,2 /var/yp/hosts.temp
   ```

6. Examine /var/yp/hosts.temp for duplicate host names. A host name can be mapped to multiple IP addresses only if the IP addresses belong to different LAN cards on the same host. If a host name appears in multiple entries that are mapped to IP addresses on different hosts, remove all the entries but one.

7. Examine the /var/yp/hosts.temp file for duplicate aliases. No alias should appear in more than one entry.

8. Move /var/yp/hosts.temp (the sorted, edited file) to /var/yp/hosts. This file is used to generate the host's map for your NIS domain.

9. Remove the /var/yp/hosts.<hostname> files from the master server.

Other Source Files

The following files can also be copied to the /var/yp directory to be used as source files for NIS maps, but first make sure that they reflect an up-to-date picture of your system environment:

- auto.home or auto_home
- auto.master or auto_master
- bootparams
- ethers
- netgroup
- netmasks
- networks
- protocols
- rpc
- service
- shadow

Unlike other source files, the /etc/mail/aliases file cannot be moved to another directory.

This file must reside in the /etc/mail directory. Make sure the /etc/mail/aliases source file is complete by verifying that it contains all the mail aliases that you want to have available throughout the domain.

Preparing the Makefile

After checking the source files and copying them into the source file directory, you now need to convert those source files into the ndbm format maps the NIS service uses. This is done automatically for you by ypinit. I describe how to set up ypinit in the next section.

The ypinit script calls the program make, which uses the Makefile located in the /var/yp directory. A default Makefile is provided for you in this directory, and it contains the commands needed to transform the source files into the desired ndbm format maps.

The function of the Makefile is to create the appropriate NIS maps for each of the databases listed under all. After passing through makedbm, the data is collected in two files, mapname.dir and mapname.pag. Both files are located in the /var/yp/<*domainname*> directory on the master server.

The Makefile builds passwd maps from the /PWDIR/passwd, /PWDIR/shadow, and /PWDIR/security/passwd.adjunct files, as appropriate.

Setting Up the Master Server with ypinit

The /usr/sbin/ypinit shell script sets up master and slave servers and clients to use NIS. It also initially runs make to create the maps on the master server. To use ypinit to build a fresh set of NIS maps on the master server, follow these steps:

1. Become root on the master server and ensure that the name service receives its information from the /etc files, not from NIS, by typing:

   cp /etc/nsswitch.files /etc/nsswitch.conf

2. Edit the /etc/hosts file to add the name and IP address of each of the NIS servers.

3. To build new maps on the master server, type:

   /usr/sbin/ypinit -m

   ypinit prompts for a list of other systems to become NIS slave servers. Type the name of the server you are working on, along with the names of your NIS slave servers. Press CTRL+D when complete.

4. ypinit asks whether you want the procedure to terminate at the first nonfatal error or to continue despite nonfatal errors. Type:

   y

If you choose y, `ypinit` exits upon encountering the first problem; you can then fix it and restart `ypinit`. This procedure is recommended if you are running `ypinit` for the first time. If you prefer to continue, you can manually try to fix all the problems that might occur, and then restart `ypinit`.

NOTE. *A nonfatal error might be displayed if some of the map files are not present. These errors do not affect the functionality of NIS.*

5. `ypinit` asks whether the existing files in the /var/yp/<*domainname*> directory can be destroyed.

    This message is displayed only if NIS was previously installed. You must answer Yes to install the new version of NIS.

6. After `ypinit` has constructed the list of servers, it invokes `make`.

    The `make` command uses the instructions contained in the Makefile located in /var/yp. The `make` command cleans any remaining comment lines from the files that you designated and then runs `makedbm` on them, creating the appropriate maps and establishing the name of the master server for each map.

7. To enable NIS as the naming service, type:

    `cp /etc/nsswitch.nis /etc/nsswitch.conf`

    This command replaces the current switch file with the default NIS-oriented switch file. You can edit this file as necessary. See the section titled "Name Service Switch" for information on the contents of this file.

Now that the master maps are created, you can start the NIS daemons on the master server.

Starting and Stopping NIS on the Master Server

To start up the NIS service on the master server, you need to start `ypserv` on the server and run `ypbind`. The daemon `ypserv` answers information requests from clients after looking them up in the NIS maps. You can start up the NIS service on the server by running the /usr/lib/netsvc/yp/ypstart script from the command line. After the NIS master server has been configured by running `ypinit`, `ypstart` is automatically invoked to start up `ypserv` whenever the system is started up.

To stop the NIS service, run the `ypstop` command on the server as follows:

`usr/lib/netsvc/yp/ypstop`

Name Service Switch

The next step in setting up the NIS service is to set up the name service switch, which involves editing the /etc/nsswitch.conf file. The name service switch controls how a client workstation or application obtains network information. The name service switch is often referred to simply as the switch. The switch determines which naming services an application uses to obtain naming information, and in what order. The switch is a file called nsswitch.conf, which is stored in each system's /etc directory.

Each workstation has a nsswitch.conf file in its /etc directory. In every system's /etc directory, you find a template file called /etc/nsswitch.nis that was installed when you loaded Solaris 2.6. This template file contains the default switch configurations used by the NIS service and local files. When Solaris 2.6 release software is first installed, if you select the default name service to be NIS, the template file is copied to /etc/nsswitch.conf. If during software installation you select "files" as the default name service, /etc/nsswitch.conf is created from nsswitch.files, which looks like this:

```
#
# /etc/nsswitch.files:
#
# An example file that could be copied over to /etc/nsswitch.conf; it
# does not use any naming service.
#
# "hosts:" and "services:" in this file are used only if the
# /etc/netconfig file has a "-" for nametoaddr_libs of "inet" transports.

passwd:     files
group:      files
hosts:      files
networks:   files
protocols:  files
rpc:        files
ethers:     files
netmasks:   files
bootparams: files
publickey:  files
# At present there isn't a 'files' backend for netgroup; the system will
#   figure it out pretty quickly, and won't use netgroups at all.
netgroup:   files
automount:  files
aliases:    files
services:   files
sendmailvars:   files
```

If you did not select NIS as your name service during software installation, you can move this file into place manually as follows:

```
cp /etc/nsswitch.nis /etc/nsswitch.conf
```

The default /etc/nsswitch.nis file looks like this:

```
#
# /etc/nsswitch.nis:
#
# An example file that could be copied over to /etc/nsswitch.conf; it
# uses NIS (YP) in conjunction with files.
#
# "hosts:" and "services:" in this file are used only if the
# /etc/netconfig file has a "-" for nametoaddr_libs of "inet" transports.

# the following two lines obviate the "+" entry in /etc/passwd and /etc/group.
passwd:     files nis
group:      files nis

# consult /etc "files" only if nis is down.
hosts:      xfn nis [NOTFOUND=return] files
networks:   nis [NOTFOUND=return] files
protocols:  nis [NOTFOUND=return] files
rpc:        nis [NOTFOUND=return] files
ethers:     nis [NOTFOUND=return] files
netmasks:   nis [NOTFOUND=return] files
bootparams: nis [NOTFOUND=return] files
publickey:  nis [NOTFOUND=return] files

netgroup:   nis

automount:  files nis
aliases:    files nis

# for efficient getservbyname() avoid nis
services:   files nis
sendmailvars:   files
```

Each line of the /etc/nsswitch.nis file identifies a particular type of network information, such as host, password, and group, followed by one or more sources, such as NIS+ tables, NIS maps, the DNS hosts table, or local /etc. The source is where the client looks for the network information. For example, the system should first look for the passwd information in the /etc/passwd file and then, if it does not find the login name there, it needs to query the NIS server.

Setting Up NIS Clients

You must perform two tasks to set up a system as a NIS client:

- Set up the nsswitch.conf file as described in the previous section.
- Configure the system to use NIS as explained next.

After setting up the nsswitch.conf file, you configure each client system to use NIS by logging in as root and running the `ypinit` command as follows:

```
ypinit -c
```

You will be asked to identify the NIS servers from which the client can obtain name service information. You can list as many master or slave servers as you want. The servers that you list can be located anywhere in the domain. It is a good practice to first list the servers closest (in network terms) to the system, followed by the more distant servers on the net.

Finally, on the NIS client, remove all the entries from the /etc/passwd file that are managed by the NIS server. Don't forget to update the /etc/shadow file. Also, remove entries from the /etc/group, /etc/hosts file, and any other network file that are now managed by NIS.

Test the NIS client by logging out and logging back in using a login name that is no longer in the /etc/passwd file and is managed by NIS. Test the host's map by pinging a system that is not identified in the local /etc/hosts file.

Setting Up NIS Slave Servers

Before setting up the NIS slave server, you must first set it up as a NIS client. After you've verified that the NIS master server is functioning properly by testing the NIS service on this system, you can set up the system as a slave server. Your network can have one or more slave servers. Having slave servers ensures the continuity of NIS services if the master server is not available. Before actually running `ypinit` to create the slave servers, you should run the `domainname` command on each NIS slave to make sure the domain name is consistent with the master server. Remember, the domain name is set by adding the domain name to the /etc/defaultdomain file. Follow these steps to set up the NIS slave server:

1. As root, edit the /etc/hosts file on the slave server to add the name and IP addresses of all the other NIS servers. This step is optional and for convenience only. At this point, I'm assuming you're not using DNS to manage hostnames (as will be explained later in this chapter). Step 3 prompts you for a hostname of the NIS server. You need an entry for this hostname in the local /etc/hosts file; otherwise, you need to specify the IP address of the NIS server.

2. Change directory to /var/yp on the slave server.

3. To initialize the slave server as a client, type the following:

   ```
   /usr/sbin/ypinit -c
   ```

   The `ypinit` command prompts you for a list of NIS servers. Enter the name of the local slave you are working on first, then the master server, followed by the other NIS slave servers in your domain, in order, from the physically closest to the furthest (in network terms).

NOTE. *You must first configure the new slave server as a NIS client so that it can receive the NIS maps from the master for the first time.*

4. Next, you need to determine if ypbind is already running. If it is running, you need to stop and restart it. Check to see if ypbind is running by typing:

   ps -ef | grep ypbind

   If a listing is displayed, ypbind is running. If ypbind is running, stop it by typing:

   /usr/lib/netsvc/yp/ypstop

   Type the following to restart ypbind:

   /usr/lib/netsvc/yp/ypstart

5. To initialize this system as a slave, type the following:

   /usr/sbin/ypinit -s <master>

   In this example, *master* is the system name of the existing NIS master server.

   Repeat the procedures described in this section for each system you want configured as a NIS slave server.

6. Now you can start daemons on the slave server and begin the NIS service. First, all existing yp processes must be stopped by typing:

   /usr/lib/netsvc/yp/ypstop

7. To start ypserv on the slave server and run ypbind, you can either restart the server or type:

   /usr/lib/netsvc/yp/ypstart

NIS+

The NIS+ is similar to NIS but with more features. NIS+ is not an extension of NIS but a new software program. NIS+ was designed to replace NIS.

NIS addresses the administrative requirements of small-to-moderate client server computing networks—those with less than a few hundred clients. NIS+ is designed for the larger networks now prevalent in which systems are spread across remote sites in various time zones and in which clients number into the thousands. In addition, the information stored in networks today changes much more frequently, and NIS had to be updated to handle this environment. Lastly, systems today require a high level of security, and NIS+ addresses many security issues that NIS did not.

NIS+ is not an objective covered in depth in the System Administration Certification exam Part II. You are asked a few general overview questions regarding NIS+ that are covered in this text, but a working knowledge of NIS+ is not required until you take the Sun Certified Network Administrator examination.

Hierarchical Namespace

NIS+ enables you to store information about workstation addresses, security information, mail information, Ethernet interfaces, and network services in central locations in which all workstations on a network can access it. This configuration of network information is referred to as the NIS+ namespace.

The NIS+ namespace is the arrangement of information stored by NIS+. The namespace can be arranged in a variety of ways to fit the needs of an organization. NIS+ can be arranged to manage large networks with more than one domain. Although the arrangement of a NIS+ namespace can vary from site to site, all sites use the same structural components: directories, tables, and groups. The components are called objects, and they can be arranged into a hierarchy that resembles a UNIX file system.

Directory objects form the skeleton of the namespace. When arranged in a treelike structure, they divide the namespace into separate parts, much like UNIX directories and subdirectories. The topmost directory in a namespace is the root directory. If a namespace is flat, it has only one directory—the root directory. The directory objects beneath the root directory are called "directories."

A namespace can have several levels of directories. When identifying the relation of one directory to another, the directory beneath is called the child directory, and the directory above is the parent.

Although UNIX directories are designed to hold UNIX files, NIS+ directories are designed to hold NIS+ objects: other directories, tables, and groups. Any NIS+ directory that stores NIS+ groups is named groups_dir, and any directory that stores NIS+ system tables is named org_dir.

NIS+ Tables

In a NIS+ environment, most namespace information is stored in NIS+ tables; think of them as being similar to NIS maps, which were described earlier. Without a name service, most network information would be stored in /etc files and almost all NIS+ tables have corresponding /etc files. With the NIS service, network information is stored in NIS maps that also mostly correspond with /etc files. All NIS+ tables are stored in the domain's org_dir NIS+ directory object except the admin and groups tables that are stored in the groups_dir directory object. The tables that come default as part of the standard distribution of NIS+ are described in Table 7-4. Users and application developers frequently create NIS+ compatible tables for their own purposes.

Table 7-4 Standard NIS+ Tables

NIS+ Table	Description
auto_home	This table is an indirect automounter map that enables a NIS+ client to mount the home directory of any user in the domain.
auto_master	This table lists all the automounter maps in a domain. For direct maps, the auto_master table provides a map name. For indirect maps, it provides both a map name and the top directory of its mount point.
bootparams	This table stores configuration information about every diskless workstation in a domain. A diskless workstation is a workstation that is connected to a network but has no hard disk.
client_info	This optional internal NIS+ table is used to store server preferences for the domain in which it resides.
cred	This table stores credential information about NIS+ principals. Each domain has one cred table, which stores the credential information of client workstations that belong to that domain and client users who are enabled to log into them.
ethers	This table stores information about the 48-bit Ethernet addresses of workstations in the domain.
group	This table stores information about UNIX user groups.
hosts	This table associates the names of all the workstations in a domain with their IP addresses. The workstations are usually NIS+ clients but they don't have to be.
mail_aliases	This table lists the domain's mail aliases recognized by sendmail.
netgroup	This table defines network-wide groups used to check permissions for remote mounts, logins, and shells. The members of net groups used for remote mounts are workstations; for remote logins and shells, the members are users.
netmasks	This table contains the network masks used to implement standard internetwork subnetting.
networks	This table lists the networks of the Internet. This table is normally created from the official network table maintained at the Network Information Control Center (NIC), although you might need to add your local networks to it.
passwd	This table contains information about the accounts of users in a domain. These users generally are, but do not have to be, NIS+ principals. However, remember that if they are NIS+ principals, their credentials are not stored here but in the domain's cred table. The passwd table usually grants read permission to the world (or to nobody). This table contains all logins except root, which is stored in the local /etc/passwd file.
protocols	This table lists the protocols used by the internetwork.
rpc	This table lists the names of RPC programs.
services	This table stores information about the services available on the internetwork.
timezone	This table lists the default time zone of every workstation in the domain.

NIS+ tables can be manipulated with AdminTool. The NIS+ master server updates its objects immediately; however, it tries to batch several updates together before it propagates them to its replicas (slaves).

NIS+ Security

NIS+ security is enhanced in two ways: First, it has the capability to authenticate access to the service, and thus, to discriminate between access that is enabled to members of the community and other network entities. Second, it includes an authorization model that enables specific rights to be granted or denied based on this authentication.

Authentication

Authentication is used to identify NIS+ principals. A NIS+ principal might be someone who is logged in to a client system as a regular user, someone who is logged in as superuser, or any process that runs with superuser permission on a NIS+ client system. Thus, a NIS+ principal can be a client user or a client workstation. Every time a principal (user or system) tries to access a NIS+ object, the user's identity and secure RPC password is confirmed and validated.

Authorization

Authorization is used to specify access rights. Every time NIS+ principals try to access NIS+ objects, they are placed in one of four authorization classes, or categories, which are summarized as:

- Owner   A single NIS+ principal
- Group   A collection of NIS+ principals
- World   All principals authenticated by NIS+
- Nobody   Unauthenticated principals

The NIS+ server finds out what access rights are assigned to that principal by that particular object. If the access rights match, the server answers the request. If they do not match, the server denies the request and returns an error message.

NIS+ authorization is the process of granting NIS+ principals access rights to a NIS+ object. Access rights are similar to file permissions. There are four types of access rights:

- Read   Principal can read the contents of the object
- Modify   Principal can modify the contents of the object
- Create   Principal can create new objects in a table or directory
- Destroy   Principal can destroy objects in a table or directory

Access rights are displayed as 16 characters, and they can be displayed with the command `nisls -l` and changed with the command `nischmod`.

The NIS+ security system enables NIS+ administrators to specify different read, modify, create, or destroy rights to NIS+ objects for each class. Thus, for example, a given class could be permitted to modify a particular column in the passwd table but not read that column, or a different class could be enabled to read some entries of a table but not others.

The implementation of the authorization scheme I just described is determined by the domain's level of security. A NIS+ server can operate at one of three security levels, which are summarized in Table 7-5.

Table 7-5   NIS+ Security Levels

Security Level	Description
0	Security level 0 is designed for testing and setting up the initial NIS+ namespace. A NIS+ server running at security level 0 grants any NIS+ principal full access rights to all NIS+ objects in the domain. Level 0 is for setup purposes only, and it should only be used by administrators for that purpose. Level 0 should not be used on networks in normal operation by regular users.
1	Security level 1 uses AUTH_SYS security. This level is not supported by NIS+, and it should not be used.
2	Security level 2 is the default. It is the highest level of security currently provided by NIS+ and the default level assigned to a NIS server. It authenticates only requests that use Data Encryption Standard (DES) credentials (see DES described in the next section). Requests with no credentials are assigned to the nobody class and have whatever access rights have been granted to that class. Requests that use invalid DES credentials are retried. After repeated failures to obtain a valid DES credential, requests with invalid credentials fail with an authentication error. (A credential might be invalid for a variety of reasons, such as the principal making the request is not keylogged in on that system, the clocks are out of sync, there is a key mismatch, and so forth.)

DES Authentication

DES authentication uses the DES and public key cryptography to authenticate both users and systems in the network. DES is a standard encryption mechanism; public key cryptography is a cipher system that involves two keys: one public and one private.

The security of DES authentication is based on a sender's capability to encrypt the current time, which the receiver can then decrypt and check against its own clock. The timestamp is encrypted with DES. Two things are necessary for this scheme to work: (1) The two agents must agree on the current time, and (2) the sender and receiver must be using the same encryption key.

If a network runs a time synchronization program, the time on the client and the server is synchronized automatically. If a time synchronization program is not available, timestamps can be computed using the server's time instead of the network time. The client asks the server for the time before starting the RPC session, and then it computes the time difference between its own clock and the server's. This difference is used to offset the client's clock when computing timestamps. If the client and server clocks become out of sync to the point where the server begins to reject the client's requests, the DES authentication system resynchronizes with the server.

The client and server arrive at the same encryption key by generating a random conversation key, and then using public key cryptography (an encryption scheme involving public and secret keys) to deduce a common key. The common key is a key that only the client and server are capable of deducing. The conversation key is used to encrypt and decrypt the client's timestamp; the common key is used to encrypt and decrypt the conversation key.

DNS

DNS is not an objective that is covered in depth on the System Administration Certification exam Part II. You need to know the definition of DNS, but a working knowledge of DNS is not required until you take the Sun Certified Network Administrator examination.

The DNS is the name service provided by the Internet for Transmission Control Protocol/Internet Protocol (TCP/IP) networks. It was developed so that workstations on the network could be identified with common names instead of Internet addresses. DNS is a program that converts domain names to their IP addresses. Without it, users would have to remember numbers instead of words to get around the Internet. The process of finding the IP address of a computer by using its host name as an index is referred to as name-to-address resolution or "mapping."

The collection of networked systems that use DNS are referred to as the DNS namespace. The DNS namespace can be divided into a hierarchy of domains. A DNS domain is simply a group of systems. Each domain is supported by two or more name servers: the primary, secondary, or cache-only server. Each domain must have one primary server and should have at least one secondary server to provide backup.

Each server implements DNS by running a daemon called `in.named`. On the client side, DNS is implemented through the "resolver." The resolver's function is to resolve users' queries. The resolver is neither a daemon nor a single program; rather, it is a set of dynamic library routines used by applications that need to know system names. After the resolver is configured, a system can request DNS service from a name server. If a system's /etc/nsswitch.conf file specifies `hosts: dns`, the resolver libraries are automatically used. If the nsswitch.conf file specifies some other name service before DNS, such as NIS, then that name service is consulted first for host information, and then only if that name service does not find the host in question are the resolver libraries used.

For example, if the hosts line in the nsswitch.conf file specifies `hosts: nis dns`, the NIS name service is first searched for host information. If the information is not found in NIS, the DNS resolver is used. Because name services, such as NIS and NIS+, contain only information about hosts in their own network, the effect of a `hosts:nis dns` line in a switch file is to specify the use of NIS for local host information and DNS for information on remote hosts out on the Internet. If the resolver queries a name server, the server returns either the requested information or a referral to another server.

Name-to-address mapping occurs if a program running on your local system needs to contact a remote computer. The program most likely knows the host name of the remote computer but might not know how to locate it, particularly if the remote system is in another company, miles from your site. To obtain the remote system's address, the program requests assistance from the DNS software running on your local system, which is considered a DNS client.

Your system sends a request to a DNS name server, which maintains the distributed DNS database. The files in the DNS database bear little resemblance to the NIS+ Host Table or even to the local /etc/hosts file, although they maintain similar information: the host names, IP addresses, and other information about a particular group of computers. The name server uses the host name your system sent as part of its request to find or "resolve" the IP address of the remote system. It then returns this IP address to your local system if the host name is in its DNS database.

If the host name is not in that name server's DNS database, this indicates that the system is outside of its authority, or, to use DNS terminology, outside the local administrative domain.

Because maintaining a central list of domain name/IP address correspondences would be impractical, the lists of domain names and IP addresses are distributed throughout the Internet in a hierarchy of authority. A DNS server that maps the domain names in your Internet requests or forwards them to other servers in the Internet is probably within close geographic proximity to your Internet access provider.

In this chapter, I covered all the name service topics that appear on the Certified Solaris Administrator Examination for Solaris 2.6, Part II. Of course, better understanding of the topics will come as you use the products described and become experienced over time. Many large networks that use a name service are heterogeneous, meaning they have more than just Solaris systems connected to it. You need to refer to the vendor's documentation for each particular system type to understand how each different operating system implements name services. You see that most are similar in their implementation, with only subtle differences. As you gain experience, and complete the Solaris Administrator Certification exams, your next goal should be to become certified as a Sun Network Administrator for Solaris. Certification in both fields is valuable for any UNIX system administrator.

CHAPTER 8

Solstice AdminSuite

The following test objectives are covered in this chapter:

- Capabilities of Solstice AdminSuite
- Using the Adminsuite of tools

I introduced Solstice AdminSuite in Chapter 1, "Installing a Server," when we installed the operating system (OS) on the server and used Host Manager to set up the AutoClients and OS server. This chapter describes the entire AdminSuite Graphical User Interface (GUI).

Solstice AdminSuite is a collection of GUI tools and commands used to perform administrative tasks, such as managing users, groups, hosts, system files, printers, disks, file systems, terminals, and modems. It's similar to AdminTool in that it aids the system administrator in tasks, such as setting up printers, serial ports, file systems, and user accounts. The main difference is that Solstice AdminSuite enables you to perform these tasks either locally or over the network from one system. It also provides additional functionality not found in AdminTool, such as setting up AutoClients and JavaStations.

Solstice AdminSuite and the Command-Line Equivalents

Just like AdminTool, Solstice AdminSuite provides tools that execute numerous commands in a single menu pick. However, you must run AdminSuite from a bitmapped screen that supports X-Windows. It's important that the system administrator understands the command-line equivalent of each task performed by AdminSuite just in case a graphics terminal is not available. Table 8-1 lists the tools available in Solstice AdminSuite along with a brief description. The table also lists the command-line equivalent of each tool provided in the AdminSuite GUI.

Table 8-1   Solstice AdminSuite Tools and the Command-Line Equivalents

AdminSuite Tool	Command-Line Equivalent	Description of Task Performed
Host Manager	admhostadd admhostdel admhostmod admhostls	Configure system information and server support for AutoClient and standalone systems, diskless and dataless clients, and JavaStations.
Group Manager	admgroupadd admgroupdel admgroupmod admgroupls	Maintain UNIX group information.
User Manager	admuseradd admuserdel admusermod admuserls	Maintain user account information.

continues

Table 8-1 Solstice AdminSuite Tools and the Command-Line Equivalents (continued)

AdminSuite Tool	Command-Line Equivalent	Description of Task Performed
Serial Port Manager	admserialdel admserialmod admserialls	Configure serial port software for terminals and modems.
Printer Manager	None	Configure print servers and clients.
Database Manager	None	Maintain network-related system files, such as aliases and hosts.
Storage Manager	None	Configure disk slices on a single disk or a group of disks. It is also used to set up file systems for a server or group of clients on a server.

Each AdminSuite tool will be described in its entirety in this chapter.

Starting the Solstice AdminSuite Tools

To get to the AdminSuite tools, you must first install the Solstice AdminSuite product. This product is not automatically installed with the OS. The process of installing the product is described in Chapter 1. Verify that AdminSuite is installed on your system by typing the following command:

```
pkginfo|grep AdminSuite
```

If the following is displayed, the Solstice AdminSuite packages are installed:

```
system      SUNWadmsm     Solstice AdminSuite Storage Manager Application
system      SUNWsadma     Solstice AdminSuite Applications
system      SUNWsadmb     Solstice AdminSuite CLI
system      SUNWsadmc     Solstice AdminSuite Core Methods
system      SUNWsadmm     Solstice AdminSuite man pages
system      SUNWsadmo     Solstice AdminSuite Object Libraries
system      SUNWsadmp     Solstice AdminSuite Data Files
system      SUNWspapp     Solstice AdminSuite print application
```

To actually use the AdminSuite tools, start the Solstice Launcher by entering the following command:

```
solstice &
```

The Solstice Launcher window opens as shown in Figure 8-1.

STARTING THE SOLSTICE ADMINSUITE TOOLS 213

Figure 8-1
The Solstice Launcher window.

In the Solstice Launcher window, click once on an icon to start a tool. Alternatively, you can use the tab key or your mouse to move from icon to icon, and press the spacebar to open a tool.

You can click on the Launcher menu item in the toolbar to display a pull-down menu with the three options shown in Figure 8-2.

Figure 8-2
The Launcher pull-down menu.

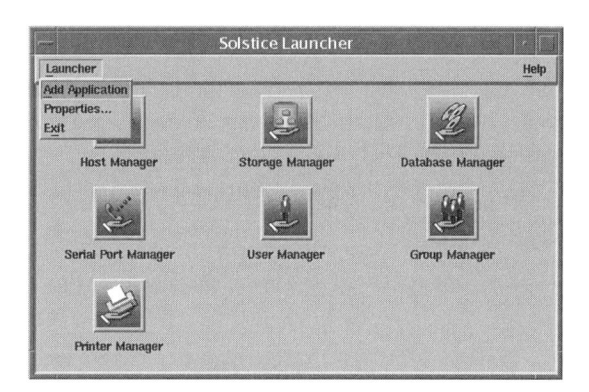

The following is a description of the three options found in the pull-down menu:

- *Add Application*—Use this option to add and register applications with the Launcher. It's possible to add your own tools to the Solstice Launcher.

- *Properties*—Use this option to customize the launcher by showing, hiding, or removing applications; reordering the icons; changing the Launcher window width; modifying application properties; and adding applications.

- *Exit*—Use this option to stop running the Solstice Launcher. This does not affect open Solstice applications.

Applications that display in the Solstice Launcher are registered. This means that you can add custom applications, such as a third party backup application to the Launcher main window. Applications are registered in three ways:

- *Private registry*—Registered applications are private to the user. Applications are registered privately with the `Add Application` command from the Launcher menu. Privately registered applications can be added or removed, and their properties can be modified from the Solstice Launcher.

- *Local registry*—Registered applications are local to the system. Applications registered locally are available to all local users of the system. Applications can only be registered locally with the `/usr/snadm/bin/soladdapp` command and can only be removed using the `soldelapp` commands. Their properties cannot be modified from the Solstice Launcher.

- *Global registry*—Registered applications are shared by all local and remote users using the Solstice Launcher in a particular /opt directory. Applications can only be registered globally with the `soladdapp` command and can only be removed using the `soldelapp` command. Their properties cannot be modified from the Solstice Launcher.

Customizing the Launcher Window

You might want to customize the applications that appear in the Solstice Launcher. The following example describes how to modify your Private Registry to customize the Launcher window for your login only. This can be done as follows:

1. Click on the Launcher menu item in the main Launcher window and select Properties from the pull-down menu.

    The Launcher: Properties window opens as shown in Figure 8-3.

Figure 8-3

The Launcher: Properties window.

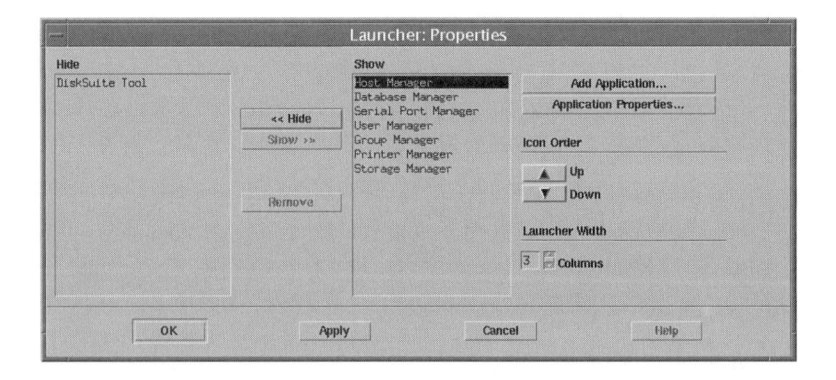

2. In the Launcher: Properties window, highlight the application that you want to hide in the launcher window, and then click on Hide. Figure 8-3 shows the Launcher: Properties window with the DiskSuite Tool on the Hide list. Repeat this process until you're finished with your selections. After you've hidden the applications, select OK. You'll return to the Solstice: Launcher window, which will now contain your customizations as shown in Figure 8-4.

Figure 8-4
The customized Launcher window.

Using the Solstice AdminSuite Tools

If you select a tool icon in the Solstice Launcher, the tool's main window opens. The main window contains two areas: a menu bar and a display area. The menu bar usually contains four menus: File, Edit, View, and Help. These items will be described in detail for each particular tool.

You can set up a log file to record each major operation completed with the Solstice AdminSuite tools. After you enable logging, the date, time, server, user ID (UID), and description for every operation are written to the specified log file. To enable logging, log in as root and follow these steps:

1. Edit the /etc/syslog.conf file and add an entry at the bottom of the file that follows this format:

    ```
    user.info filename
    ```

    The filename must be the absolute path name of the file, for example, /var/log/adminsuite.log.

2. Create the log file if it does not already exist using the touch command as follows:

    ```
    touch /var/log/filename
    ```

3. To make the changes in /etc/syslog.conf take effect, stop and start the syslog service as follows:

   ```
   /etc/init.d/syslog stop
   /etc/init.d/syslog start
   ```

   Solstice AdminSuite operations will now be logged to the file you specified.

Now we'll take at look at each individual tool in AdminSuite.

Host Manager

We took a detailed look at Host Manager in Chapters 1 and 2, when I described how to set up and maintain server and client support. Refer to these chapters for information on the Host Manager tool.

User Manager

User manager is a GUI that enables you to manage user accounts in a NIS or NIS+ domain or in a local system. Use the User Manager to perform the following tasks:

- Add, modify, or delete a user account
- Display and sort user-account information

Startup User Manager by clicking on the User Manager icon in the Solstice Launcher window. The User Manager window opens with the User Manager: Load window on top of it as shown in Figure 8-5.

Figure 8-5
The User Manager: Load window.

Select your naming service, check that the domain or host name is correct, and click on OK. The User Manager main window displays the list of users for the context you chose, as shown in Figure 8-6.

Figure 8-6

The User Manager main window.

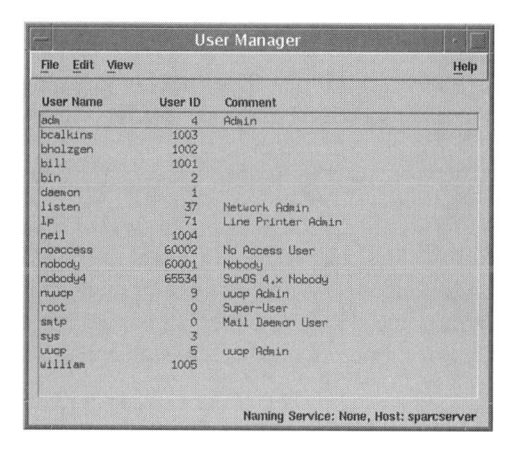

Setting Up User Account Defaults

If you'll be adding several new user accounts, you might want to create a set of defaults that each user will share. If you have a standard value that you employ repeatedly for users, you can set that value as a default so that you do not have to enter it each time you add a user. The defaults you select will be the initial default values assigned to the new account whenever you add a new user. To get into the Set Add Defaults window, click on Edit in the menu bar located in the User Manager window, and then click on Set Defaults. The Set Add Defaults window opens as shown in Figure 8-7.

Figure 8-7

The Set Add Defaults window.

You can set the following defaults:

- *Primary Group*—Specifies a group ID number or group name that the OS will assign to files created by the user. Users in the same group can then access these files, assuming they have correct permissions set.

NOTE. *Group 10 (staff) is the default primary group that is appropriate for most users.*

- *Secondary Groups* (Optional)—Specifies one or more additional groups that the user can also belong to. You can specify either a group ID number or group name. If you specify more than one group, separate them with commas.
- *Login Shell*—Specifies a login shell (Bourne, Korn, or C shell) for the user. You can also select Other to specify a shell not in the list.
- *Password*—Specifies a password scheme for the user. The following table describes the password options.

Cleared until first login	The account will not have a password. The user will be prompted for a new password at the first login. The user must set a password after first logging in.
Account is locked	Account is locked. The user will not be able to log in until the administrator assigns a password.
No password—setuid only	Account cannot be logged in to, but account programs are allowed to run.

- *Min Change* (Optional)—Specifies the minimum number of days allowed between password changes. This can be used to prevent a user from changing a password and immediately changing it back to the original password. This option is not available if you are using the NIS name service.
- *Max Change* (Optional)—Specifies the maximum number of days the user can go without having to set up a new password. If the password is not changed within this number of days, the user account is locked until you modify the user account's Password field to *Normal Password* or *Cleared until first login*. This option is not available if you are using the NIS name service.
- *Max Inactive* (Optional)—Specifies the maximum number of days the user account can be inactive before the user account is locked. The user account remains locked until you modify the user account's Password field to *Normal Password* or *Cleared until first login*. This option is not available if you are using the NIS name service.

- *Expiration Date* (Optional)—Specifies the day, month, and year when the user account expires and is locked. The user account remains locked until you modify the user account's Password field to *Normal Password* or *Cleared until first login*.

- *Warning* (Optional)—Specifies when the user will start receiving a warning message about their password expiring.

- *Create Home Dir*—Specifies whether to automatically create the user's home directory.

- *Server*—Specifies the name of the system that contains the home directory.

- *Skeleton Path*—Specifies the path that contains the user initialization files that you have created for the user. The files are copied into the user's home directory. The default directory is /etc/skel.

- *AutoHome Setup*—Specifies whether or not to create an Autofs entry for the user's home directory. If you create an Autofs entry, the user's home directory will be automatically mounted.

- *Permissions*—Specifies the permissions to set on the user's home directory.

- *Mail Server*—Specifies the name of the system that contains the user's mailbox.

Adding a New User Account

To add a new user account, click on Edit in the menu bar of the User Manager main window and select Add from the popup.

The User Manager: Add window opens as shown in Figure 8-8.

Fill in the appropriate boxes and when they are complete, click on OK. Refer to the section titled "Setting Up User Account Defaults" for information on each field. In addition to the fields described in the preceding section, you will also see the following fields in the User Manager: Add window:

- *User Name*—Specifies a login name to identify an individual user. A user name must be a unique name composed of uppercase or lowercase alphabetical characters (A–Z, a–z) or digits (0–9). A user name must be one to eight characters long and include at least one lowercase letter. In addition, the first character of a user's name must be a letter.

- *User ID (UID)*—Specifies a unique number by which the OS can identify a user. In Solaris 2.6, the maximum value is 2147483647. The UIDs 60001 (nobody) and 65534 (nobody4) are reserved and are not to be used.

Figure 8-8

The User Manager: Add window.

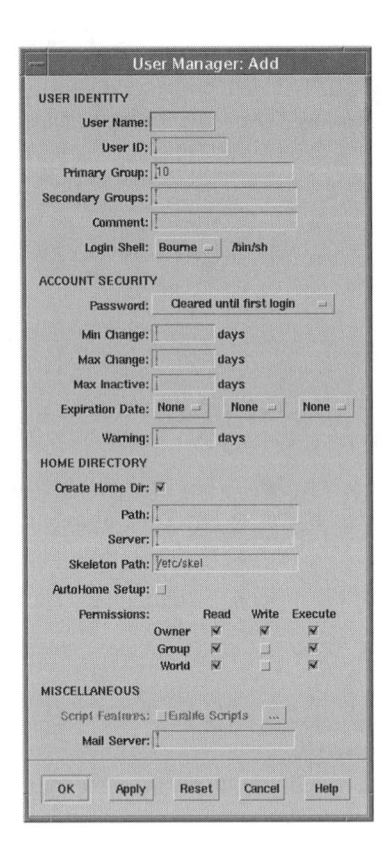

NOTE. *It is strongly recommended that UIDs be kept under 60000 to minimize software incompatibilities. Some software packages, such as third-party PC-NFS packages, can't handle UIDs over 60000.*

- *Comment* (Optional)—Specifies notes about this user account, such as a user's full name, phone number, or department.

- *Normal Password*— Displays the Set Password window, which allows you to assign a password to the account when adding the user.

- *Path*—Specifies the path for the user's home directory. By convention, this is /export/home/<*user-name*>.

Another option presented in the popup menu is the capability to copy an existing account. Simply highlight an existing account in the User Manager main window and select Copy from the popup menu. The User Manager: Copy window opens with blank User Name and User ID fields. The rest of the fields are filled in with the settings from the user you chose to copy.

Modify a User Account

To make changes to a user account, highlight the account you want to modify by clicking on the account name in the User Manager main window. Click on Edit in the menu bar and select Modify from the menu.

The User Manager: Modify window opens as shown in Figure 8-9.

Figure 8-9

The User Manager: Modify window.

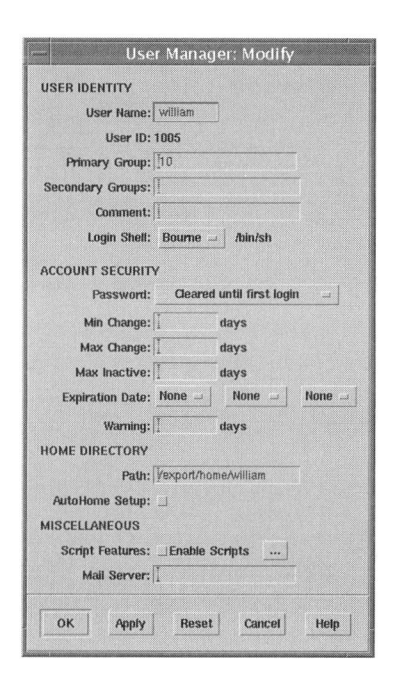

Change the appropriate boxes and click on OK after it's complete. Refer to the section titled "Setting Up User Account Defaults" for information on each field.

Delete a User Account

To delete a user account, highlight the account that you want to delete by clicking on the account name in the User Manager main window. Click on Edit in the menu bar of the User Manager main window and select Delete from the pull-down menu.

The User Manager: Delete window opens to confirm the removal of the user account as shown in Figure 8-10.

Figure 8-10

The User Manager: Delete window.

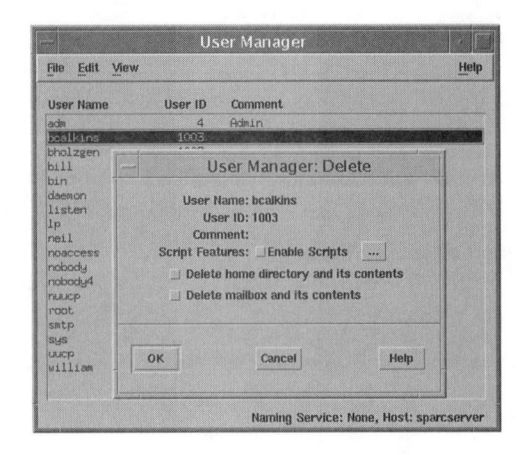

In the User Manager: Delete window, you are presented with a few options before deleting the account.

- Click on the Script Features box to specify scripts to be run before or after the account is deleted from the system. You can specify whether to run the scripts before or after the account is deleted.

- Click on the first check box to delete the user's home directory and its contents.

- Click on the second check box to delete the user's mailbox and its contents.

Click on OK if you are ready to delete the user account. The user account entry is deleted from the User Manager main window.

Group Manager

To add, modify, or delete groups, click on the Group Manager Icon in the Solstice Launcher main window. The Group Account Manager window opens with the Load window on top of it as shown in Figure 8-11.

Figure 8-11

The Group Manager: Load window.

Select the name service and click on OK. The Group Manager main window opens as shown in Figure 8-12.

Figure 8-12

The Group Manager main window.

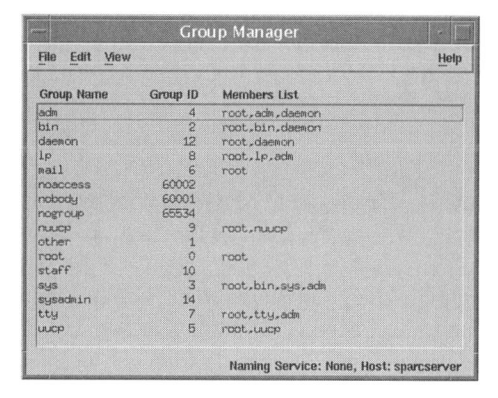

To add a group, click on Edit from the menu bar located at the top of the Group Manager main window and select Add from the pull-down menu. The Group Manager: Add window opens as shown in Figure 8-13.

Figure 8-13

The Group Manager: Add window.

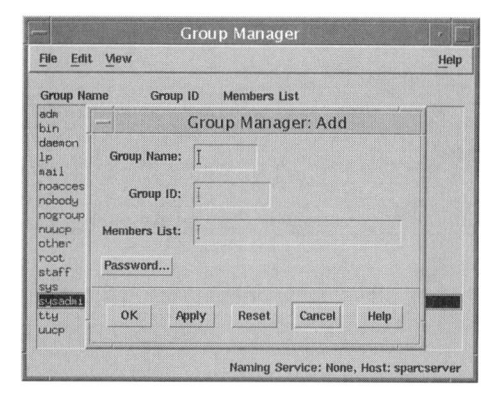

In the Group Manager: Add window, you are presented with four items, two of which are mandatory and two are optional. They are described as follows:

- *Group Name*—Type the name of the new group in the Group Name text box. A group name contains lowercase alphabetical characters (a–z) and digits (0–9). A group name can be 1–9 characters long.

- *Group ID*—Specify the group ID (GID) for the new group. This GID must be a non-negative decimal integer between 100 and 2147483647. GIDs from 0–99 are reserved by SunOS for future applications and GIDs 60002 (noaccess) and 65534 (nogroup) are reserved.

NOTE. *It is strongly recommended that GIDs be kept below 60000 to minimize software incompatibilities. Some software packages, such as third party PC-NFS packages, can't handle GIDs over 60000.*

- *Members List* (Optional)—Specify the users or groups who belong to this group. If there is to be more than one member in the list, separate the names with a comma. Spaces are not allowed.

  Example: neil,glenda,nicole

- *Password* (Optional)—Displays the password window that enables you to enter the group password.

To modify a group, highlight the group name in the Group Manager main window, click on Edit in the menu bar, and select Modify from the popup menu. The Group Manager: Modify window opens containing the selected group entry as shown in Figure 8-14.

Figure 8-14

The Group Manager: Modify window.

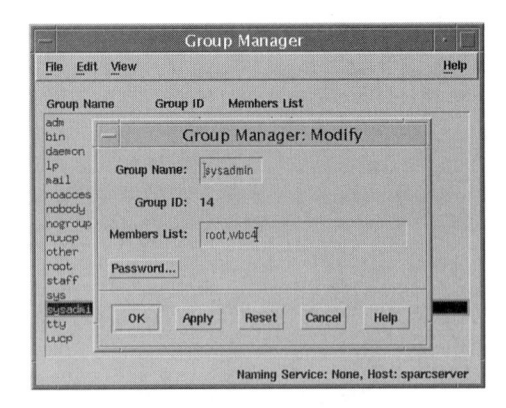

You can modify either the group's name or the users in the group. User names must be separated by commas.

Modify the group's password by clicking on the Password button. Enter the group password, and then verify it in the fields provided in the Password dialog box.

Click on OK after the modifications are complete.

Serial Port Manager

The Serial Port Manager configures the serial port software to work with terminals and modems by calling the `pmadm` command and supplying the appropriate information. Serial Port Manager allows you to:

- Display serial port information

- Use templates for common terminal and modem configurations
- Configure, modify, or delete multiple ports at the same time

The Serial Port Manager consists primarily of two windows: the Serial Port Manager main window, Figure 8-15, and the Serial Port Manager: Modify window, Figure 8-16. To access the Serial Port Manager main window, click on the Serial Port Manager icon in the Launcher window. The Serial Port main window opens as shown in Figure 8-15.

Figure 8-15

The Serial Port main window.

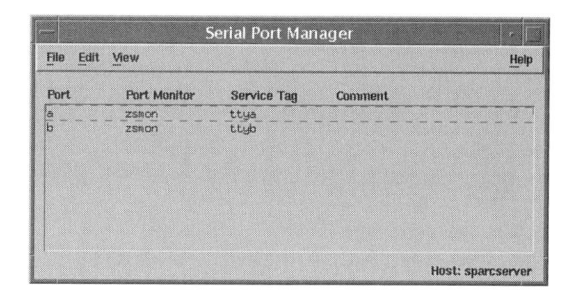

In this window, three pull-down menus enable you to

- Select the port that you want to modify
- Delete modems and terminals
- View serial ports for different hosts
- Exit the Serial Port Manager

The three pull-down menus are described in Table 8-2.

Table 8-2 Pull-Down Menus

Pull-Down Menu	Options	Description
File	Exit	Closes the Serial Port Manager tool.
Edit	Modify	Opens the Serial Port Manager: Modify window.
	Delete	Removes the port monitor and service tag configuration for the selected port.
View	Host	Brings up the Host window, which enables you to select from a list of available hosts.

The option that is most commonly used is the Modify option in the Edit pull-down menu. To modify a port, highlight the port you want to modify, click on Edit, and then click on Modify. To configure multiple ports at the same time using Serial Port Manager, highlight more than one port.

The Serial Port Manager: Modify window opens as shown in Figure 8-16.

Figure 8-16
The Serial Port Manager: Modify window.

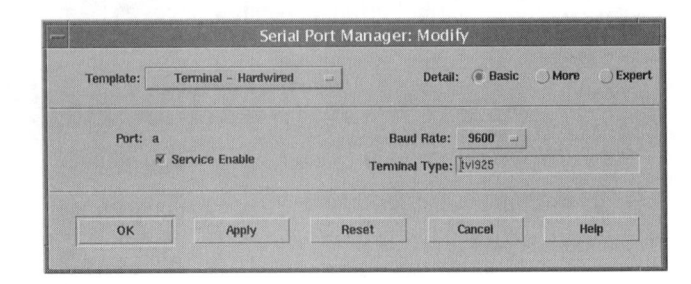

In this window, you have many options to choose from, including templates for commonly used terminal and modem configurations. The templates can be viewed by selecting the Template button, which allows you to choose one of the following template options as shown in Figure 8-17.

Figure 8-17
The Serial Port templates.

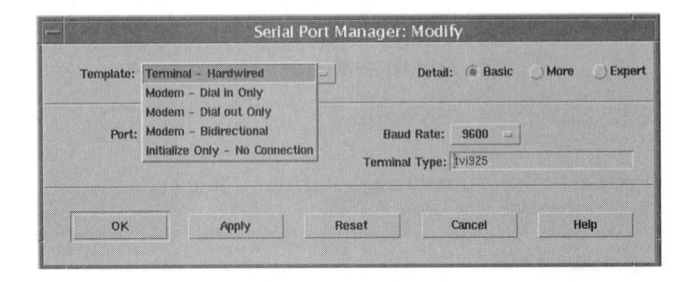

The template selections are described in Table 8-3.

Table 8-3 Serial Port Templates

Option	Description
Terminal—Hardwired	Users can log in via a terminal directly connected to the system.
Modem—Dial in only	Users can dial into the modem, but can't dial out.
Modem—Dial Out Only	Users can dial out from the modem, but can't dial in.

Option	Description
Modem—Bi-directional	Users can dial in or out from the modem.
Initialize Only—No Connection	The port service is initialized but not configured. Use this to initialize the port connection without actually connecting a device to the port.

The Serial Port Manager: Modify window has three levels of detail that can be displayed: Basic, More, and Expert. Figure 8-18 shows the Expert level of detail.

Figure 8-18
The Serial Port Manager: Modify window—Expert-level detail.

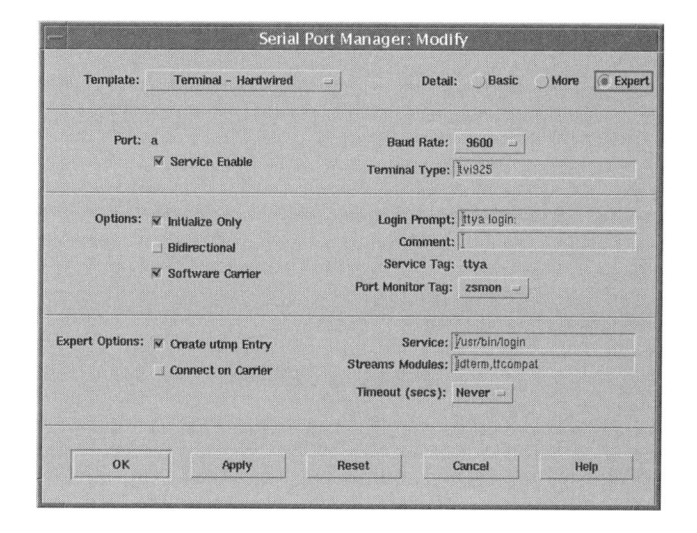

Each option in the window is described in Table 8-4. Chapter 12 in *The Solaris 2.6 Administrator Certification Training Guide, Part I* provides detail in setting up serial ports for modems and terminals.

Table 8-4 Serial Port Manager Options

Option	Description
Port	Lists the port or ports you selected from the Serial Port main window.
Service	Specifies that the service for the port is turned on (enabled).
Baud Rate	Specifies the line speed used to communicate with the terminal. The line speed represents an entry in the /etc/ttydefs file.
Terminal Type	Shows the abbreviation for the type of terminal; for example, ansi or vt100. Similar abbreviations are found in /etc/termcap. This value is set in the $TERM environment variable.

continues

Table 8-4 Serial Port Manager Options (continued)

Option	Description
Option: Initialize Only	Specifies that the port software is initialized but not configured.
Option: Bi-directional	Specifies that the port line is used in both directions.
Option: Software Carrier	Specifies that the software-carrier detection feature is used. If the option is not checked, the hardware-carrier detection signal is used.
Login Prompt	Shows the prompt displayed to a user after a connection is made.
Comment	Shows the comment field for the service.
Service Tag	Lists the service tag associated with this port, which is typically an entry in the /dev/term directory.
Port Monitor Tag	Specifies the name of the port monitor to be used for this port. The default monitor is typically correct.
Create utmp Entry	Specifies that a utmp entry is created in the accounting files upon login.
Connect on Carrier	Specifies that a port's associated service is invoked immediately after a connect indication is received.
Service	Shows the program that is run upon connection.
Streams Modules	Shows the STREAMS modules that are pushed before the service is invoked.
Timeout (secs)	Specifies the number of seconds before a port is closed if the open process on the port succeeds and no input data is received.

Print Client Software

Before discussing how to use Printer Manager to set up printers, it's important for us to take a look at The SunSoft Print Client software and how it compares with the lp print service described in Part I of this training guide. Let me begin by describing a print server and a print client, and then I'll describe the SunSoft print process by illustrating the path of a typical print request.

The Print Server

The print server is a system that has a local printer connected to it and makes the printer available to other systems on the network. The SunSoft print client commands use the BSD (Berkley Standard Distribution) printing protocol. The main advantage of this protocol is that it can communicate with a variety of print servers such as

- SunOS 4.x BSD (lpd) print servers

- SunOS 5.x SVR4 (LP) print servers
- Any other print server or printer that accepts the BSD printing protocol

The BSD printing protocol is an industry standard. It is widely used and it provides compatibility between different types of systems from various manufacturers. Sun has chosen to support the BSD printing protocol to provide interoperability in the future. The System V protocol, on the other hand, is not as widely used and does not provide compatibility with BSD print servers.

The print server is set up using the Solstice AdminSuite Printer Manager tool described later in this chapter.

The Print Client

The print client is a system that can send print requests to a print server. A system becomes a SunSoft print client when you install the SunSoft print client software and enable access to remote printers on the system. After you install the Print Client software on a system, some of the print commands in Solaris are replaced by SunSoft print client commands. These commands have the same names, accept the same command-line options, generate the same output, and work with the same tools as the standard Solaris print commands. The difference, however, is that the SunSoft commands perform their tasks using a method that improves printing performance by providing more options to locate printer configuration information. The print configuration resources are a key component of the SunSoft Print Client software. They increase printing efficiency because of the method they use to locate printer information.

The SunSoft print client commands check the following resources to locate printers and printer configuration information:

- The command-line interface
- A printer alias file in the user's home directory
- Local (print client) configuration files
- A network (shared) configuration file, if you use a name service

In contrast, the standard print commands in Solaris use fewer options to locate printer information. In addition, the standard Solaris print commands do not check information on the network and they do not support a name service.

The SunSoft print client commands enable clients to submit requests directly to the print server.

The SunSoft print client sends its requests to the print server's queue; the client does not have a local queue. The client writes the print request to a temporary spooling area only if the print server is not available or an error occurs. This streamlined path to the server decreases the print client's use of resources, reduces the chances for printing problems, and improves performance.

In contrast, the standard Solaris print commands depend on a local print daemon to communicate with the print server. The standard Solaris print commands write every print request to a local spooling area on the print client and then notifies another set of processes to transfer the request, even if the print server is available and there are no error conditions.

Processing a Print Request

The following steps outline how the SunSoft Print Client software processes a print request:

1. A user submits a print request from a SunSoft print client by using a SunSoft print client command.

2. The print client command then checks a hierarchy of print configuration resources to determine where to send the print request.

3. The print client command sends the print request directly to the appropriate print server. A SunSoft print server can be any server that accepts BSD printing protocol, including SVR4 (LP) print servers and BSD print servers (such as the SunOS 4.x BSD print server).

4. The print server sends the print request to the appropriate printer.

5. The print request is printed.

Printer Manager

Use the Printer Manager to set up and manage the SunSoft print client software. The following tasks can be performed using Printer Manager.

- *Install a printer on a print server*—Installs a printer on the system to which it is attached. This procedure tells the system about the printer so that it can act as a print server. If you use a name service, this task also makes the printer available to all SunSoft print clients.

- *Install a network printer*—Installs a printer on your network that provides access to all network users.

- *Give Print clients access*—Gives SunSoft print clients access to a printer that is installed on a print server.

- *Modify Printer Information*—Modifies the current configuration information for a printer.

To start up Printer Manager, select the Printer Manager icon from the Launcher window. The Printer Manager window opens with the Printer Manager: Load window on top of it, as shown in Figure 8-19.

Figure 8-19
The Printer Manager: Load window.

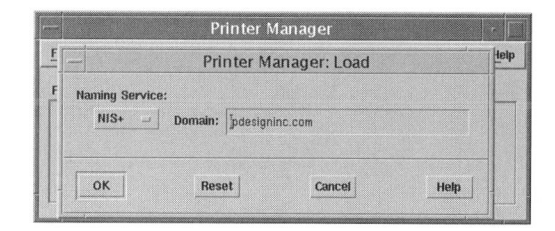

Select the correct naming service from the pull-down menu and then click on OK; the Printer Manager main window opens as shown in Figure 8-20.

Figure 8-20
The Printer Manager main window.

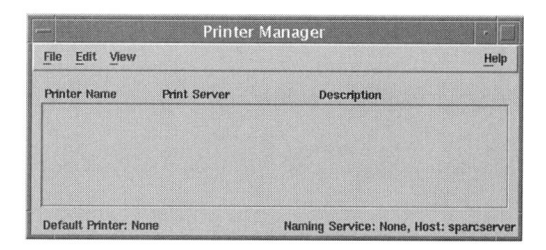

Installing a Printer

If you use Printer Manager to install a printer on a system, you define the characteristics of the printer and identify the users who are permitted to access it. The system on which you install the printer becomes the print server.

Installing a printer means something different depending on whether you use a name service. If you are using a name service, Printer Manager adds the printer in the NIS or NIS+ master file, and the printer then is available to all SunSoft print clients. If you're not using a name service, Printer Manager adds the printer in the print server's configuration files only and the print clients do not know about the printer.

To install a new printer, connect the printer to the system and turn on the power to the printer. Start the Printer Manager as described earlier, click on Edit in the menu bar, and select either Install Local Printer or Install Network Printer from the pull-down menu. In the example, I'm going to install a local printer.

The Install Local Printer window opens as shown in Figure 8-21.

Figure 8-21

The Install Local Printer window.

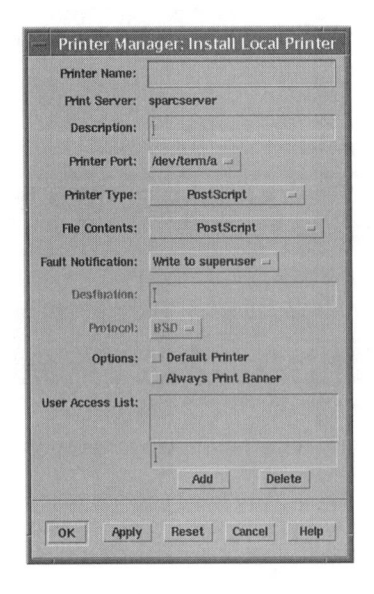

Fill in the fields and click on Apply if finished.

NOTE. *Selecting Apply allows you to save your changes and stay in the same window to add additional printers. Clicking on OK saves your changes and takes you out of the window back to the Printer Manager main window.*

The information that should be entered into the fields is as follows:

- *Printer Name*—Specifies a name for the printer. The printer name can include uppercase or lowercase alphabetical characters (A–Z), digits (0–9), minus signs, and underscores. A printer name can be a maximum of 14 characters long, and the name must be unique within the network. The printer name must start with an alphabetic (A–Z, a–z) character.

- *Print Server*—Specifies the name of the system to which the printer is physically connected. The system manages local and remote print requests for the printer.

- *Description* (Optional)—Specifies a description for the printer that helps to identify it. The description that you assign a printer should contain information that will help users to identify the printer. You might include the department where the printer is located, the type of printer, or the manufacturer.

Example: Printer in Computer Room

The description must start with an alphabetic character (A–Z, a–z) and cannot contain a colon (:), a semicolon (;), an ampersand (&), or a double quote (").

- *Printer Port*—Specifies the port to which the printer is connected (printer device name). If you select Other, you need to enter a port name that the print server recognizes.

- *Printer Type*—Specifies a generic name for the type of printer. The printer type identifies the terminfo database entry that contains various control sequences for the printer. Supported printer types correspond to printers listed in the /usr/share/lib/terminfo directory.

- *File Contents*—The File Contents entry tells the LP print service the type of file contents that can be printed directly, without filtering. To print without filtering, the necessary fonts must be available in the printer. PostScript is the default. In Printer Manager, you can select a specific type of file contents from the pull-down menu. Not all available types of file contents are listed on the menu. You must use the `lpadmin` command to specify file content types that are not included on the Printer Manager pull-down menu.

- *Fault Notification*—Specifies how the superuser (root) is to be notified in case of a printer error. "Write to superuser" will display a message in the print server's root console window, and "Mail to superuser" will send email to root.

- *Options–Default Printer*—Specifies whether to set the printer as the default printer, which is where print requests are sent if you do not specify a printer. If you are using NIS or NIS+, this option will set the default printer for all the SunSoft print clients in the name service.

    If an application doesn't provide a specific printer destination or if you don't provide a printer name when using a print command, `lp` searches for the default printer in a specific order:

    1. LPDEST variable

    2. PRINTER variable

    3. _default in .printers file

    4. _default in /etc/printers.conf file

- *Always Print Banner*—A banner page identifies who submitted the print request, the print request ID, and when the request was printed. A banner page can also have an optional title that the requester can use to better identify a printout. This option specifies whether to give users control over printing a banner page. If disabled, users can use a command option (`-o nobanner`) to prevent a banner page from printing. If enabled, a banner page always prints.

- *User Access List* (Optional)—Lists the users who are allowed access to the printer. If you leave this box blank, all users can submit print requests to the printer. If you add one or more user names, only those users can access the printer.

You might want to control which users can access some or all the available printers. For example, you might want to prevent some users from printing on a high-quality color printer to minimize expense.

If selecting Install Network Printer from the Print Manager main window, you'll be presented with the Install Network Printer window shown in Figure 8-22.

Figure 8-22

The Install Network Printer window.

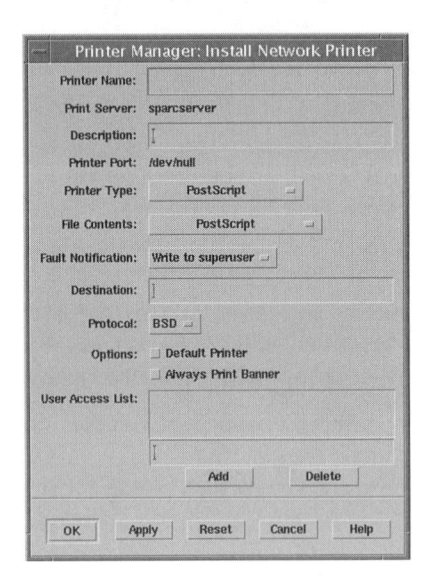

The following is a description of some of the additional options you can select:

- *Destination*—The name of the system to which the printer is connected.

- *Protocol*—Select BSD or TCP. This sets the over-the-wire protocol to the printer. Default is BSD, and BSD should always be selected unless you're told otherwise by the manufacturer. You'll select the TCP option for printers that don't support BSD.

NOTE. *If setting up network printers, it is always best to use the printer manufacturer's spooling software to setup and maintain network printers that have their own IP address. Often free software is available from the manufacturer of the network card for the printer. If the software is available in both System V and BSD, obtain the BSD version.*

If you're finished filling in the fields, click on OK and you'll return to the Print Manager main window where you should see the printer listed that you just added.

Modify a Printer

To modify a printer, highlight the printer in the Print Manager main window, select Edit from the menu bar, and click on Modify from the pull-down menu. If modifying a network printer, the Modify Network Printer window opens. If modifying a local printer, the Modify Local Printer window opens as shown in Figure 8-23.

Figure 8-23

The Print Manager: Modify Window

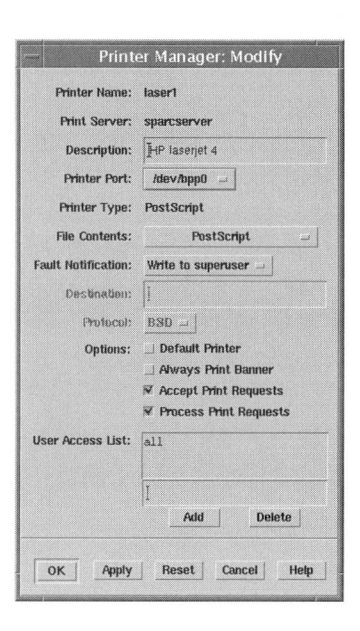

Make your changes in this window and click on OK when finished. You'll return to the Print Manager main window.

Delete a Printer

To delete a printer, highlight the printer you want to delete in the Print Manager main window, click on Edit from the menu bar, and select Delete from the pull-down menu. You'll receive a warning message asking if you really want to delete the printer, click on OK, and you'll return to the Print Manager main window. The printer will now be deleted from the list of printers.

Database Manager

Database Manager is used to manage the network-related system files. With Database Manager, you can edit system files in a system's /etc directory, NIS name service, or the NIS+ name service. Using Database Manager to add an entry to a system file usually managed by another tool can save time. For example, Host Manager requires you to enter the Ethernet address in the /etc/ethers file when adding a standalone system although you might just want to use this system for remote login only. An entry in the /etc/hosts file is all that is required for remote logins. If you use Database Manager to add the entry to the /etc/hosts file, you won't be prompted for additional information and the process will go much quicker.

The network-related system files that can be modified with Database Manager are described in Table 8-5.

Table 8-5   System Files

File	Description
aliases	Aliases in ASCII format for the local host. Or, for a NIS+ or NIS file, aliases available for use across the network.
auto.home	Entries for client systems to mount their auto_home (NIS+) home directories automatically; an indirect or /etc automounter map.
bootparams	Entries client systems need to start up from the network.
ethers	Ethernet addresses of network client systems.
group	Entries that define group access.
hosts	Entries for systems on the network and their associated IP addresses.
locale	The default locales used by network clients.
netgroup	Entries for netgroups, a group of systems granted identical access to network resources for security and organizational reasons.
netmasks	Network mask values used to implement IP subnetting.
networks	Information about available networks.
passwd	User account and password entries.
protocols	Information about Internet protocols used in your network.
rpc	Entries for available RPC services (by name) and their associated program numbers and aliases.
services	Information about network services and their port numbers.
timezone	Entries for systems and their geographic region and time zone used at installation.

The following steps describe how to use Database Manager to manage network services files.

1. Click on the Database Manager icon located in the Solstice Launcher window. The Database Manager: Load window opens as shown in Figure 8-24.

Figure 8-24

The Database Manager: Load window.

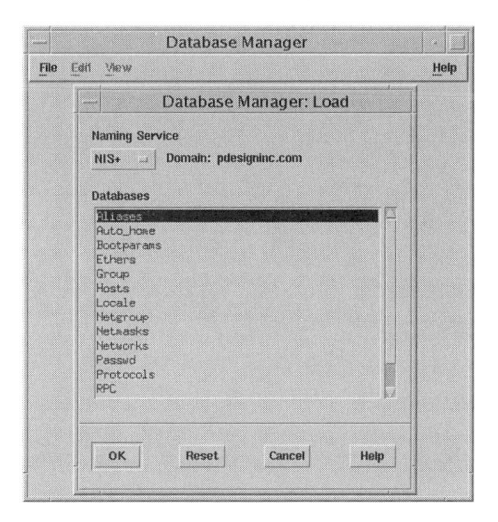

2. Select the file you want to modify from the Databases box, select your name service from the pull-down menu, and then select OK. A window opens with the contents of that database for you to modify.

   In the following example, I entered the wrong Ethernet address when adding an AutoClient system; therefore, I'm going to quickly change the entry in the /etc/ethers file. This is much quicker than deleting the entry and reentering all the client information in the Host Manager tool. I'm simply going to modify an entry in the "Ethers" database.

3. I'll start by clicking on Database Manager in the Launcher window. After the Database Manager: Load window appears, I'm going to select None as my name service and I'm going to highlight the Ethers database as shown in Figure 8-25.

Figure 8-25
Modify the Ethers Database.

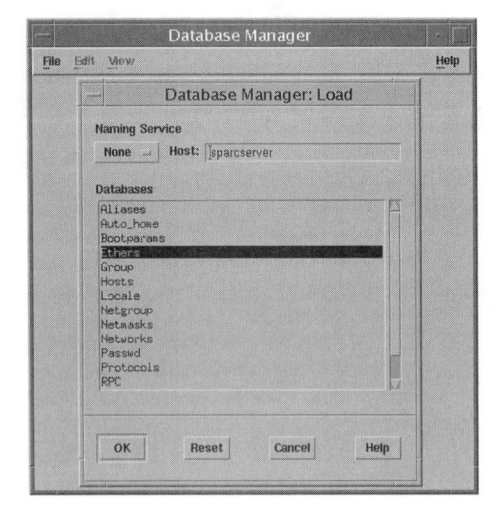

4. Click on OK if you are finished making your selection and the Ethers Database window opens as shown in Figure 8-26.

Figure 8-26
The Ethers Database window.

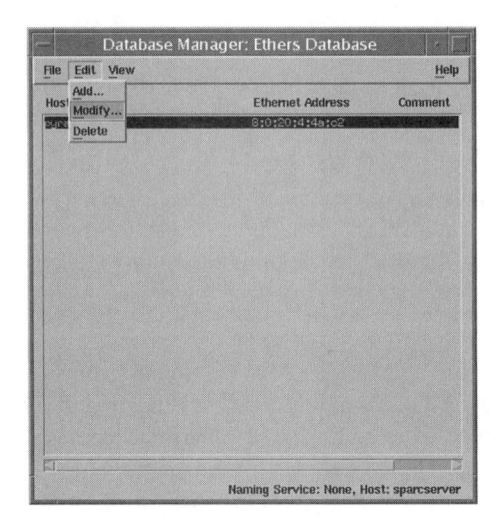

5. Highlight the entry you want to modify, click on Edit in the menu bar, and select Modify from the pull-down menu.

6. The Database Manager: Modify window opens as shown in Figure 8-27. Modify the entry in the Ethernet Address box and click on OK.

Figure 8-27

The Database Manager: Modify window.

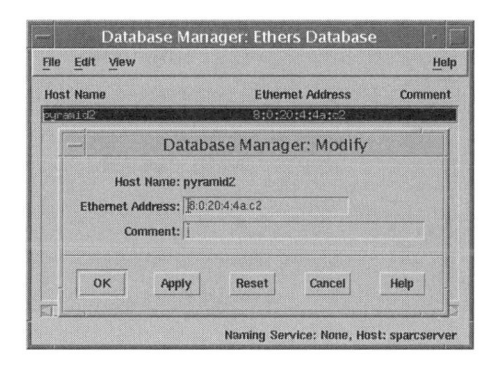

7. You'll return to the Database Manager: Ethers Database window and the entry will reflect the new Ethernet address. Select File from the menu bar and select Exit from the pull-down menu to return to the Solstice Launcher window.

Storage Manager

The Storage Manager application contains two tools, File System Manager and Disk Manager. These tools enable you to manage disk configurations and file systems on servers that are on your network. Because setting up file systems and disk drives are covered in more depth in earlier chapters, I'll briefly describe the function of Storage Manager here.

The Storage Manager, shown in Figure 8-28, is accessed by selecting the Storage Manager icon located in the Launcher window.

The Load Context window opens when you start Storage Manager, and you must select a host in the Host Chapter before you can use File System Manager or Disk Manager. Sun uses several terms throughout the Storage Manager that might seem confusing; therefore, I'll define some of these terms in Table 8-6.

Table 8-6 Storage Manager Definition of Terms

Term	Definition
Context	Describes the environment or components of the object whose properties you are going to view and edit. For the File System Manager, the context includes what name service to modify and how to view and modify the file systems on a server.
Current Context	The server you are going manage and how you are going to view the server's file systems.
Context Type	Indicates the name of the tool with which the current context is associated.

continues

Table 8-6　Storage Manager Definition of Terms (continued)

Term	Definition
Chapter	Represents the properties of an object. You can view and change the properties within a chapter by opening it.
Host Chapter	Use this chapter to specify a different system on which to manage file systems or disks. Specify a remote host to manage disks or file systems on a remote system.
Property Viewer	Displays the object or context properties you can view and/or modify.
Property Book	The mechanism by which you identify, view, and modify the properties of editable objects.

Figure 8-28

The Storage Manager: Load Context window.

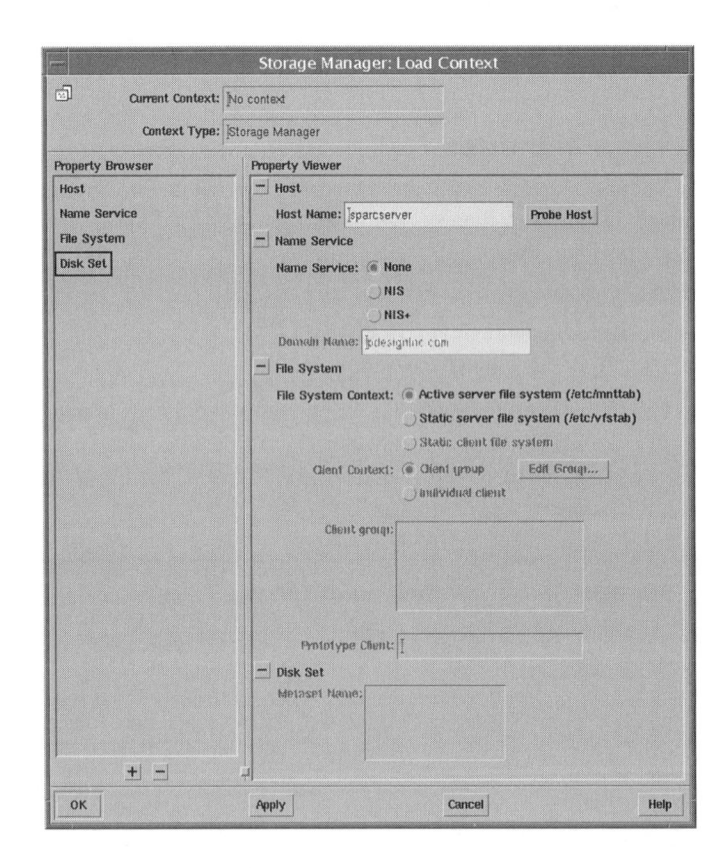

You'll begin by entering a host in the Host Name box and clicking on Apply at the bottom of the window. The File System Manager window opens for the host specified as shown in Figure 8-29.

Figure 8-29

The File System Manager window.

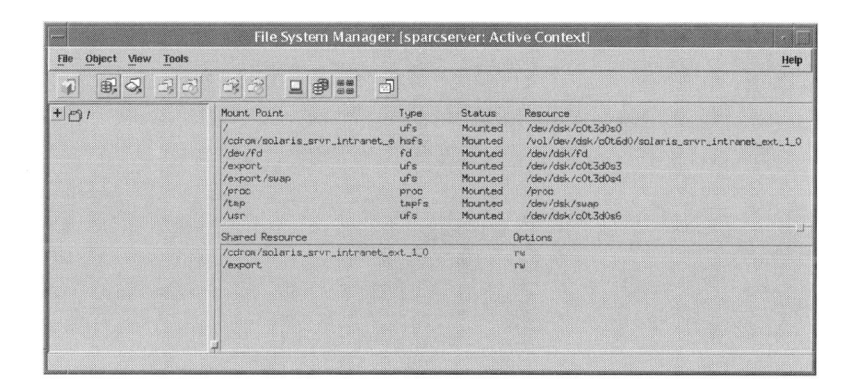

File System Manager is a tool that enables you to create and modify file systems, mount points, and directories using two types of windows, the main window, and a Property Book. The main window displays a hierarchical view of directories and file systems, as well as the mount points and shared resources for the current context. The Property Book displays the chapters and their properties for a selected directory or file system that you can view or modify.

Specifically, File System Manager is a tool that enables you to perform the following tasks:

- Create new file systems.
- Modify file system options in the /etc/vfstab file.
- Manage /etc/vfstab files on a single or group of diskless clients or AutoClient systems.
- Mount or unmount file systems.
- Share or unshare file systems.
- Include a file system in existing automounter maps.
- Convert a directory into a mount point.

Also in Storage Manager is Disk Manager, a tool that enables you to view and edit disk partitions and slices. Select this tool by clicking on Tools in the File System Manager window and selecting Disk Manager from the pull-down menu. The Disk Manager window opens as shown in Figure 8-30.

Figure 8-30
The Disk Manager window.

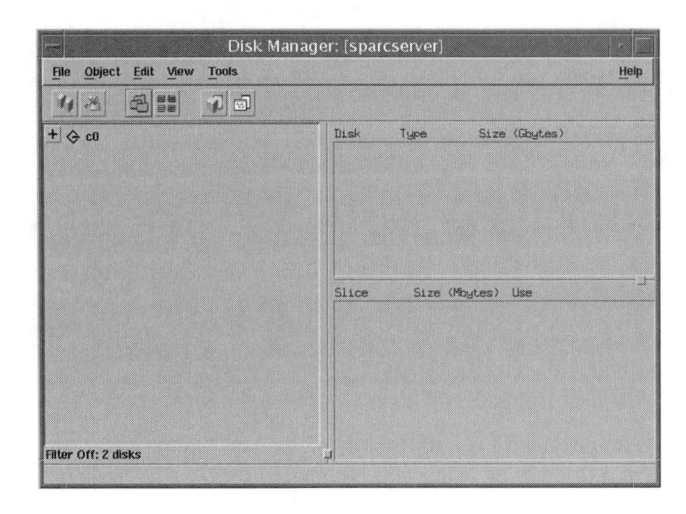

Specifically, you can perform the following tasks with Disk Manager:

- Assign a volume name to a disk.
- View and modify fdisk partitions on x86 platforms.
- Show and set the active fdisk partition on x86 platforms.
- View and modify slice geometry on SPARC and x86 platforms.
- Copy a disk's characteristics to one or more disks of the same type.

Solstice AdminSuite provides an easy-to-use, graphical interface for managing your systems from anywhere on the network. The tools and commands in the GUI are much faster than using numerous Solaris commands to perform the same tasks. Spend some time getting familiar with the AdminSuite tools. At any time while in the GUI, click on the Help button to obtain more information on using this tool.

APPENDIX A

Web Start

Web Start is Sun's Java-based installation program that simplifies and accelerates the installation of Solaris Software. Web Start uses technology from InstallShield, which is widely recognized as the provider of de facto install technology for Microsoft Windows applications. This tool lets network administrators use a familiar Web browser utilizing a point-and-click interface to install all the software bundled with Solaris. Through Solaris Web Start, you select and install all the software your machine requires, including the Solaris software group and Solstice utilities. In addition, Web Start is the only install utility that also installs the other software provided on the additional CDs. It's much like the Solaris interactive installation program described in Part I of the *Solaris 2.6 Administrator Certification Training Guide* but with a much more user-friendly interface. Solaris Web Start uses the JumpStart utility to read the configuration profile automatically, thus installing the Solaris software and the other selected products with minimal intervention.

If you're setting up a machine that includes a frame buffer, keyboard, and monitor, you can run Web Start directly from that machine. If you only have a character-based terminal connected via the serial port, you can still start up to the CD-ROM and enter the system identification information.

After the system identification is complete, you have your choice of how you want to continue the installation: You can either continue using the character-based Interactive Installation, as explained in Chapter 1, "Installing a Server," or use Web Start, with its graphical user interface, by utilizing a bit-mapped terminal connected to a system (or PC) over the network. This process is explained later in this chapter.

Minimum System Requirements for Solaris Web Start

If you want to run Solaris Web Start, your computer must have

- At least 48MB of RAM.
- A 1.05 GB startup disk just to run Solaris Web Start, after which the program determines whether your system has enough disk space to install the products you selected. 2 GBs of disk space is recommended for installing server software.

Modes of Operation

There are two ways to use Solaris Web Start: in local mode or in client-server mode.

Local Mode

If you run Solaris Web Start locally on the machine that you're setting up, it writes the profile to disk and uses that profile information when you select and confirm the Install Now option. Your computer system must include a CD-ROM drive, frame buffer, keyboard, and monitor if you are to use this mode.

To start up Web Start in local mode, simply start up from the Solaris 2.6 software CD using the following command at the startup PROM:

```
ok boot cdrom - browser
```

NOTE. *Be sure to include a space before and after the hyphen.*

After the system starts up from the CD, follow the instructions on the screen.

Client-Server Mode

Use the client-server mode if the system does not have a bitmapped graphics display. In this mode, Solaris Web Start runs on the machine being configured, but Java applets in Web Start interact with you on your desktop Web browser. You can run Web Start from any system connected to the network that has a Web browser like Netscape Navigator or Microsoft Internet Explorer. Client-server mode is useful for installing software on a "headless server," which does not include a frame buffer for bitmapped graphics.

Solaris Web Start's client-server mode lets you take advantage of the ease and convenience of a browser-based installation, even if the machine on which you're loading the software doesn't support a graphical user interface.

If the system has no monitor at all, connect a PC or dumb terminal, such as a VT-100, to the system's serial port. Use a null modem cable to connect the terminal to the serial port on the Sun system. I use a laptop with a communications package, such as ProComm™ or HyperTerminal in Windows 98™. Configure the PC for a direct-connection from Com1 to serial port A on the back of your Sun system. When the system is powered on, it detects that the keyboard and monitor are missing and defaults to using serial port A. You'll get the familiar "ok" prompt on your PC. To get into client-server mode, start up from the CD the same way described earlier for getting into local mode:

```
ok boot cdrom - browser
```

A system identification tool asks you to supply system and network information about the machine that you're adding to the network. This is a standard part of Sun's installation process and was described in Part I of the *Solaris 2.6 Administrator Certification Training Guide*.

After you've completed entering the system identification information, Solaris Web Start "figures out" that your machine lacks graphical support and displays the following message:

```
You cannot run Solaris Web Start on this system—it requires a bitmapped graphics
display.

------------------------
You have two options:
------------------------

[1] Continue running Solaris Web Start using a web-browser window on another machine
connected over the network.
[2] Run the Solaris interactive installation.

Options other than Solaris Web Start only install Solaris software on your computer.
Solaris Web Start installs both Solaris software and co-packaged products.

Solaris Web Start provides a suite of online information to guide you through product
selection and installation. If you change your mind, you can exit from Solaris Web
Start at any time and return to the Solaris interactive installation.

Type 1 or 2 then press the Return key=>1
```

To switch to the Interactive Installation program and continue using this terminal, select Option 2.

If you choose to proceed using Web Start, you'll be instructed to provide a password. This authentication password is distinct from any others you might have. The password restricts who can use Web Start to install software over the network on your machine.

```
Before Solaris Web Start can begin, you must choose a special
Solaris Web Start authentication password for user 'webstart'.

Adding password for webstart
Enter password:
Re-enter password:
```

Web Start next explains how you can run your installation over the network by going to another machine and pointing your Web browser program at a special Uniform Resource Locator (URL).

The URL, however, is different for each system that you are setting up, because it contains the hostname that has been assigned to the new system, in this case, 'sparc1'.

```
-----------------------------------
To continue with Solaris Web Start
-----------------------------------

Step 1. Go to another machine connected to this network.
```

Step 2. On the other machine, start the HotJava(TM) or another supported web-browser program.

Step 3. Point the browser at this URL: http://sparc1/start.html

Step 4. When you are prompted to enter a user name and password, respond by typing: 'webstart' for the user name and the authentication password you chose earlier.

The next line that appears on this console is a status message. Ignore it and proceed with the browser install.

Jun 21 13:27:21 sws[1226]: SWS-1.0 server started.

If you follow these steps on a remote system, you'll soon see the Solaris Web Start welcome page appear in your Web browser, as shown in Figure A-1.

Figure A-1
The Web Start Welcome page.

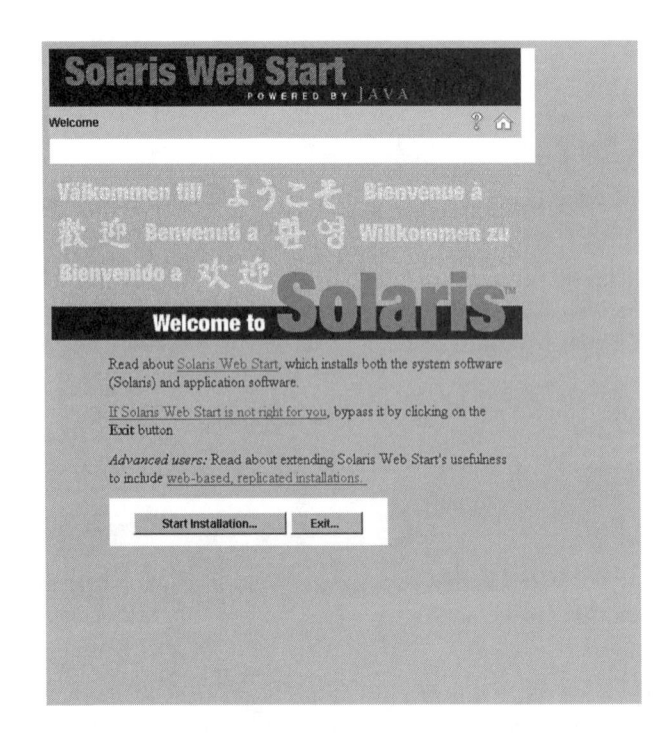

Click on the Start Installation button, and Web Start begins the installation process by opening a window that asks you to set the root password, as shown in Figure A-2.

Figure A-2
The Password Setup window.

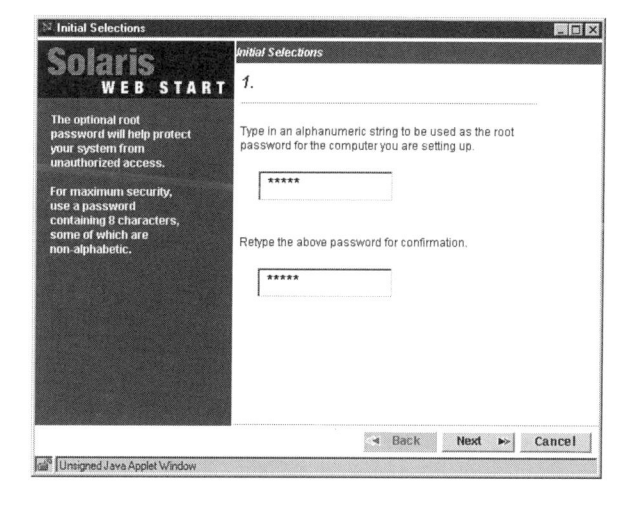

Enter the password twice and click on the button labeled Next. A confirmation window, as shown in Figure A-3, opens.

Figure A-3
The Confirmation window.

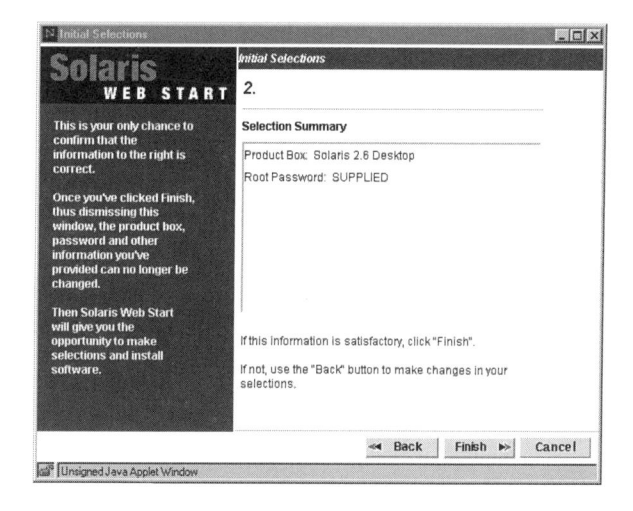

Click on the Finish button, and Web Start begins the installation process by opening the selection window shown in Figure A-4.

Figure A-4
The Web Start Selection window.

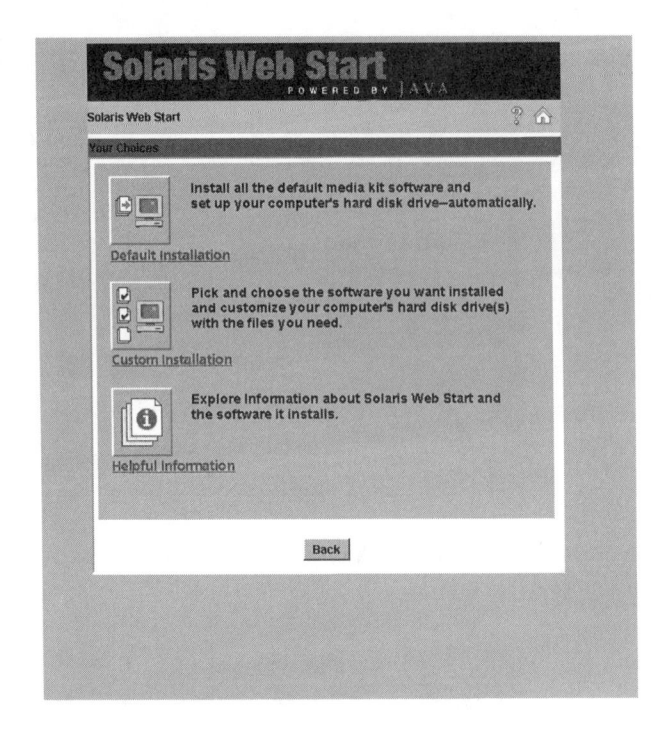

The following sections describe the options that are presented in the Selection window.

Web Start Default Installation Selection

The Default Installation option in Web Start is the easiest way to install system and co-packaged additional software on your computer. Just click the Default Installation button shown in Figure A-4 and the Default Installation Configuration window opens, as shown in Figure A-5.

Figure A-5
The Default Installation Configuration window.

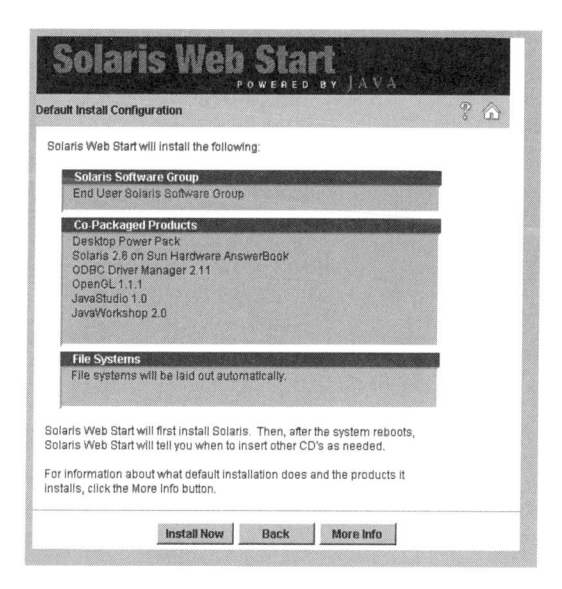

Click on the Install Now button, and Web Start

- Creates root and swap partitions on the system disk.
- Creates an /opt partition for the co-packaged software utilities.
- Installs the entire Solaris Software Group on server systems and the End User Software Group on desktop systems.
- Installs all the software that comes with the Solaris Server plus Intranet Extension product boxes. The software that is packaged in other product boxes varies, and the co-packaged software automatically installed also varies. Check the products listed in the Web Start interface for details.
- Installs AnswerBook2 documentation on server systems. On desktops, the documentation that is installed varies. Check the products listed in the Web Start interface for details.

Limitations of the Default Installation

If you are installing software on a system that has multiple disks, the Default Installation option sets up only the system disk. Other disks are not recognized by the operating system unless you manually set up and mount file systems on them and create entries for them in /etc/vfstab after the Web Start installation.

If you want Web Start to set up all the disks in your system, use the Customized Installation option described next and then choose to lay out the file system manually.

Web Start Custom Installation

Use this option to customize the software installation. Unlike the default installation in which software selections and file systems are already defined, this option lets you select the installation of software and the creation of file systems. The customized installation is much like the Interactive Software Installation described in Part I with the following exceptions:

- Solaris Web Start does not perform software upgrades. It is designed to install software on a new computer.
- Solaris Web Start installs entire software clusters and does not provide the flexibility of selecting/deselecting particular packages within a cluster.
- Solaris Web Start installs Solstice utility and other software in the /opt directory and does not allow you to choose an alternate location.
- Solaris Web Start installs the full versions of all software packages. It does not install "light" or "nil" versions of any software.
- Solaris Web Start lets you choose a system disk, but it does not let you move the root partition off the system disk afterward.

If you need to do any of the previously listed installations, use the Solaris Interactive Installation program instead of Solaris Web Start.

After you've decided to proceed with the custom installation, click on the Custom Installation button in the Web Start Selection window (see Figure A-4). The Customize window opens and you are presented with three options, as shown in Figure A-6.

Figure A-6
The Customize window.

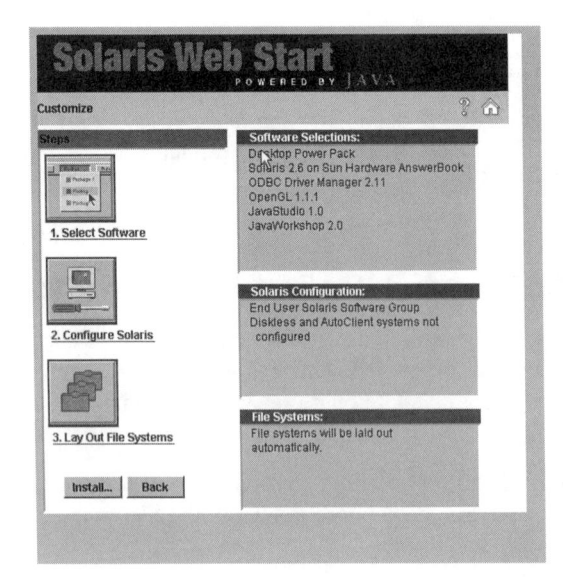

WEB START CUSTOM INSTALLATION

The options are as follows:

1. Select Software

    If you select this button, you are presented with the Software Selection window, as shown in Figure A-7.

Figure A-7
The Software Selection window.

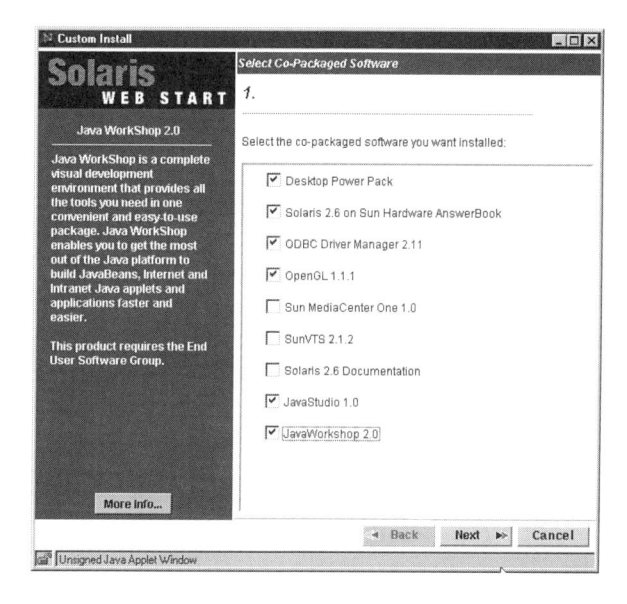

Use this option to select the co-packaged software that you want to install. The software includes such packages as "Desktop Power Pack" and "OpenGL." When you position your cursor over each option, a brief description of that product appears in the frame on the left side of the window. If you click on the More Info button, another window opens describing the software package in more detail, as well as the system requirements to run it.

After you are finished, select Next, and a window displaying the selected options opens. Select Finish and you'll return to the Customize window.

2. Configure Solaris

    Use this option to select the software group you want installed, such as the "End User Software Group" or the "Developer Software Group." After you've made your selection, the Solaris 2.6 Configuration window opens, as shown in Figure A-8.

Figure A-8

The Solaris 2.6 Configuration window.

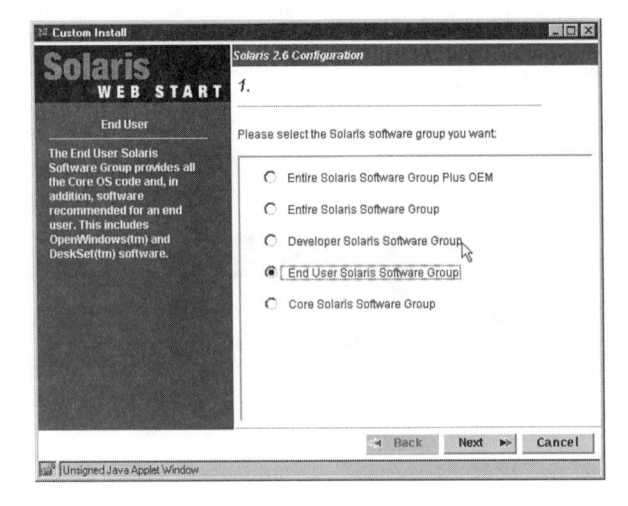

Select the software group and click on Next. Verify your selections in the confirmation message box that appears, and then click on the Finish button to return to the Customize window.

3. Lay Out File Systems

   After selecting this option, you are presented with the Lay Out File Systems window, as shown in Figure A-9.

Figure A-9

The Lay Out File Systems window.

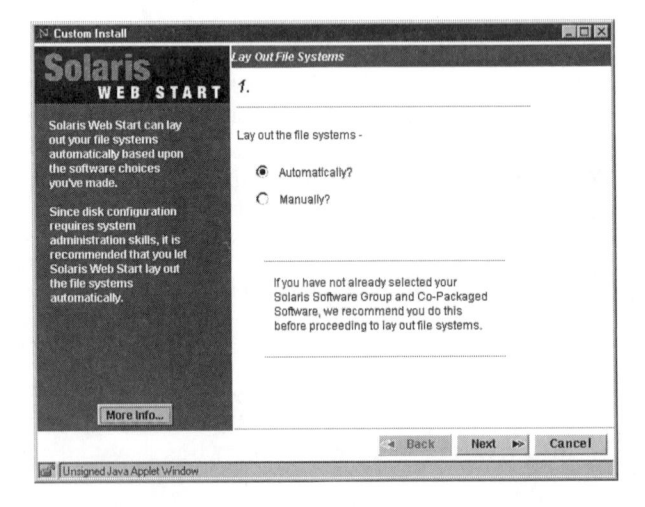

To have the installation program layout the file systems automatically, select the option labeled Automatically?. The file systems are laid out automatically based on the software selections that you have made; therefore, this step should be performed last. Select the button labeled Next to continue, and a Layout Summary window opens as shown in Figure A-10.

Figure A-10
The Layout Summary window.

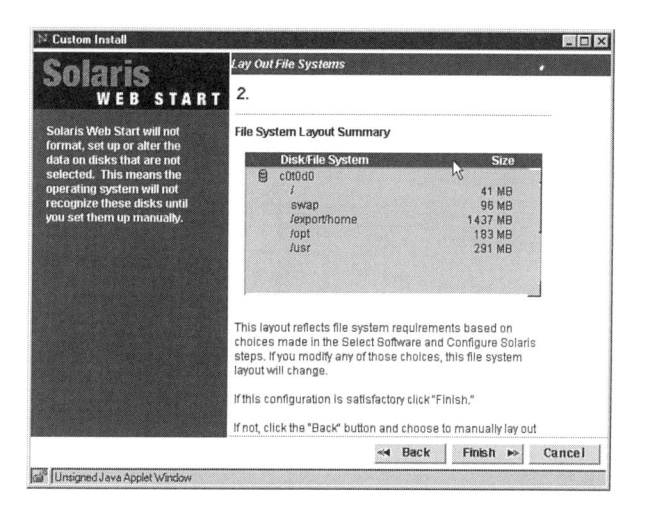

If, however, you want to manually configure the disks and file systems, select the option labeled Back to return to the Lay Out File Systems Window (see Figure A-9) and select the option labeled Manually. After selecting the Next button, the prompts displayed in the windows that follow allow you to select the disks and create the file systems.

When to Lay Out File Systems Manually

If you do not have experience in laying out file systems, let Web Start lay out the file systems for you automatically. Web Start does so in a way that mirrors Interactive Installation. The major difference between Web Start and the Interactive Installation is that Web Start lays out enough space (in /opt) for all the selected co-packaged software products—not just Solaris.

The file system configurations automatically provided by Web Start is adequate for most situations. However, you might consider laying out file systems manually if:

- Other products that are not included in your Solaris product box need to be installed. These products must share the same file systems (root, /usr, and /swap) used by the co-packaged software in the product box.

- It has been your experience that the file systems provided by the Interactive Installation program do not work for your situation.

After you are finished selecting software, configuring Solaris, and laying out the file systems, click on the Install button. You are presented with one more window summarizing the current install configuration as shown in Figure A-11.

Figure A-11
The Install Summary window.

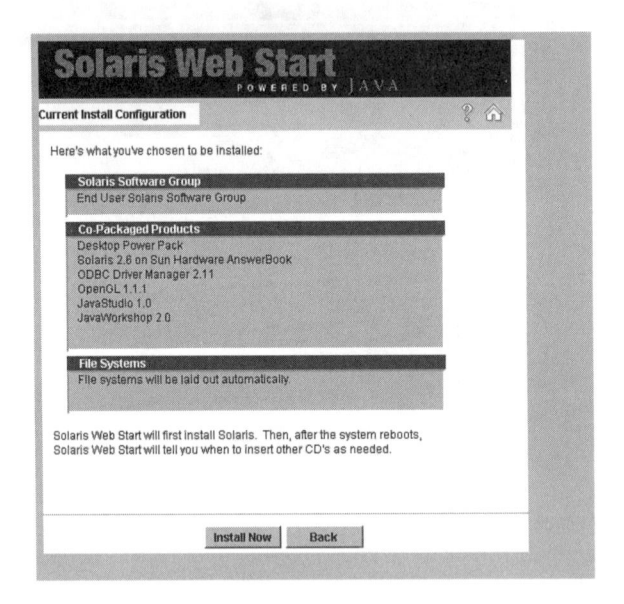

Confirm your selections and start the install by clicking on the Install Now button. Web Start first installs Solaris, and then, after the system restarts, it tells you when to load the other CDs as needed.

Web Start Helpful Information

The Helpful Information and More Info buttons located on the Web Start windows are your sources of information about the Web Start program, as well as the software products that it installs.

This completes the discussion of the Web Start installation utility. Look for further developments in this package, specifically in the area of wizards. Solaris Web Start wizards enhance application software written for the Solaris platform. Application vendors are already starting to use Web Start wizards, which allow their applications to be installed from a Java desktop environment, or remotely from a Java-enabled Web browser, to any Solaris server or desktop on the network.

INDEX

Symbols

\ (backslash), 173
(number sign), 173
/ (slashes), device path names (OpenBoot), 77

A

access rights, NIS+ authorization, 206
accessing servers, 21
actions, vold.conf (volume manager), 144-146
adb (absolute debugger) command, kernels, 104-105
add drv command, 117-119
add install client command, 37-39
Add OS Services window, AutoClient servers, 27
adding
    AutoClients to servers, 30-32
    groups, Group Manager (Solstice AdminSuite tools), 223-224
    user accounts, User Manager (Solstice AdminSuite tools), 219-220
admclientpatch command, 33

AdminSuite, 15, 211
    command-line equivalents, 211-212
    Database Manager, 16
    Group Manager, 16
    Host Manager, 16
    installing, 18-21, 212
        pre-installation checklist, 18-19
    Printer Manager, 16
    Serial Port Manager, 16
    Storage Manager, 17
    tools, Solstice Launcher window, 212-214
    User Manager, 16

AdminSuite tools, 215
    Database Manager, 236
        service files, 237-239
        system files, 236
    Group Manager, 222
        adding groups, 223-224
        modifying groups, 224
    logging, 215-216
    Printer Manager, 230-231
        deleting printers, 235
        installing printers, 231-235
        modifying printers, 235
    Serial Port Manager, 224
        modifying ports, 226
        options, 227-228
        Serial Port main window, 225
        Serial Port Manager: Modify window, 226-227
    Storage Manager, 239-240
        Disk Manager window, 241-242
        File System Manager window, 241
    User Manager, 216
        adding new user accounts, 219-220
        deleting user accounts, 221-222
        modifying user accounts, 221
        setting up user account defaults, 217-219

AdminTool, 206
aliases, device aliases (OpenBoot), 80-81
applications, registering Solstice Launcher window, 214
architecture, OpenBoot, 75-76
assigning passwords, OpenBoot, 86-87
authentication
    DES, 207-208
    NIS+, 206
authorization, NIS+, 206
auto-boot?
    boot configuration variables, OpenBoot, 92
    NVRAM variables, 81
auto-configuration, 114-116
    benefits of, 115
AutoClient
    benefits of, 22
    disk space, 23
    Host Manager, 23
    patching admclientpatch command, 33
    servers
        Add OS Services window, 27
        adding to, 30-32
        Set Media Path window, 27
        setting up, 25-29
AutoClient clients, 7-8
AutoClient systems, 7
    how they work, 24-25
    maintaining patches, 35
    patching, 32-35
    starting, 32
AutoClients, maintaining patches, 33-35
autofs, 169-171
    automount command, 169-170
    automount service, 169-170
    automountd daemon, 170

direct maps, 175-176
  failover, 178
  fields, 176
  selecting servers, 177
indirect maps, 179-180
  fields, 180
  home directories, 180-181
maps, 172
  modifying, 182
master maps, 172-175
automount, 182-183
automount command, autofs, 169-170
automount service, autofs, 169-170
automountd daemon, autofs, 170
automounter. *See* **autofs**
autosync command, AutoClient systems, 24

B

backup media, profiles, 56
banner command, OpenBoot diagnostics, 88
begin scripts, 54-55
benefits of
  auto-configuration, 115
  AutoClient, 22
  NFS, 155
  volume manager, 142
  WebNFS, 166
boot command
  filenames, 95
  ok prompt, starting systems, 93-94
  OpenBoot, 92-93
boot device, profiles, 56-57

boot-command
  boot configuration variables, OpenBoot, 92
  NVRAM variables, 81
boot-device
  boot configuration variables, OpenBoot, 92
  NVRAM variables, 81
boot-file
  boot configuration variables, OpenBoot, 92
  NVRAM variables, 82
bootblocks, 94
bootstrap procedure, 90
browsers, WebNFS, 168-169
BSD (Berkley Standard Distribution) printing protocol, 228

C

category arguments, help command (OpenBoot), 77
changing configuration variables, NVRAM, 82-85
check command, 37
check script, rules files, 52-54
client arch, profiles, 57
client root, profiles, 57
client swap, profiles, 58
client-server mode, Web Start, 246-249
clients, 7
  AutoClient, 8
  AutoClient clients, 7
  dataless clients, 7
  diskless clients, 7
  install servers, 69
  JavaStation, 7

NFS, 156
NIS, 187
NIS clients, configuring, 201-202
setting up, 67
starting up, 70
cluster, profiles, 58-59
command-line equivalents, Solstice AdminSuite, 211-212
commands
    adb, kernels, 104-105
    add_drv, 117-119
    add_install_client, 37, 39
    admclientpatch, 33
    automount, autofs, 169-170
    autosync, 24
    banner, OpenBoot diagnostics, 88
    boot, OpenBoot, 92-93
    check, 37
    dev .., device trees, 79
    dev /, device trees, 80
    dev device-path, device trees, 79-80
    dev node-name, device trees, 79
    devalias, OpenBoot, 80
    devalias alias, OpenBoot, 80
    devalias alias device-path, OpenBoot, 80
    device-end, device trees, 80
    device-path find device, device trees, 80
    device-path select-dev, device trees, 80
    devlinks, 125
    df, 151-152
    dfmounts, NFS, 165
    dfshares, 161
    disks, 123
        logical device names, 124
    dmesg, 108-109, 113-114
        instance names, 117
    drvconfig, 117, 119

eeprom, UNIX, 84
.enet-addr, OpenBoot diagnostics, 88
esp, 123
fdformat, 148-149
for browsing device trees, OpenBoot, 79-80
fsck, 151
fstyp, 135-136
fuser, 141
help, OpenBoot, 76-77
.idprom, OpenBoot diagnostics, 88
installboot, 94
labelit, 131
ls, device trees, 80
make, NIS, 193
makedbm, NIS, 193
mkfs, 129-131, 135
modinfo, kernels, 96
mount, 136-139
    direct maps, 179
    NFS, 162-164, 166
newfs, 129, 131
NIS, 193
nischmod, 207
nisls -1, 207
nvalias, 81
nvalias alias device-path, NVRAM, 85
nvunalias, 81
nvunalias alias, NVRAM, 85
password, NVRAM variables, 83
patchadd -c, 43
pfinstall, 37, 65
pkginfo, 192
ports, 123
printenv, NVRAM variables, 83
probe-scsi, OpenBoot diagnostics, 87
.properties, device trees, 79
prtconf, 109
prtvtoc, 136

pwd, device trees, 80
rmmount, 146
set-default variable, NVRAM variables, 83
set-defaults, NVRAM variables, 83
setenv variable value, NVRAM variables, 83
setup install server, 37-39, 43, 68
share, 158-160, 162
shareall, 160
show-devs
    OpenBoot, 78-79
    OpenBoot diagnostics, 88
show-devs [*device-path*], device trees, 80
show-sbus, OpenBoot diagnostics, 88
showmount, autofs, 171-172
soladdapp, 214
.speed, OpenBoot diagnostics, 88
SunSoft print client commands, 229
sysdef, 109-113
    instance names, 119
    kernels, 97-101, 103-104
tapes, 123
test device-specifier, OpenBoot diagnostics, 87
test-all [*device-specifier*], OpenBoot diagnostics, 87
.traps, OpenBoot diagnostics, 88
tunefs, 133-134
/usr/sbin/share, 159
umount, 140-141
    NFS, 165
uname -i, 95
unshare, 162
.version, OpenBoot diagnostics, 88
volcancel, 146
volcheck, 146
volcopy, 132-133
vold, 146
volmissing, 146
watch-clock, OpenBoot diagnostics, 87
watch-net, OpenBoot diagnostics, 87
ypcat, NIS, 193
ypinit, NIS, 193
yppoll, NIS, 193
yppush, NIS, 193
ypset, NIS, 193
ypstart, NIS, 193
ypstop, 199
    NIS, 193
ypwhich, NIS, 193

configuration variables
    NVRAM, 85
        changing, 82-85
        OpenBoot, 81-82
    OpenBoot, console, 89-90
    SPARC, 82
    startup process, OpenBoot, 91-92
    UNIX, 85

configuring
    NIS clients, 201-202
    NIS master server, 192-194
    NIS slave servers, 202-203

console, OpenBoot configuration variables, 89-90

constructing file systems
    labelit command, 131
    mkfs command, 129-131
    volcopy command, 132-133

customized installation, Web Start, 252-255

customizing
    JumpStart installation, 38-39
        install servers, 43
        startup servers, 39-42
    Solstice Launcher window, 214-215

D

daemons
  automountd, autofs, 170
  NFS, 158
  NIS, 192-193

Database Manager
  Solstice AdminSuite, 16, 212
  Solstice AdminSuite tools, 236
    service files, 237-239
    system files, 236

dataless clients, 7

Default Installation option, Web Start, 250-251

defaults, user accounts (User manager), 217-219

deleting
  printers, Printer Manager (Solstice AdminSuite tools), 235
  user accounts, User Manager (Solstice AdminSuite tools), 221-222

DES authentication, 207-208

dev .. command, device trees, 79

dev / command, device trees, 80

dev device-path command, device trees, 79-80

dev node-name command, device trees, 79

devalias alias command, OpenBoot, 80

devalias alias device-path command, OpenBoot, 80

devalias command, OpenBoot, 80

device-path find-device command, device trees, 80

device-path select-dev command, device trees, 80

device aliases, OpenBoot, 80-81

device drivers, 107

device names, OpenBoot, 77-78

device trees, OpenBoot, 75
  commands
    for browsing, 79-80
    show-devs, 78-79

device-arguments, device names (OpenBoot), 78

device-end command, device trees, 80

devices
  auto-configuration, 114-116
  instance names, 116-118
    dmesg command, 117
  logical device names, 122-123
    disks command, 124
    dsk directory, 124
    /rdsk directory, 125
    reconfigure start up, 125
  major device numbers, 120-122
  meta devices, 126-127
  minor device numbers, 120-122
  vold.conf, volume manager, 143-144

devlinks command, 125

df command, 151
  file systems, 152

dfmounts command, NFS, 165

dfshares command, 161

diag-device
  boot configuration variables, OpenBoot, 92
  NVRAM variables, 82

diag-file
  boot configuration variables, OpenBoot, 92
  NVRAM variables, 82

diag-switch?
  boot configuration variables, OpenBoot, 92
  NVRAM variables, 82

diagnostics, OpenBoot, 87-88
    commands, 87
    system information commands, 88-89
direct maps, 175-176
    failover, 178
    fields, 176
    mount command, 179
    mount points, 175-176
    multiple locations, 176
    replication of file systems, 176
    servers, selecting, 177
directories
    indirect maps, 180-181
    volume manager, 142
disabling
    vold, 147
    volume manager, 146-147
disk config files, 66
Disk Manager window, Storage manager (Solstice AdminSuite tools), 241-242
disk space, servers (AutoClient), 23
diskless clients, 7
disks command, 123
diskspace, minfree values, 133-134
dmesg command, 108-109, 113-114
DNS (Domain Name System), 185, 208-209
    name-to-address mapping, 209
domains, planning (NIS), 191-192
dontuse, profiles, 59
driver-name, device names (OpenBoot), 78
drvconfig command, 117, 119
drvconfig utility, 121
dsk directory, logical device names, 124

E

eeprom, 56
eeprom command, UNIX, 84
enabling
    logging, Solstice AdminSuite tools, 215-216
    WebNFS access, 168
.enet-addr command, OpenBoot diagnostics, 88
Enterprise Volume Manager, 126
Equipment, starting, 73-74
esp command, 123
/etc files, 185-186
/etc/dfs/dfstab files, 158
/etc/mnttab, mouting file systems, 139-140
/etc/system file, kernels, 96-97

F

failover, direct maps, 178
Fcode interpreter, OpenBoot, 75
fcode-debug?, NVRAM variables, 82
fdformat command, 148-149
fields
    direct maps, 176
    indirect maps, 180
File System Manager window, Storage Manager (Solstice AdminSuite tools), 241
file systems
    constructing
        labelit command, 131
        mkfs command, 129-131
        volcopy command, 132-133

df command, 152
fragmentation, 152
fsck command, 151
large versus small, 136
mounting
   /etc/mnttab, 139-140
   mount command, 136-139
NFS
   mounting, 162
   sharing, 158-161
replication, 176
tuning
   fstyp command, 135-136
   mkfs command, 135
   tunefs command, 133-134
ufs, 132-133
unmounting, 175
   fuser command, 141
   umount command, 140-141
Web Start, laying out, 254-255
WebNFS, 167

filenames, boot command, 95

files, tar, 148

filesys, profiles, 59-61

finish scripts, 54

formatting default disk devices with SunOS labels, 150

Forth, programmable user interfaces (OpenBoot), 76

fragmentation, file systems, 152

fsck command, 151

fsname, 133

fstyp command, 135-136

functions of OpenBoot, 75

fuser command, 141

G-H

global registry, Solstice Launcher, 214

Group Manager
Solstice AdminSuite, 16, 211
Solstice AdminSuite tools, 222
   adding groups, 223-224
   modifying groups, 224

help command, OpenBoot, 76
with category arguments, 77

Helpful Information button, Web Start, 256

Host Manager
AutoClient, 23
Solstice AdminSuite, 16, 211
startup servers, 40-42

I

.idprom command, OpenBoot diagnostics, 88

indirect maps, 179-180
fields, 180
home directories, 180-181

input-device
configuration variables, OpenBoot console, 89
NVRAM variables, 82

install servers
clients, setting up, 69
customized JumpStart installation, 43

install type, profiles, 61

installboot command, 94

installing
    JumpStart, 38-39
        example, 68-69
        install servers, 43
        startup servers, 39-40, 42
    printers, Printer Manager (Solstice AdminSuite tools), 231-235
    software
        interactive installation process, 10-14
        JumpStart. *See* JumpStart
    Solaris 2.6 on servers, 8-10
    Solstice AdminSuite, 18-21, 212
        pre-installation checklist, 18-19
    Web Start. *See* Web Start

InstallShield, 241

instance names, 107, 116-118
    add_drv command, 117-119
    dmesg command, 117
    drvconfig command, 117, 119
    sysdef command, 119

interactive installation process, installing software, 10-14

J

JavaStation, 7

JumpStart, 37
    installing, 38-39
        example, 68-69
        install servers, 43
        startup servers, 39-42

JumpStart directories, 68
    profile servers, 44

JumpStart utility, 241

K-L

/kernel directory, 115-116

kernels, 95
    /etc/system file, 96-97
    commands
        adb, 104-105
        modinfo, 96
        sysdef, 97, 99-101, 103-104
    instance names, 116

labelit command, 131

launching
    AutoClient systems, 32
    NIS master servers, 199
    systems, 73-74
        from ok prompt, 93-94

laying out file systems, Web Start, 254-256

layout constraint, profiles, 61-62

limitations of Default Installation option, Web Start, 251

links to directories, volume manager, 142

local mode, Web Start, 246

local registry, Solstice Launcher, 214

locale, profiles, 63

lockd, NFS daemons, 158

logging, enabling (Solstice AdminSuite tools), 215-216

logical device names, 107, 122-123
    disks command, 124
    dsk directory, 124
    /rdsk directory, 125
    reconfigure start up, 125

ls command, device trees, 80

M

maintaining patches, AutoClient Systems, 33-35
major device numbers, 120-122
make command, NIS, 193
makedbm command, NIS, 193
Makefiles, NIS master servers, 198
managing user logins, NIS, 194
maps
    autofs, 172
    direct maps, 175-176
        failover, 178
        fields, 176
        mount command, 179
        mount points, 175-176
        multiple locations, 176
        replication of file systems, 176
        servers, selecting, 177
    indirect maps, 179-180
        fields, 180
        home directories, 180-181
    master maps, 172-175
    modifying, 182
    NIS, 188-191
master group files, NIS master servers, 195-196
master host files, NIS master servers, 196-197
master maps, 172-175
master servers, NIS, 187
    configuring, 192-194
    creating
        master group files, 195-196
        master host files, 196-197
        passwd files, 194-195
        source files, 197-198
    name service switches, 200-201
    preparing Makefiles, 198
    setting up with ypinit, 198-199
    starting, 199
    stopping, 199
MCL (multi-component lookup), WebNFS, 167
meta devices, 126-127
minfree values, 133-134
minor device numbers, 120-122
mkfs command, 129-131, 135
modes of operation, Web Start
    client-server mode, 245-247
    local mode, 246
modifying
    groups, Group Manager (Solstice AdminSuite tools), 224
    maps, 182
    ports, Serial Port Manager (Solstice AdminSuite tools), 226
    printers, Printer Manager (Solstice AdminSuite tools), 235
    system files, Database Manager (Solstice AdminSuite), 236
    user accounts, User Manager (Solstice AdminSuite tools), 221
modinfo command, kernels, 96
More Info button, Web Start, 256
mount command, 136-139
    direct maps, 179
    NFS, 162-164, 166
mount points, 175-176
mountd, NFS daemons, 158

mounting
    autuofs. *See* autofs
    file systems
        /etc/mnttab, 139-140
        mount command, 136-139
    NFS file systems, 162
    remote file systems, NFS, 162-166
    vold, 150-151

multi-component lookup (MCL), 167

N

name service switches, NIS master servers, 200-201

name services, 185
    DNS, 185
    /etc files, 185-186
    NIS, 185-186
        structure of, 186-188
    NIS+, 185

name-to-address mapping, DNS, 209

namespaces, NIS+, 204

naming conventions, physical device names, 108, 114
    dmesg command, 113-114
    prtconf command, 109
    sysdef command, 110-113

Network File System. *See* **NFS**

Network Information Service Plus. *See* **NIS+**

Network Information Service. *See* **NIS**

newfs command, 129, 131

NFS (Network File System), 155
    autofs, 169, 171
        automount service, 169-170
        automountd daemon, 170
        showmount command, 171-172
    benefits of, 155
    daemons, 158
    dfmounts command, 165
    dfshares command, 161
    file systems, mounting, 162
    mount command, 162-164, 166
    remote file systems, mounting, 162-166
    security, 161-162
    setting up, 158-161
    share command, 158-160, 162
    shareall command, 160
    showmount command, 171-172
    Solaris, 156
    umount command, 165
    unshare command, 162
    WebNFS, 166-167
        access, enabling, 168
        benefits of, 166
        browsers, 168-169
        file systems, 167
        remote file access, 166

NFS clients, 156

NFS servers, 155

NFS URLs, browsers, 168-169

NFS version 2, 156

NFS version 3.0
    Solaris 2.5, 156-157
    Solaris 2.6, 157

nfsd, NFS daemons, 158

NIS (Network Information Service), 185-186
   commands, 193
   daemons, 192-193
   maps, 188-189, 191
      default maps, 189-191
   master servers
      configuring, 192-194
      creating master group files, 195-196
      creating master host files, 196-197
      creating passwd files, 194-195
      creating source files, 197-198
      name service switches, 200-201
      preparing Makefiles, 198
      setting up with ypinit, 198-199
      starting, 199
      stopping, 199
   structure of, 186-187
      clients, 187
      determining number of servers, 188
      determining which hosts will be servers, 188
      master server, 187
      slave servers, 187
   user logins, managing, 194

NIS+ (Network Information Service Plus), 185, 203-204
   authentication, 206
   authorization, access rights, 206
   name spaces, 204
   security, 206
      levels of, 207
   tables, 204-206

NIS clients, configuring, 201-202
NIS domains, planning, 191-192
NIS slave servers, configuring, 202-203

nischmod command, 207
nisls _1 command, 207
Nonvolatile Random Access Memory chip (NVRAM chip), 74
num clients, profiles, 63
nvalias alias device-path command, NVRAM, 85
nvalias command, 81
NVRAM
   commands, 85
   configuration variables, 85
      changing, 82-85
   OpenBoot, configuration variables, 81-82

NVRAM (Nonvolatile Random Access Memory) chip, 74
nvramrc, 81
   NVRAM variables, 82
nvunalias alias command, NVRAM, 85
nvunalias command, 81

O

OBP (OpenBoot PROM), 74
oem-banner, NVRAM variables, 82
oem-banner?, NVRAM variables, 82
oem-logo, NVRAM variables, 82
oem-logo?, NVRAM variables, 82
ok OpenBoot prompt, 83
ok prompt, starting systems, 93-94
OpenBoot
   architecture, 75
      features of, 75-76
   bootstrap procedure, 90

commands
  boot, 92-93
  devalias, 80
  devalias alias, 80
  devalias alias device-path, 80
  for browsing device trees, 79-80
  help, 76
  help (with category argument), 77
  show-devs, 78-79
console, configuration variables, 89-90
device aliases, 80-81
device names, 77-78
diagnostics, 87-88
  commands, 87
  system information commands, 88-89
Forth, 76
functions, 75
how to get there, 74
NVRAM, configuration variables, 81-82
NVRAM chip, 74
ok OpenBoot prompt, 83
operating system kernel, 75
programmable user interfaces, Forth, 76
security
  passwords, 86-87
  security-mode, 86
  variables, 85
startup process, 90, 94
  configuration variables, 91-92
UNIX configuratio variables, 85

OpenBoot PROM (OBP), 74

operating system kernel, OpenBoot, 75

options, Serial Port Manager (Solstice AdminSuite tools), 227-228

OS servers, 7

output-device
configuration variables, OpenBoot console, 89
NVRAM variables, 82

P

package, profiles, 63

parameters, 144

partitioning profiles, 63-64

passwd files, NIS master servers, 194-195

password command, changing NVRAM variables, 83

passwords
security variables, OpenBoot, 86-87
Web Start, client-server mode, 246-248

patchadd _c command, 43

patching AutoClient systems, 32-35
admclientpatch command, 33

pfinstall command, 37, 65

physical device names, 107-108, 114
dmesg command, 113-114
prtconf command, 109
sysdef command, 110-113

pkginfo command, 192

planning NIS domains, 191-192

platform-names, uname _i command, 95

plug-in device drivers, OpenBoot, 75

ports, modifying (Serial Port Manager, Solstice AdminSuite tools), 226

ports command, 123

powering on
AutoClient systems, 32
NIS master servers, 199
systems, 73-74
  from ok prompt, 93-94

pre-installation checklist, installing Solstice AdminSuite, 18-19

prerequisites for servers, 8

print clients, 229-230

print commands, SunSoft print client commands, 229

print requests, processing SunSoft Print Client software, 230

print servers, 228-229

printenv command, changing NVRAM variables, 83

Printer Manager
  Load window, 231
  Solstice AdminSuite, 16, 212
  Solstice AdminSuite tools, 230-231
    deleting printers, 235
    installing printers, 231-235
    modifying printers, 235

printers
  deleting, Printer Manager (Solstice AdminSuite tools), 235
  installing, Printer Manager (Solstice AdminSuite tools), 231-235
  modifying, Printer Manager (Solstice AdminSuite tools), 235

private registry, Solstice Launcher, 214

probe-scsi command, OpenBoot diagnostics, 87

processing print requests, SunSoft Print Client software, 230

profile diskettes, 44-45

profile servers
  JumpStart directories, 44
  setting up, 44, 68-69

profiles, 55
  backup media, 56
  boot device, 56-57
  client arch, 57
  client root, 57
  client swap, 58
  cluster, 58-59

  dontuse, 59
  filesys, 59-61
  install type, 61
  layout constraint, 61-62
  locale, 63
  num clients, 63
  package, 63
  partitioning, 63-64
  root device, 64
  system type, 64
  testing, 65-67
  use disk, 64

Programmable Read-Only Memory (PROM), 74

programmable user interfaces, OpenBoot, 76

programming languages, Forth, 76

PROM (Programmable Read-Only Memory), 74

.properties command, device trees, 79

protocols
  BSD printing protocols, 228
  System V, 229

prtconf command, 109

prtvtoc command, 136

pwd command, device trees, 80

Q-R

/rdsk directory, logical device names, 125

reconfigure start up, logical device names, 125

registering applications, Solstice Launcher, 214

remote file systems, mounting (NFS), 162-166

removing shared resources, 162
replication, file systems, 176
rmmount command, 146
root device, profiles, 64
rpcbind, NFS daemons, 158
rule keywords, rules files, 49-50, 52
rule values, rules files, 49-50, 52
rules files, 45, 52
    begin scripts, 54-55
    check scripts, 52-54
    example, 46-48
    finish scripts, 54
    requirements for, 49
    rule keywords, 49-50, 52
    rule values, 49-50, 52
    syntax, 48-49
    validating, 52-54

S

sbus-probe-list, NVRAM variables, 82
Scaleable Processor Architecture (SPARC), 75
screen-#columns
    configuration variables, OpenBoot console, 89
    NVRAM variables, 82
screen-#rows
    configuration variables, OpenBoot console, 89
    NVRAM variables, 82
scripts, rules files
    begin scripts, 54-55
    check scripts, 52-54
    finish scripts, 54

security
    DES authentication, 207
    NFS, 161-162
    NIS+, 206
        levels of, 207
    OpenBoot
        passwords, 86-87
        security-mode, 86
        variables, 85
security-#badlogins
    NVRAM variables, 82
    security variables, OpenBoot, 85
security-mode
    NVRAM variables, 82
    security variables, OpenBoot, 85-86
security-password
    NVRAM variables, 82
    security variables, OpenBoot, 85
    See wordname command, device trees, 80
selecting servers, direct maps, 177
Serial Port main window, Serial Port Manager (Solstice AdminSuite tools), 225
Serial Port Manager
    serial port templates, 226-227
    Solstice AdminSuite, 16, 212
    Solstice AdminSuite tools, 224
        modifying ports, 226
        options, 227-228
        Serial Port main window, 225
        Serial Port Manager: Modify window, 226-227
Serial Port Manager: Modify window, Serial Port Manager (Solstice AdminSuite tools), 226-227
serial port templates, Serial Port Manager, 226-227

servers, 7
    accessing, 21
    AutoClient
        disk space, 23
        setting up, 25-29
    AutoClient clients, 7
    AutoClients, adding, 30-32
    clients, 7
    direct maps, selecting, 177
    master servers, 187
        configuring, 192-194
        master group files, creating, 195-196
        master host files, creating, 196-197
        name service switches, 200-201
        passwd files, creating, 194-195
        preparing Makefiles, 198
        setting up with ypinit, 198-199
        source files, creating, 197-198
        starting, 199
        stopping, 199
    NFS, 155
    NIS, 188
    NIS slave servers, configuring, 202-203
    prerequisites for, 8
    Solaris 2.6, installing, 8-10
service files, Database Manager (Solstice AdminSuite tools), 237-239
Set Media Path window, AutoClient servers, 27
set-default *variable* command, changing NVRAM variables, 83
set-defaults command, changing NVRAM variables, 83
setenv *variable value* command, changing NVRAM variables, 83
setup install server command, 37, 39, 43, 68

share command, 158-160, 162
shareall command, 160
shared resources
    NFS, 158-161
    removing, 162
sharing file systems, NFS, 158-161
show-devs command
    OpenBoot, 78-79
    OpenBoot diagnostics, 88
show-devs [*device-path*] command, device trees, 80
show-sbus command, OpenBoot diagnostics, 88
showmount command, autofs, 171-172
slave servers, NIS, 187
software
    installing
        interactive installation process, 10-14
        Web Start. *See* Web Start
    SunSoft Print Client software, 228
soladdapp command, 214
Solaris 2.5, NFS version 3.0, 156-157
Solaris 2.6
    NFS version 3.0, 157
    Servers, installing, 8-10
Solaris Web Start, 244
    customized installation, 252-255
    Default Installation option, 250-251
    file systems, laying out, 252, 254-255
    Helpful Information button, 256
    modes of operation
        client-server mode, 246-250
        local mode, 246
    More Info button, 256
    system requirements, 245

Solstice AdminSuite, 15, 211
   command-line equivalents, 211-212
   Database Manager, 16
   Group Manager, 16
   Host Manager, 16
   installing, 18-21, 212
      pre-installation checklist, 18-19
   Printer Manager, 16
   Serial Port Manager, 16
   Storage Manager, 17
   tools, Solstice Launcher window, 212-214
   User Manager, 16
Solstice AdminSuite tools, 215
   Database Manager, 236
      service files, 237-239
      system files, 236
   Group Manager, 222
      adding groups, 223-224
      modifying groups, 224
   logging, 215-216
   Printer Manager, 230-231
      deleting printers, 235
      installing printers, 231-235
      modifying printers, 235
   Serial Port Manager, 224
      modifying ports, 226
      options, 227-228
      Serial Port main window, 225
      Serial Port Manager: Modify window, 226-227
   Storage Manager, 239-240
      Disk Manager window, 241-242
      File System Manager window, 241
   User Manager, 216
      adding new user accounts, 219-220
      deleting user accounts, 221-222
      modifying user accounts, 221
      setting up user account defaults, 217-219

Solstice DiskSuite, 126
Solstice Launcher window
   AdminSuite tools, 212
      pull-down menu options, 213-214
   applications, registering, 214
   customizing, 214-215
source files, NIS master servers, 197-198
SPARC (Scaleable Processor Architecture), 75
   configuration variables, 82
special parameters, 144
.speed command, OpenBoot diagnostics, 88
starting
   AutoClient systems, 32
   NIS master servers, 199
   systems, 73-74
      from ok prompt, 93-94
startup process, OpenBoot, 90, 94
   configuration variables, 91-92
startup programs, kernels, 95
   adb command, 104-105
   /etc/system file, 96-97
   sysdef command, 97, 99-101, 103-104
startup servers
   customized JumpStart installation, 39-42
   Host manager, 40-42
statd, NFS daemons, 158
stopping NIS master servers, 199
Storage Manager
   Solstice AdminSuite, 17, 212
   Solstice AdminSuite tools, 239-240
      Disk Manager window, 241-242
      File System Manager window, 241
Storage Manager: Load Context window, 239

structure of NIS, 186-187
    clients, 187
    determining number of servers, 188
    determining which hosts will be servers, 188
    master server, 187
    slave servers, 187

SunOS 4.x BSD (lpd) print servers, 228

SunOS 5.x SVR4 (LP) print servers, 229

SunSoft print client, print servers, 228

SunSoft print client commands, 229

SunSoft Print Client software, 228
    print requests, processing, 230

Sunsoft print clients, 229-230

superblock, 133

symname parameters, 144

sysadmin group, 19

sysdef command, 109-113, 119
    kernels, 97, 99-101, 103-104

system files, Database Manager (Solstice AdminSuite tools), 236

system identification, Web Start (client-server mode), 246-248

system information commands, OpenBoot diagnostics, 88-89

system requirements, Web Start, 245

system type, profiles, 64

System V protocol, 229

systems, starting, 73-74
    from ok prompt, 93-94

T

tables, NIS+, 204-206

tapes command, 123

tar files, 148

templates, serial port templates (Serial Port manager), 226-227

test *device-specifier* command, OpenBoot diagnostics, 87

test-all [*device-specifier*] command, OpenBoot diagnostics, 87

testing profiles, 65-67

tools
    Solstice AdminSuite, 215
        Solstice Launcher window, 212-214
    Solstice AdminSuite tools, 215
        Database Manager, 236-239
        Group Manager, 222-224
        logging, 215-216
        Printer Manager, 230-235
        Serial Port Manager, 224-228
        Storage Manager, 239-242
        User Manager, 216-222

.traps command, OpenBoot diagnostics, 88

troubleshooting volume manager, 147-151

tunefs command, 133-134

tuning file systems
    fstyp command, 135-136
    mkfs command, 135
    tunefs command, 133-134

U

ufs file systems, 132-133

umount command, 140-141
    NFS, 165

uname -i command, 95

unit-address, device names (OpenBoot), 78

UNIX
    /etc files, 185-186
    OpenBoot configuration variables, 85

unmounting file systems, 175
   fuser command, 141
   umount command, 140-141
unshare command, 162
URLs, Web Start (client-server mode), 247
use disk, profiles, 64
use-nvramrc?, NVRAM variables, 82
user accounts, User Manager (Solstice AdminSuite tools)
   adding, 219-220
   deleting, 221-222
   modifying, 221
   setting defaults, 217-219
user logins, managing (NIS), 194
User Manager
   Solstice AdminSuite, 16, 211
   Solstice AdminSuite tools, 216
      adding new user accounts, 219-220
      deleting user accounts, 221-222
      modifying user accounts, 221
      setting up user account defaults, 217-219
/usr/sbin/share command, 159
utilities
   drvconfig, 121
   JumpStart, 241

V

validating rules files, 52-54
variables
   configuration variables
      changing, 82-85
      NVRAM (OpenBoot), 81-82
      OpenBoot console, 89-90
      OpenBoot startup process, 91-92
      SPARC, 82
   Security, OpenBoot, 85

.version command, OpenBoot diagnostics, 88
volcancel command, 146
volcheck command, 146
volcopy command, 132-133
vold
   disabling, 147
   mounting, 150-151
   volume manager, 147
vold command, 146
vold daemon, volume manager, 143
vold.conf
   actions, 144-146
   devices to use, 143-144
volmissing command, 146
volname, 133
volume manager, 142
   benefits of, 142
   commands, 146
   directories, 142
   disabling, 146-147
   troubleshooting, 147-151
   vold, 147
   vold daemon, 143
   vold.conf
      actions, 144-146
      devices, 143-144

W

watch-clock command, OpenBoot diagnostics, 87
watch-net command, OpenBoot diagnostics, 87
Watchdog Reset, 74

Web Start, 244
   customized installation, 252-255
   Default Installation option, 250-251
   file systems, laying out, 252, 254-255
   Helpful Information button, 256
   modes of operation
      client-server mode, 246-250
      local mode, 246
   More Info button, 256
   system requirements, 245
WebNFS, 166-167
   access, enabling, 168
   benefits of, 166
   browsers, 168-169
   file systems, 167
   remote file access, 166

X-Y-Z

YP (Yellow Pages), NIS, 185-186
   commands, 193
   daemons, 192-193
   maps, 188-189, 191
      default maps, 189-191
   master servers
      configuring, 192-194
      creating master group files, 195-196
      creating master host files, 196-197
      creating passwd files, 194-195
      creating source files, 197-198
      name service switches, 200-201
      preparing Makefiles, 198
      setting up with ypinit, 198-199
      starting, 199
      stopping, 199
   structure of, 186-187
      clients, 187
      determining number of servers, 188
      determining which hosts will be servers, 188
      master server, 187
      slave servers, 187
   user logins, managing, 194
ypcat command, NIS, 193
ypinit command
   NIS, 193
   NIS master servers, 198-199
yppoll command, NIS, 193
yppush command, NIS, 193
ypset command, NIS, 193
ypstart command, NIS, 193
ypstop command, 199
   NIS, 193
ypwhich command, NIS, 193

Books for Professionals

UNIX/Linux Titles

Solaris Essential Reference
By John P. Mulligan
1st Edition
350 pages, $24.95
ISBN: 0-7357-0023-0

Looking for the fastest, easiest way to find the Solaris command you need? Need a few pointers on shell scripting? How about advanced administration tips and sound, practical expertise on security issues? Are you looking for trustworthy information about available third-party software packages that will enhance your operating system? Author John Mulligan—creator of the popular Unofficial Guide to Solaris Web site (sun.icsnet.com)—delivers all that and more in one attractive, easy-to-use reference book. With clear and concise instructions on how to perform important administration and management tasks and key information on powerful commands and advanced topics, *Solaris Essential Reference* is the reference you need when you know what you want to do and you just need to know how.

Linux System Administration
By M Carling and James T. Dennis
1st Edition
450 pages, $29.99
ISBN: 1-56205-934-3

As an administrator, you probably feel that most of your time and energy is spent in endless firefighting. If your network has become a fragile quilt of temporary patches and workarounds, then this book is for you. For example, have you had trouble sending or receiving your email lately? Are you looking for a way to keep your network running smoothly with enhanced performance? Are your users always hankering for more storage, more services, and more speed? *Linux System Administration* advises you on the many intricacies of maintaining a secure, stable system. In this definitive work, the author addresses all the issues related to system administration, from adding users and managing file permissions to Internet services and Web hosting to recovery planning and security. This book fulfills the need for expert advice that will ensure a trouble-free Linux environment.

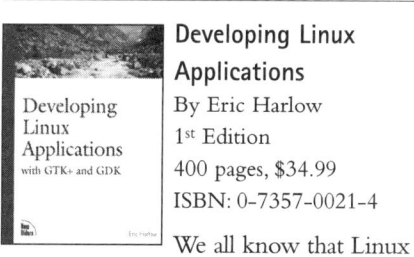

Developing Linux Applications
By Eric Harlow
1st Edition
400 pages, $34.99
ISBN: 0-7357-0021-4

We all know that Linux is one of the most powerful and solid operating systems in existence. And as the success of Linux grows, there is an increasing interest in developing applications with graphical user interfaces that really take advantage of the power of Linux. In this book, software developer Eric Harlow gives you an indispensable development handbook focusing on the GTK+ toolkit. More than an overview on the elements of application or GUI design, this is a hands-on book that delves deeply into the technology. With in-depth material on the various GUI programming tools and loads of examples, this book's unique focus will give you the information you need to design and launch professional-quality applications.

Linux Firewalls

By Robert Ziegler
1st Edition
400 pages, $39.99
ISBN: 0-7357-0900-9

New Riders is proud to offer the first book aimed specifically at Linux security issues. While there are a host of general UNIX security books, we think it is time to address the practical needs of the Linux network. Author Robert Ziegler takes a balanced approach to system security, discussing topics like planning a secure environment, firewalls, and utilizing security scripts. With comprehensive information on specific system compromises, and advice on how to prevent and repair them, this is one book that Linux administrators should have on their shelves.

GIMP Essential Reference

by Alex Harford
1st Edition
400 pages, $24.95
ISBN: 0-7357-0911-4

GIMP Essential Reference is designed to fulfill a need for the computer expert. It is made to bring someone experienced in computers up to speed with the GNU Image Manipulation Program. It provides essential information on using this program effectively. This book is targeted at you if you want to efficiently use the GIMP. *GIMP Essential Reference* will show you how to quickly become familiar with the advanced user interface using a table-heavy format that will allow users to find what they're looking for quickly.

GIMP Essential Reference is for users working with GIMP who know what they want to accomplish, but don't know exactly how to do it.

KDE Application Development

by Uwe Thiem
1st Edition
216 pages, $39.99
ISBN: 1-57870-201-1

KDE Application Development offers a head start into KDE and Qt. The book will cover the essential widgets available in KDE and Qt, and it offers a strong start without the "first try" annoyances that sometimes make strong developers and programmers give up. This book explains KDE and Qt by writing a real application from the very beginning stages, where it can't do anything but display itself and offer a button to quit. Then it will finally bring the user to a full-featured application. The process of developing such an application takes the potential KDE developer through all stages of excitement.

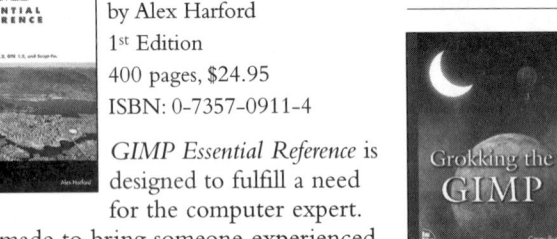

Grokking the GIMP

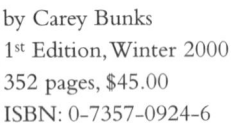

by Carey Bunks
1st Edition, Winter 2000
352 pages, $45.00
ISBN: 0-7357-0924-6

This titles is a technical and inspirational reference covering the intricacies of the GIMP's feature set. Even if you have little background in image manipulation, you can succeed at using the GIMP to achieve your goals, using this book as a guide. Keeping in mind that all tools are not created equal, author Carey Bunks provides an in-depth look at the GIMP's most useful tools. The content focuses on the intermediate to advanced topics of interest to most users, like photo touchup and enhancement, compositing, and animations. Invaluable is the conceptual approach of the author, in which he avoids the cookbook approach to learning image manipulation and helps you become self-sufficient.

Samba Administration

by John Terpstra
1st Edition, Summer 2000
400 pages, $35.00
ISBN: 0-7357-0903-3

The world of today's system administrators is filled with many different types of network operating systems, protocols, and hardware configurations all under the requirements of demanding and sometimes less than savvy users. Many administrators turn to the Samba product to help them share services between systems.

Samba Administration provides the sysadmin with the necessary technical background on the SMB architecture, compiling the source and installation, managing clients and servers, and dealing with the inexplicable.

Inside Linux

by Michael Tobler
1st Edition, Spring 2000
700 pages, $39.99
ISBN: 0-7357-0940-8

With in-depth complete coverage on the installation process, editing and typesetting, graphical user interfaces, programming, system administration, and managing Internet sites, *Inside Linux* is the only book "smart" users new to Linux will need. If you have an understanding of computer technology and are looking for just the right reference to fit your sophisticated needs, this book guides you to a high level of proficiency with all the flavors of Linux, and helps you with crucial system administration chores. *Inside Linux* is different than other books available because it's a unique blend of a how-to and a reference guide.

Development Titles

GTK+/Gnome Application Development

By Havoc Pennington
1st Edition
400 pages, $34.99
ISBN: 0-7357-0078-8

GTK+/Gnome Application Development provides the experienced programmer the knowledge to develop X Window applications with the powerful GTK+ toolkit. The author provides the reader with a checklist of features every application should have, advanced GUI techniques, and the ability to create custom widgets. The title also contains reference information for more experienced users already familiar with usage, but requires knowledge of function prototypes and detailed descriptions. These tools let the reader write powerful applications in record time.

Python Essential Reference

By David Beazley
1st Edition
300 pages, $34.95
ISBN: 0-7357-0901-7

This book describes the Python programming language and its library of standard modules. Python is an informal language that has become a highly valuable software development tool for many computing professionals. This language reference covers Python's lexical conventions, built-in datatypes, control flow, functions, statements, classes, and execution model. This book also covers the contents of the Python library as bundled in the standard Python distribution.

glibc: A Comprehensive Reference to GNU/Linux libC

by Jeff Garzik
1st Edition, Spring 2000
500 pages, $40.00
ISBN: 1-57870-202-X

glibc comprises over 1,800 functions. This title is a complete reference work encompassing a single-volume version that gives quick coverage to each function. It includes a searchable index to provide added value, and it is slated to become an Open Source title available for free download online. The book content consists of an index of functions by category (networking, threading, string, etc.), and then an alphabetical function listing.

Lotus Notes and Domino Titles

Domino System Administration

By Rob Kirkland
1st Edition
880 pages, $49.99
ISBN: 1-56205-948-3

Your boss has just announced that you will be upgrading to the newest version of Lotus Notes and Domino when it ships. As a Premium Lotus Business Partner, Lotus has offered a substantial price break to keep your company away from Microsoft's Exchange Server. How are you supposed to get this new system installed, configured, and rolled out to all of your endusers? You understand how Lotus Notes works—you've been administering it for years. What you need is a concise, practical explanation about the new features, and how to make some of the advanced stuff really work. You need answers and solutions from someone like you, who has worked with the product for years, and understands what it is you need to know. *Domino System Administration* is the answer—the first book on Domino that attacks the technology at the professional level, with practical, hands-on assistance to get Domino running in your organization.

Lotus Notes & Domino Essential Reference

By Dave Hatter and
Tim Bankes
1st Edition
700 pages, $45.00
ISBN: 0-7357-0007-9

You're in a bind because you've been asked to design and program a new database in Notes that will keep track of and itemize a myriad of inventory and shipping data for an important client. The client wants a user-friendly interface, without sacrificing speed or functionality. You are experienced (and could develop this app in your sleep), but feel that you need to take your talents to the next level. You need something to facilitate your creative and technical abilities, something to perfect your programming skills. Your answer is waiting for you: *Lotus Notes & Domino Essential Reference*. It's compact and simply designed. It's loaded with information. All of the objects, classes, functions, and methods are listed. It shows you the object hierarchy and the overlaying relationship between each one. It's perfect for you. Problem solved.

Networking Titles

Cisco Router Configuration & Troubleshooting

By Mark Tripod
1st Edition
300 pages, $34.99
ISBN: 0-7357-0024-9

Want the real story on making your Cisco routers run like a dream? Why not pick up a copy of *Cisco Router Configuration & Troubleshooting* and see what Mark Tripod has to say? His company is the one responsible for making some of the largest sites on the Net scream, like Amazon.com, Hotmail, USAToday, Geocities, and Sony. In this book, he provides advanced configuration issues, sprinkled with advice and preferred practices. You won't see a general overview on TCP/IP—he talks about more meaty issues like security, monitoring, traffic management, and more. In the troubleshooting section, Mark provides a unique methodology and lots of sample problems to illustrate. By providing real-world insight and examples instead of rehashing Cisco's documentation, Mark gives network administrators information they can start using today.

Understanding Data Communications

By Gilbert Held
6th Edition
550 pages, $34.99
ISBN: 0-7357-0036-2

Updated from the highly successful fifth edition, this book explains how data communications systems and their various hardware and software components work. Not an entry-level book, it approaches the material in a textbook format, addressing the complex issues involved in internetworking today. A great reference book for the experienced networking professional, written by noted networking authority, Gilbert Held.

DCE/RPC over SMB

by Luke Leighton
1st Edition
400 pages, $45.00
ISBN: 1-57870-150-3

When Microsoft's systems were locked into offices and chained to small LANs, they were relatively safe. Now, as they've been unleashed onto the Internet, they are more and more vulnerable to attack. Security people, system and network administrators, and the folks writing tools for them all need to be familiar with the packets flowing across their networks. It's the only way to really know how much trouble a system is in. This book describes how Microsoft has taken DCE/RPC (Distributed Computing Environment / Remote Procedure Calls) and implemented it over SMB (Server Message Block) and TCP/IP. SMB itself runs over three transports: TCP/IP, IPX/SPX, and NETBEUI.

Luke Leighton presents Microsoft Developer NT system calls (including what some such calls would be, if they were documented) and shows what they look like over-the-wire by providing example C code to compile and use. This gives administrators and developers insights into how information flows through their network, so that they can improve efficiency, security, and heterogeneous transfers.

Intrusion Detection: An Analyst's Handbook

by Stephen Northcutt
1st Edition
350 pages, $39.99
ISBN: 0-7357-0868-1

Get answers and solutions from someone who has been in the trenches with *Network Intrusion Detection: An Analyst's Handbook*. Author Stephen Northcutt, original developer of the Shadow intrusion detection system and former Director of the United States Navy's Information System Security Office at the Naval Security Warfare Center, lends his expertise to intrusion detection specialists, security analysts, and consultants responsible for setting up and maintaining an effective defense against network security.

NEW RIDERS CERTIFICATION TITLES

TRAINING GUIDES
NEXT GENERATION TRAINING

MCSE Training Guide: Networking Essentials, Second Edition
1-56205-919-X, $49.99, 9/98

MCSE Training Guide: TCP/IP, Second Edition
1-56205-920-3, $49.99, 10/98

MCSE Training Guide: Internet Information Server 4, 2E
0-7357-0865-7, $49.99, 5/99

MCSE Training Guide: Windows NT Server 4, Second Edition
1-56205-916-5, $49.99, 9/98

MCSE Training Guide: SQL Server 7 Administration
0-7357-0003-6, $49.99, 5/99

A+ Certification Training Guide, 2E
0-7357-0907-6, $49.99, 11/99

MCSE Training Guide: Windows NT Server 4 Enterprise, Second Edition
1-56205-917-3, $49.99, 9/98

MCSE Training Guide: SQL Server 7 Database Design
0-7357-0004-4, $49.99, 5/99

TRAINING GUIDES
FIRST EDITIONS

MCSE Training Guide: Systems Management Server 1.2, 1-56205-748-0

MCSE Training Guide: SQL Server 6.5 Administration, 1-56205-726-X

MCSE Training Guide: SQL Server 6.5 Design and Implementation, 1-56205-830-4

MCSE Training Guide: Windows 95, 70-064 Exam, 1-56205-880-0

MCSE Training Guide: Windows NT Workstation 4, Second Edition
1-56205-918-1, $49.99, 9/98

MCSD Training Guide: Solution Architectures
0-7357-0026-5, $49.99, 3/99

MCSE Training Guide: Internet Explorer 4, 1-56205-889-4

MCSE Training Guide: Microsoft Exchange Server 5.5, 1-56205-899-1

MCSD Training Guide: Visual Basic 5, 1-56205-850-9

MCSE Training Guide: Windows 98
1-56205-890-8, $49.99, 2/99

MCSD Training Guide: Visual Basic 6 Exams
0-7357-0002-8, $69.99, 3/99

Microsoft Corporation is a registered trademark of Microsoft Corporation in the United States and other countries. New Riders Publishing is an independent entity from Microsoft Corporation, and is not affiliated with Microsoft Corporation in any manner.

NEW RIDERS CERTIFICATION TITLES

FAST TRACKS

The Accelerated Path to Certification Success

Fast Tracks provide an easy way to review the key elements of each certification technology without being bogged down with elementary-level information.

These guides are perfect for when you already have real-world, hands-on experience. They're the ideal enhancement to training courses, test simulators, and comprehensive training guides.

No fluff—simply what you really need to pass the exam!

MCSE Fast Track: Networking Essentials
1-56205-939-4,
$19.99, 9/98

MCSE Fast Track: Windows 98
0-7357-0016-8,
$19.99, 12/98

MCSE Fast Track: TCP/IP
1-56205-937-8,
$19.99, 9/98

MCSE Fast Track: Windows NT Server 4
1-56205-935-1,
$19.99, 9/98

MCSE Fast Track: Windows NT Server 4 Enterprise
1-56205-940-8,
$19.99, 9/98

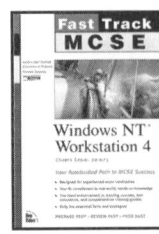

MCSE Fast Track: Windows NT Workstation 4
1-56205-938-6,
$19.99, 9/98

A+ Fast Track: Core/Hardware Exam & DOS/Windows Exam
0-7357-0028-1,
$34.99, 3/99

MCSE Fast Track: Internet Information Server 4
1-56205-936-X,
$19.99, 9/98

MCSE Fast Track: SQL Server 7 Administration
0-7357-0041-9,
$29.99, 4/99

MCSE/MCSD Fast Track: SQL Server 7 Database Design
0-7357-0040-0,
$29.99, 6/99

MCSD Fast Track: Visual Basic 6 Exam 70-175
0-7357-0018-4,
$19.99, 12/98

MCSD Fast Track: Visual Basic 6 Exam 70-176
0-7357-0019-2,
$19.99, 12/98

MCSD Fast Track: Solution Architectures
0-7357-0029-X,
$29.99, 9/99

Network+ Fast Track:
0-7357-0904-1,
$29.99, 7/99

NEW RIDERS CERTIFICATION TITLES

TESTPREPS

PRACTICE, CHECK, PASS!

Questions. Questions. And more questions. That's what you'll find in our New Riders *TestPreps*. They're great practice books when you reach the final stage of studying for an exam. We recommend them as supplements to our *Training Guides*.

What makes these study tools unique is that the questions are the primary focus of each book. All the text in these books support and explain the answers to these questions.

- ✓ **Scenario-based questions** challenge your experience.
- ✓ **Multiple-choice questions** prep you for the exam.
- ✓ **Fact-based questions** test your product knowledge.
- ✓ **Exam strategies** assist you in test preparation.
- ✓ **Complete yet concise explanations of answers** make for better retention.
- ✓ **Two practice exams** prepare you for the real thing.
- ✓ **Fast Facts** offer you everything you need to review in the testing center parking lot.

Practice, practice, practice—pass with New Riders TestPreps!

MCSE TestPrep: Networking Essentials, Second Edition
0-7357-0010-9, $19.99, 12/98

MCSE TestPrep: Windows 98
1-56205-922-X, $19.99, 11/98

MCSE TestPrep: Windows 95, Second Edition
0-7357-0011-7, $29.99, 12/98

MCSE TestPrep: Windows NT Server 4, Second Edition
0-7357-0012-5, $19.99, 12/98

MCSE TestPrep: Windows NT Server 4 Enterprise, Second Edition
0-7357-0009-5, $19.99, 11/98

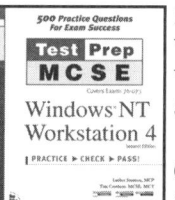

MCSE TestPrep: Windows NT Workstation 4, Second Edition
0-7357-0008-7, $19.99, 11/98

MCSE TestPrep: TCP/IP, Second Edition
0-7357-0025-7, $19.99, 12/98

A+ Certification TestPrep
1-56205-892-4, $19.99, 12/98

MCSD TestPrep: Visual Basic 6 Exams
0-7357-0032-X, $29.99, 1/99

TESTPREPS

FIRST EDITIONS

MCSE TestPrep: SQL Server 6.5 Administration, 0-7897-1597-X

MCSE TestPrep: SQL Server 6.5 Design and Implementation, 1-56205-915-7

MCSE TestPrep: Windows 95 70-64 Exam, 0-7897-1609-7

MCSE TestPrep: Internet Explorer 4, 0-7897-1654-2

MCSE TestPrep: Exchange Server 5.5, 0-7897-1611-9

MCSE TestPrep: IIS 4.0, 0-7897-1610-0

HOW TO CONTACT US

IF YOU NEED THE LATEST UPDATES ON A TITLE THAT YOU'VE PURCHASED:

1) Visit our Web site at www.newriders.com.

2) Click on the Downloads link.

3) There you'll find available updates for your title.

IF YOU ARE HAVING TECHNICAL PROBLEMS WITH THE BOOK OR THE CD THAT IS INCLUDED:

1) Check the book's information page on our Web site according to the instructions listed above, or

2) Email us at nrfeedback@newriders.com, or

3) Fax us at 317-581-4663 ATTN: Tech Support.

IF YOU HAVE COMMENTS ABOUT ANY OF OUR CERTIFICATION PRODUCTS THAT ARE NON-SUPPORT RELATED:

1) Email us at nrfeedback@newriders.com, or

2) Write to us at New Riders, 201 W. 103rd St., Indianapolis, IN 46290-1097, or

3) Fax us at 317-581-4663.

IF YOU ARE OUTSIDE THE UNITED STATES AND NEED TO FIND A DISTRIBUTOR IN YOUR AREA:

Please contact our international department at international@mcp.com.

IF YOU WISH TO PREVIEW ANY OF OUR CERTIFICATION BOOKS FOR CLASSROOM USE:

Email us at nrmedia@newriders.com. Your message should include your name, title, training company or school, department, address, phone number, office days/hours, text in use, and enrollment. Send these details along with your request for desk/examination copies and/or additional information.

WE WANT TO KNOW WHAT YOU THINK

To better serve you, we would like your opinion on the content and quality of this book. Please complete this card and mail it to us or fax it to 317-581-4663.

Name _____

Address _____

City _____ State _____ Zip _____

Phone _____ Email Address _____

Occupation _____

Which certification exams have you already passed? _____
_____
_____
_____

Which certification exams do you plan to take? _____
_____
_____
_____

What influenced your purchase of this book?
❑ Recommendation   ❑ Cover Design
❑ Table of Contents   ❑ Index
❑ Magazine Review   ❑ Advertisement
❑ Reputation of New Riders ❑ Author Name

How would you rate the contents of this book?
❑ Excellent   ❑ Very Good
❑ Good   ❑ Fair
❑ Below Average   ❑ Poor

What other types of certification products will you buy/have you bought to help you prepare for the exam?
❑ Quick reference books   ❑ Testing software
❑ Study guides   ❑ Other

What do you like most about this book? Check all that apply.
❑ Content   ❑ Writing Style
❑ Accuracy   ❑ Examples
❑ Listings   ❑ Design
❑ Index   ❑ Page Count
❑ Price   ❑ Illustrations

What do you like least about this book? Check all that apply.
❑ Content   ❑ Writing Style
❑ Accuracy   ❑ Examples
❑ Listings   ❑ Design
❑ Index   ❑ Page Count
❑ Price   ❑ Illustrations

What would be a useful follow-up book to this one for you?_____

Where did you purchase this book? _____

Can you name a similar book that you like better than this one, or one that is as good? Why?_____
_____
_____

How many New Riders books do you own? _____

What are your favorite certification or general computer book titles? _____
_____

What other titles would you like to see us develop?_____
_____

Any comments for us? _____
_____
_____

SOLARIS 2.6 ADMINISTRATOR CERTIFICATION TRAINING GUIDE, PART II   1-57870-086-8

Fold here and tape to mail

Place
Stamp
Here

New Riders
201 W. 103rd St.
Indianapolis, IN 46290